Sport Psychology

David Tod,
Joanne Thatcher
and Rachel Rahman

**PALGRAVE
INSIGHTS** IN
PSYCHOLOGY

SERIES EDITORS:
**NIGEL HOLT
& ROB LEWIS**

palgrave
macmillan

First published 2010 by
PALGRAVE MACMILLAN

Palgrave Macmillan in the UK is an imprint of Macmillan Publishers Limited, registered in England, company number 785998, of Houndmills, Basingstoke, Hampshire RG21 6XS.

Palgrave Macmillan in the US is a division of St Martin's Press LLC, 175 Fifth Avenue, New York, NY 10010.

Palgrave Macmillan is the global academic imprint of the above companies and has companies and representatives throughout the world.

Palgrave® and Macmillan® are registered trademarks in the United States, the United Kingdom, Europe and other countries.

ISBN: 978–0–230–24987–5

This book is printed on paper suitable for recycling and made from fully managed and sustained forest sources. Logging, pulping and manufacturing processes are expected to conform to the environmental regulations of the country of origin.

A catalogue record for this book is available from the British Library.

A catalog record for this book is available from the Library of Congress.

Sport Psychology

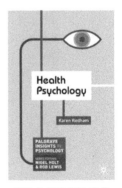

Contents

List of figures

List of tables

Note from series editors

The psychology of sport and exercise has an interesting history and has its origins in biological sciences and the psychology of motivation. You can see from a quick glance at the contents page of this book that the topic has matured significantly from these beginnings. It is extremely unusual now to find a sportsperson who is not connected professionally with a sport and exercise psychologist, and those who prepare professionals and amateur sportspeople will find the psychology of sport and exercise to be an important part of their own training.

David Tod, Jo Thatcher and Rachel Rahman are a formidable writing team and have put together a book that manages to be interesting and engaging while remaining well informed and carefully considered. We approached them to write for this series because of their strong reputation, and their drive and passion for their subject. Where there is passion for a subject there is motivation and an interested and interesting perspective and we certainly see these in this book.

- *Some of you will be reading this book in preparation for a university course.* It may be that you have chosen to study psychology, sport science, physiology or perhaps sports therapy. The writing team develop and deliver courses such as these and are aware of the existing literature and the pressures faced by students. They have produced a book to meet your needs.
- *Some of you will be reading this book while at university.* By now you will have realized that reading lists are never terribly brief and you will find other books identified as being worthy of your attention. This book should certainly be one of the books you read. It is more

than a gentle introduction to the topic and will form an invaluable addition to your collection that we are certain you will return to time and again.

- *Some of you will be reading this book as part of a pre-university course such as A-level.* We know from experience that A-levels place unique demands upon a student and those preparing students for the examinations. Students should use this book to develop their understanding and really stretch and challenge themselves to aim for the highest marks possible. Teachers can use this book to better develop the material available in their chosen course textbooks and to encourage their students to really understand the topic with up-to-date research and theory. The Reading Guide at the end of the book tells you where different A-level specifications appear.

The courses upon which the material here is relevant are numerous and growing, both in number and popularity. Psychologists, sociologists, sport scientists, medics, sports therapists, physiologists and physiotherapists will all find useful information here. If reading because of an interest in sport, either as an amateur or a professional, we are sure you will find the approach interesting and instructive. We commend this book to you strongly and are pleased to have it in this series.

NIGEL HOLT AND ROB LEWIS
Series Editors

Chapter 1

Introduction

Jane is a coach for a secondary school female netball team. The team has won its last five games. The players are talking about how they must surely win the competition and they are the best team around. Jane is wondering if the players are overconfident and how she might change the players' attitudes, especially as next month they will be playing some of the better teams in the competition, against whom her team have struggled in previous years.

Tom is in his early forties, and he has noticed he is putting on weight and getting tired and out of breath each time he walks up a hill to the building where he works. Although he played a lot of sport until his mid-thirties, in the past few years he hasn't played much or exercised regularly because his job keeps him busy. He finds it hard to motivate himself and believes that other people will think he looks silly if he gets into workout clothes because of his weight. He isn't sure how he can overcome his lack of motivation and worries about his appearance.

Gillian is an exercise instructor who organizes a community walking programme for a local county council. Gillian notices that the majority of walkers who come along each week are retired females. She would like to find ways to attract a greater variety of individuals including men and people of different ages and ethnicities to the weekly walks.

John plays football each week for a local club team. He is the team's centre forward and for the last few weeks hasn't been scoring many goals. He has started to get nervous before games and finds himself getting tense. He is worried that if he doesn't start scoring more goals, the coach will replace him with another player.

The situations above are examples of the types of issues that people involved in sports, exercise or physical activity face in their personal and professional lives. The field of sport and exercise psychology provides knowledge and strategies that may help the people above and others resolve their issues and help themselves and others perform better, get fitter and have more fun. In this chapter, you will learn a definition of sport and exercise psychology, its scope and application, and how it is underpinned by scientific knowledge.

In this chapter, we will examine:
- A definition of sport and exercise psychology
- The scope of the discipline
- The people who use sport and exercise psychology knowledge
- The scientific basis of sport and exercise psychology

👁 What is sport and exercise psychology?

A common theme in the situations above involved the way people's behaviours, thoughts and feelings influenced their sport and exercise participation. For example, John wanted to improve his performance (behaviour), reduce his worries and negative thoughts (his thinking), and lower his anxiety (feelings). Understanding people's behaviours, thoughts and feelings in sport and exercise contexts is one central focus of **sport and exercise psychology**, which may be defined as the study of people and their behaviour in sport and exercise settings (Gill and Williams, 2008). We use the term 'sport and exercise' in this book broadly and embrace all forms of physical activity, not just competitive sport or fitness programmes at leisure centres. Other forms of physical activity are included, such as informal non-competitive sports, outdoor pursuits, and school physical education (PE) classes.

The discipline is an applied science, and a second central focus is the application of sport and exercise psychology knowledge to help people. Learning about people and their behaviour in sport and exercise, and then applying that knowledge, can yield many benefits for various individuals. As examples, athletes might learn ways to improve their performances, enjoy their sports more, and live happier lives. Exercise participants can use strategies to ensure they have more fun, stick to their exercise programmes, and improve their physical and mental health. PE teachers can use sport and exercise psychology knowledge to help their students learn sports skills quicker, develop positive attitudes towards physical activity, and learn life skills.

When sport and exercise psychology is discussed in the newspapers, on the television and the radio, it is often in relation to elite athletes, such as people talking about why the English football team won or lost a recent game, or explaining why British athletes have done so well at the latest Olympics. Sport and exercise psychology knowledge, however, can assist many people involved in sport and exercise, not just elite athletes. Male and female athletes and exercise participants of all ages, abilities, ethnicities and sexual orientations can benefit from sport and exercise psychology knowledge.

The history of sport and exercise psychology can be traced back over 100 years, with the publication of the first recognized study exploring the influence of other riders on individuals' cycling times (Triplett, 1898). Its emergence as a scientific discipline, however, occurred in the 1960s and 70s, when it became a separate topic within the sport and exercise sciences, typically called physical education at that time (Weinberg and Gould, 2007). Since the 1960s and 70s, the sport and exercise sciences and mainstream psychology have been the two major disciplines that have influenced sport and exercise psychology. Table 1.1 lists some of the areas in the sport and exercise sciences and psychology that have influenced and continue to influence sport and exercise psychology. Knowledge from both parent disciplines helps sport and exercise psychologists to understand and help their clients in the most effective ways.

Sport and exercise science subdisciplines	Psychology subdisciplines
Exercise physiology	Clinical and counselling psychology
Biomechanics	Organizational psychology
Sports medicine	Developmental psychology
Motor learning	Personality psychology
Sport and exercise sociology	Psychophysiology
Sport and exercise pedagogy	Abnormal psychology
Coaching science	Health psychology

Table 1.1 Subdisciplines in the sport and exercise sciences and psychology, influencing sport and exercise psychology

Summary

Sport and exercise psychology involves the study of people and their behaviour in sport and exercise settings. As an applied science, the discipline also involves the application of knowledge to help people. The two parent disciplines influencing sport and exercise psychology include mainstream psychology and the sport and exercise sciences. The benefits of sport and exercise psychology are available for a range of people, not just elite athletes.

👁 The scope of sport and exercise psychology

Broadly, sport and exercise psychologists are interested in two key questions:

- How do psychological factors influence participation and performance in sport and exercise?
- What are the psychological effects from participating in sport and exercise (Williams and Straub, 2010)?

Examples of specific topics associated with the first question include:

- Do recreational runners improve their fitness levels quicker when they set goals?
- Does self-confidence help weightlifters learn correct technique?
- Are any personality traits associated with sporting success?

Answers to these types of specific questions allow sport and exercise psychologists to develop knowledge, strategies and interventions to help people gain more benefits from their participation.

Examples of specific topics associated with the second question include:

- Does participating in weekly aerobic classes reduce levels of depression?
- Can sports like football, basketball and cricket teach people how to work in teams?
- Do sports like rugby union and boxing teach people to be aggressive?

Answers to these specific questions help sport and exercise psychologists discuss the value of sport and exercise for individuals, communities and society.

To help appreciate the scope of the discipline further, it is useful to discuss the three focus areas of the Association of Applied Sport Psychology, one of the largest international professional organizations in the field. The three focus areas are health and exercise psychology, performance psychology, and social psychology:

- Professionals in the *health and exercise psychology focus area* are interested in applying psychological principles to the development and maintenance of health-enhancing behaviours over the lifespan, including play, physical activity and structured exercise, and the psychological and emotional consequences of those activities. Professionals are also interested in the role of exercise in disease remediation, injury rehabilitation and stress reduction. Topics in this book that might be related to this focus area include mental health, physical health and drugs.
- Professionals interested in the *performance psychology focus area* are interested in the research and practice related to performance enhancement in exercise and sport. These individuals are also interested in the effects of sport and exercise psychology interventions on athletes' and exercise participants' wellbeing, for example the influence of imagery on basketball free throw percentages or the role of positive feedback on cardiac rehabilitation patients' exercise adherence. Examples of topics covered in this book include self-talk, imagery and anxiety management.
- In the *social psychology focus area*, professionals are interested in the individual and group processes involved in sport and exercise settings. They also focus on the application of social psychological principles in examining factors related to the sport participant, coach, team and spectator. Examples of topics from the social psychology focus area covered in this book include group cohesion and leadership.

Summary

Sport and exercise psychologists are interested in two key questions:

1 How do psychological factors influence sport and exercise participation and performance?
2 What are the psychological effects of sport and exercise participation?

The three focus areas of the Association of Applied Sport Psychology include performance psychology, health and exercise psychology, and social psychology.

◉ Who uses sport and exercise psychology knowledge?

Sport and exercise psychologists use their knowledge of the discipline to perform three major roles in their professional lives: research, teaching and consulting. For sport and exercise psychology to be viewed as a credible applied scientific discipline, professionals need to conduct good quality research and develop a body of knowledge that people in the teaching and consulting roles can share with students and athletes (Anderson et al., 2002). For example, professionals have conducted many studies on the influence of imagery on motor skill learning and performance, and from these studies, theories describing why imagery can improve motor skill execution and guidelines for helping people make effective use of the technique have emerged (Murphy et al., 2008).

University lecturers, tutors at further education colleges and PE teachers are examples of individuals who perform the teaching role. In addition to helping people learn about sport and exercise psychology knowledge, teachers motivate and inspire individuals to become involved in the discipline and become the professionals of the future. For example, a PE teacher might design a class to help students learn about the influence of imagery on motor skill execution.

Many individuals involved in sport and exercise have specific issues and problems with which they need assistance, such as athletes who want help managing anxiety or fitness instructors who wish to help clients adhere to exercise programmes. Sport and exercise psychology professionals performing the consulting role provide assistance to help others with their issues and problems. For example, a sport and exercise psychologist might assist a beginning cricket player to use imagery to help learn the forward defensive shot.

Sport and exercise psychologists may play each of the three roles during the course of their professional lives. Being involved in one of the roles might help people when they undertake another role. For example, a person who conducts research on group cohesion in hockey may then have the knowledge to help teams in that sport play together better and develop camaraderie. As another example, people who consult with exercise participants might understand what types of research are worth doing.

There are other people who also use sport and exercise psychology knowledge to help them in different ways. Examples include coaches, fitness instructors, athletes, exercise participants, PE teachers, outdoor education leaders, leisure centre managers, and sports medicine specialists. People in local county councils, national government and privates businesses, who wish to encourage and help people exercise and play sport, will also have an interest in learning sport and exercise psychology knowledge.

Summary

Many different types of people use sport and exercise psychology knowledge for personal reasons or to help others. Sport and exercise psychologists use the knowledge to help them undertake research, teach students, and consult with clients.

The scientific underpinning of sport and exercise psychology

Sport and exercise psychology knowledge has been generated through scientific research. When thinking of **science**, people may have an image of white lab coats, chemistry experiments, Bunsen burners, and rats running mazes; however, sport and exercise psychologists conducting research seldom play with rats or Bunsen burners. They are more likely to ask people to fill in questionnaires or undertake some type of intervention or exercise programme. Science is a way of learning about the world, in this case, learning about how psychological processes operate in sport and exercise. The **scientific method** is a systematic process that allows sport and exercise psychologists to develop knowledge through controlled and rigorous observation, with the goals of describing, explaining, predicting and controlling behaviour in sport and exercise (Thomas et al., 2005).

One major aim among scientists is to develop a **theory**, or a systematic and related set of facts that explain a topic of interest. **Social Learning Theory** is an example that many people think helps explain athletes' and exercise participants' behaviour (e.g. Bandura, 1977a). According to the theory, people learn suitable and unsuitable behaviour through either reward and punishment or **modelling** (watching how other people act). If football players, for example, are praised by their coach for displaying sportsmanship during a game, they are likely to carry on acting in such a fashion. As another example, if children see their favourite cricket players verbally abusing opponents, they may start engaging in the same behaviour. Modelling is especially powerful if the people being watched are rewarded for their behaviour.

A good theory can be a powerful way of understanding behaviour. Human behaviour is complex and there are many factors that influence why we do what we do. For example, people's sporting performances are influenced by many variables including their skills, mood, anxiety, confidence and motivation. Performance might also be influenced by opponents, officials, spectators, equipment, the weather, and the game or event's importance. A good theory can help sport and exercise psychologists understand, predict and manage behaviour. For example, by drawing on Social Learning Theory, a sport and exercise psychologist might assist a tennis coach to teach players to engage in fair play and treat opponents with respect. Below is an example of how useful a good theory can be, in this case, Locke and Latham's (2002) Goal-setting Theory.

Thinking scientifically → **making use of a good theory**

Christina was a junior Olympic weightlifter who wanted to prepare for a competition she had in three months' time. To make the most of her preparation, she asked Simon, a sport and exercise psychologist, to help her to use goal setting. Simon knew that effective consultants base their work on sound research and theory. He drew on Locke and Latham's (2002) Goal-setting Theory to help him with Christina. According to the theory, specific difficult goals are more effective than vague easy ones. Simon talked with Christina and her coach to help them identify specific measurable goals, such as the amount of weight she would lift during training and competition. Together, Simon, Christina and her coach also established difficult goals that would challenge her each training session and at the competition. Even though the goals were difficult, Simon made sure Christina was confident, because Goal-setting Theory states that self-confidence increases people's commitment to their targets and increases the likelihood they will achieve them. Also, for goals to be most effective, people need feedback about their progress. One form of feedback available to Christina was the amount of weight on the bar, and Simon had Christina keep a diary to record how she got on at each training session. Over time, Christina could see her progress and readjust her goals to keep them difficult but realistic. Simon also asked the coach to give Christina feedback each training session about her lifting technique so she knew if she was performing the skills most efficiently. By drawing on Goal-setting Theory to guide his work, Simon was able to help Christina make effective use of goal setting.

Typically, when conducting research, sport and exercise psychologists follow a four-step process, known as the scientific method (Thomas et al., 2005). The four-step process is illustrated in Figure 1.1, and goes something like this:

- In *step 1*, to develop the question, researchers identify the variables or factors they want to observe. For example, if interested in the influence of exercise on body image in males, investigators will specify the type of exercise they are examining, such as the influence of weight training, and they will select a body image measure. The typical way to measure body image is through questionnaires, but other methods are available, such as interviews.
- The **hypotheses** formed in *step 2* are researchers' expected results. Probably, in the above example, the researchers anticipate that weight training will increase the males' body image. Questions and hypotheses are generally framed within the current research and doing so helps ensure a study extends knowledge. For example, the investigators may have read the existing research and found that no one has examined whether weight training improves secondary school male students' body image. The researchers might then decide to use secondary school male students as participants.
- Before researchers start collecting data (*step 3*), they need to develop a good quality study. With respect to the current example, the researchers might measure body image in a large group of male students, and then randomly place them into either a weight-training group or a control group that does not exercise. The researchers will probably measure body image again after the weight-training intervention. Any changes in body image can then be assessed. If results show the weight trainers' body image improved, whereas the control participants' body image did not change (see step 4), and the only difference between the two groups was whether they engaged in weight training or not, then the researchers can conclude that weight training improves body image in secondary school male students.
- In *step 4*, the researchers will probably use a statistical test to analyse the results and answer the question: did weight training influence body image? Then the investigators will try to interpret the results by suggesting an explanation. If the students' body image improved, the researchers might suggest that body image

improved because weight training increased their muscle size and they looked more muscular and athletic – a body shape portrayed in the media as being the ideal for males. After completing the study, the researchers will tell other sport and exercise psychologists about it, so they can use it when working with clients or help them decide if more research needs to be conducted.

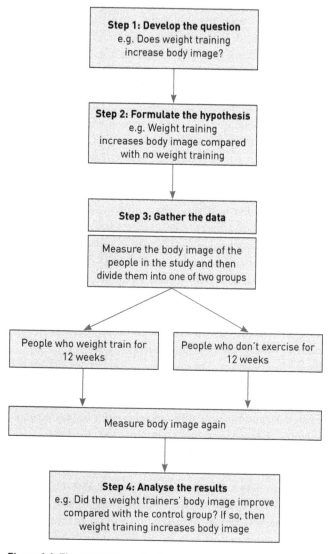

Step 1: Develop the question
e.g. Does weight training increase body image?

Step 2: Formulate the hypothesis
e.g. Weight training increases body image compared with no weight training

Step 3: Gather the data

Measure the body image of the people in the study and then divide them into one of two groups

People who weight train for 12 weeks

People who don't exercise for 12 weeks

Measure body image again

Step 4: Analyse the results
e.g. Did the weight trainers' body image improve compared with the control group? If so, then weight training increases body image

Figure 1.1 The scientific method

It might seem strange to briefly describe science and the scientific method in a textbook on sport and exercise psychology. The brief discussion, however, illustrates that knowledge in the discipline has developed through a logical and systematic process involving careful thought and has been reviewed by experts in the field. There are many people in the sport and fitness industries making a lot of weird and wonderful claims about the psychological aspects of sport and exercise; for example articles in fitness magazines often claim that exercise improves appearance, confidence and sexual attractiveness. It can be difficult for athletes, coaches, fitness leaders and exercise participants to decide which claims are accurate and which deserve to be rejected. Knowing that sport and exercise psychologists base their work on scientific research can give these people confidence that they are learning worthwhile information and strategies.

Summary

Responsible sport and exercise psychologists base their work on scientific knowledge. Science is a way of learning about a topic of interest in a systematic and logical way and the scientific method is based on four steps: identifying a question; developing a hypothesis; collecting data; and analysing and interpreting the results. When sport and exercise psychologists base their work on scientific knowledge, their clients can be confident they are learning useful information.

◉ Using sport and exercise psychology knowledge

Although it can be challenging to apply scientific knowledge about the psychological processes involved in sport and exercise to specific situations, it can be achieved, and, ideally, it forms the basis of practitioners' professional behaviours. Such application can be realized through reflection and active experimentation (Anderson et al., 2004). For example, a netball coach who wishes to encourage her players to undertake extra training outside team sessions might read the information on motivation in this book. After reflecting on the content, she might identify ways to encourage players to undertake extra training. The coach will then try out her ideas and will keep a record of those players who do, and do not, undertake extra training. After a period of time, the coach will evaluate how successful her attempts have been and decide whether to continue or change her approach. It is unlikely that every strategy the coach uses will work well and she will probably benefit from being flexible and willing to change strategies so they better suit the players. With reflection and experimentation, it is likely that she will eventually identify strategies that encourage players to undertake extra training.

Summary

To make the most of reading this book, you might think about your own sport and exercise participation and identify a topic covered in one of the chapters that could help you with a challenge or an issue. With reflection, active experimentation and evaluation, you might find a way to improve your performance or have more fun.

Conclusion

Compared with other sciences, like physics, psychology and physiology, sport and exercise psychology is still relatively new, having established itself in only the last 40 years (Williams and Straub, 2010). Among the different sport and exercise sciences, however, it is often popular with students because most people have some familiarity and experience with topics like confidence, motivation and group cohesion. Sport and exercise psychology is the study of people and their behaviours. Sport and exercise psychologists are interested in people's behaviours, thoughts and feelings. Many other people, such as coaches, fitness instructors and PE teachers are interested in sport and excise psychology as well, because helping individuals understand and manage their thoughts, feelings and behaviours may allow them to improve their performance and have more enriching experiences when playing and participating in sport and physical activity.

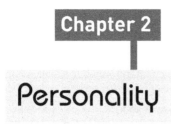

Chapter 2

Personality

When sport and exercise psychology was becoming an established academic discipline during the 1960s and 70s, personality was a popular research topic. Sport and exercise psychologists were interested in seeing if differences in personality, such as extraversion, could predict sporting behaviour and performance. More than 1,000 studies were published during this time period (Fisher, 1984). In more recent years, interest in personality has waned, because few consistent or useful conclusions have emerged (Vealey, 2002). Understanding personality, however, is useful for people involved in sport and exercise, including exercise leaders and coaches. Learning about people's personalities, and getting to know them as individuals, helps coaches and exercise leaders do their jobs more effectively because they can tailor their services to athletes' and clients' needs and preferences. For example, if an athletics coach knows her runners respond to encouragement, she can ensure she gives them positive feedback.

In this chapter, we will examine:
- Definitions of personality and related ideas, such as traits and states
- Different approaches to studying personality
- How personality is measured
- The relationship different personality dimensions have with sport performance and behaviour

What is personality?

When students are asked to list words they think of when they hear the term **personality**, they typically write 'characteristics', 'individual', 'different' and 'unique'. Then if you ask the students to define personality, using only the words on their lists, their descriptions normally include two ideas:

- personality consists of the characteristics that make people who they are
- each individual's personality is unique.

This exercise illustrates that most people have some understanding of what personality is about. Personality refers to the collection of an individual's characteristics, or thoughts, feelings and behaviours, that make them different from others (Carducci, 2009; Vealey, 2002). When thinking about personality, people often focus on social characteristics, such as introversion or extraversion. Personality also includes perceptual, cognitive and behavioural characteristics (Gill and Williams, 2008).

Regarding structure, personality may be separated into three levels: psychological core, typical responses and role-related behaviour (Hollander, 1971):

1   The **psychological core** is the most internal, deepest and stable level, and includes our beliefs, attitudes, motivations, needs and values.
2   **Typical responses** refers to the way people usually respond to others, events and situations they encounter; for example a typical response in many Western countries is to shake hands when people meet each other.
3   The **role-related behaviour** dimension is the most changeable aspect of personality and refers to the ways individuals behave based on their perceptions of their social environments.

As folks live their daily lives, their social environments change and they take on different roles. For example, individuals reading this chapter in a classroom might be acting the role of student. After school, they might then play the role of athlete as they participate in a sport. Once they go home, they might be a son, daughter, brother, sister or friend, depending on the people with whom they interact. They may play multiple roles at the same time. To play each role successfully, people need to change their behaviour. For example, people may need to demonstrate leadership behaviour to be a good sports captain, but when playing the role of student, they may display less leadership behaviours.

Summary

Personality is the blend of characteristics (thoughts, feelings and behaviours) that make individuals unique. One approach to personality suggests there are three levels including psychological core, typical responses, and role-related behaviour.

◉ Personality theories

Several different theories have been used to study personality in sport and exercise. One central aim of these approaches has been to identify the causes of athletes' and exercise participants' behaviours. These approaches can be identified as being person, environment, or interaction focused (Vealey, 2002). According to person-focused approaches, people's dispositional characteristics cause their behaviour. In environment-focused approaches, situational factors influence behaviour. According to interactional approaches, people's characteristics, the environment and the interaction between the two best predict behaviour. In the following sections, five of the common theories used to understand personality in sport and exercise are presented.

Person-focused theories

Psychodynamic theories

Central to psychodynamic theories is the idea that the interactions and conflicts among conscious and unconscious mental processes (such as motivations and needs) determine behaviours and personalities (Hewstone et al., 2005), and these approaches originated with Sigmund Freud. According to Freud (1916/1973), people's personalities are made up of the id, the ego and the superego:

- The **id** is the source of mental energy and has two drives: Eros, or the drive for life, love and sex, and Thantos, the drive for death and aggression. The id seeks to satisfy people's urges and drives for pleasure.
- The **ego** represents individuals' rational thinking aspects and tries to delay the id's attempts to satisfy urges until suitable occasions.
- The **superego** represents internalized moral standards learned from parents and society.

The ego mediates the id's and superego's interactions. The conflicts among these three personality structures results in anxiety. If unable to deal with anxiety consciously, people engage in unconscious defence mechanisms, in which they deny, change or falsify reality. According to Freud, personalities are shaped during childhood through the way people deal with developmental challenges. The Oedipus complex or challenge, for example, involves males (typically aged three to five years) becoming attracted to their mothers and resentful of their fathers. These boys then experience anxiety or fear that their fathers will punish them.

Most sport and exercise psychologists ignore psychodynamic approaches, because they are often difficult theories to test and do not give enough emphasis to the environment's influence on behaviour (Hewstone et al., 2005). Some sport and exercise psychologists, however, acknowledge the contributions of psychodynamic theories, such as the recognition that athletes are not always aware of why they behave the way they do and the role of unconscious needs and motivations (Hill, 2001).

Trait theories

Traits refer to consistent and enduring aspects of personality or behaviour (Hewstone et al., 2005). For example, trait anxiety refers to individuals' tendencies to see non-dangerous events as threatening and to respond with high levels of anxiety. Traits exist on a continuum. Each person, for example, has some level of trait anxiety ranging from low to high. Although traits are relatively enduring ways of behaving, **states** refer to right-now feelings, thoughts and behaviours that may change quickly as the environment changes.

There are numerous trait theories. Hans Eysenck (1988), for example, developed a well-known Trait Theory and his questionnaire, the Eysenck Personality Questionnaire (EPQ), has been used in sport. Eysenck's theory consisted of three personality dimensions: extraversion-introversion, neuroticism-stability, and psychoticism-superego. As you can see in Figure 2.1, Eysenck used the extraversion-introversion and neuroticism-stability dimensions to group various traits together into four personality types: **melancholic, choleric, phlegmatic** and **sanguine**. From Figure 2.1, it is possible to see the types of personality traits associated with extraversion, **introversion**, neuroticism and **stability**. **Psychoticism** is associated with being egocentric, aggressive, impersonal, cold, lacking empathy, impulsive and lacking in concern for others, whereas superego is related to the opposite of these traits.

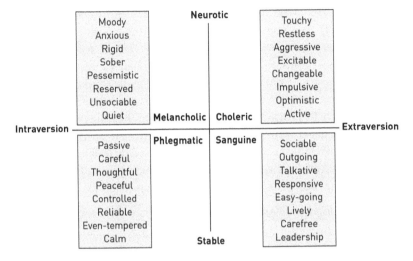

Figure 2.1 Eysenck's (1988) Trait Theory

More recently, the Five Factor Model has gained acceptance among many psychologists and consists of five dimensions thought to represent personality, under which sets of similar traits are grouped (Costa and McCrae, 1992):

- **Neuroticism** represents the tendency to experience psychological distress
- **Extraversion** includes the tendency to be sociable and experience positive emotions
- **Openness to experience** refers to an appreciation for the arts, emotions, adventures, unusual ideas, imagination, curiosity and various experiences
- **Agreeableness** describes the degree to which people are cooperative and compassionate towards others
- **Conscientiousness** refers to the tendency to be organized, diligent and scrupulous.

As will be discussed below, many sport and exercise psychologists consider that the trait approach has been of limited help to understanding and predicting behaviour in sport.

Environment-focused theories
Learning theories

Learning theories argue that the environment influences behaviour. B.F. Skinner (1978) was one well-known learning theory proponent, who believed it was not necessary to refer to internal factors, such as unconscious motives or traits, to understand behaviour. Instead, people's behaviour was the result of reward and punishment. People would more likely engage in behaviours for which they had been rewarded previously, and avoid those acts for which they had been punished. Learning theory helps people to influence behaviour in sport and exercise, such as coaches wishing to teach athletes to train with intensity and direction. Most sport and exercise psychologists, however, do not think learning approaches help understand the relationship between personality and sport (Vealey, 2002).

Social learning theories

According to social learning approaches, people behave according to how they have learned to respond to other people and events around them. According to Bandura (1977a), for example, there are two mechanisms by which people learn: modelling and direct reinforcement. For example, if college cricketers observe international players verbally abusing (or sledging) their opposition, they may begin to sledge their own opponents. If the college players find their opponents intimidated, or if they get positive feedback from coaches and teammates, then they may continue sledging. Through modelling and social reinforcement the college cricketers have learned a new behaviour.

Interactional-focused approaches

Most sport and exercise psychologists do not think that personal or situational factors alone best predict behaviour. Instead they believe that behaviour is best understood by considering personal factors, situational factors and the interactions between the two (Vealey, 2002). One central feature of interactional approaches involves understanding how individuals perceive themselves and their environments (Vealey, 2002). According to interactional approaches, personality dimensions, such as confidence, or environmental factors, such as coaching style, are insufficient to predict behaviour; it also helps to assess athletes' interpretations and perceptions of these variables. Interactional approaches have become popular among sport and exercise psychologists and many of the topics in this book are based on the interactional perspective.

Summary

Researchers have drawn on several different theories to study personality and behaviour in sport and exercise. These approaches can be identified as person, environment, or interaction focused. Currently, most sport and exercise psychologists argue that understanding personal factors, environmental factors and the interactions between the two results in the best understanding of personality, or individuals' behaviour, thoughts and feelings in sport and exercise.

◉ Measuring personality

Typically, there are three reasons psychologists may wish to measure aspects of personality (Carducci, 2009):

1 Personality measures help them to gain meaningful knowledge about people, such as their tendency to get anxious before competition.
2 Personality measures help to collect information in ways that allow them to communicate knowledge about an individual's personality to others.
3 Personality measures may help sport and exercise psychologists predict behaviour.

Knowing that an athlete tends to get anxious before competition, for example, may lead to predictions about how the individual will behave prior to an important event. The following paragraphs present the major ways sport and exercise psychologists attempt to measure personality.

Standardized questionnaires

The use of standardized questionnaires is the most common way sport and exercise psychologists measure personality dimensions. These measures consist of questions, presented in the same way to people, to which they respond in the same manner, often through the use of a Likert scale, as illustrated in Figure 2.2. Psychologists believe that if the questions and ways of responding are standardized, then differences between individuals represent aspects of their personality (Carducci, 2009). An example of a standardized questionnaire used in sport and exercise psychology research is the 16 Personality Factor Inventory (16PF; Cattell and Cattell, 1995). The 16PF assesses 16 traits that can be grouped under five global factors, including extraversion, anxiety, tough-mindedness, independence and self-control.

Although general questionnaires provide useful information about personality, some psychologists argue that sport-specific inventories predict athletes' and exercise participants' behaviour better because they consider both the person and the specific contextual factors associated with sport (Weinberg and Gould, 2007). There are many sport-specific standardized questionnaires available to measure any number of personality dimensions. One example is The Sport Psychology Attitudes – Revised Form (SPA-RF) questionnaire, shown in Figure 2.2 (Martin et al., 2001). The SPA-RF assesses individuals' attitudes towards sport psychology consulting. Sport and exercise psychologists might use the SPA-RF if they are interested in predicting which athletes and exercise participants are most open and receptive to receiving help with their psychological issues.

There are advantages and disadvantages to using standardized questionnaires (Carducci, 2009). Standardized questionnaires are easy to administer and score. Also, everybody is treated the same way. Standardization reduces administrator subjective bias when scoring, which helps increase reliability. Standardized questionnaires, however, rely on testtakers to respond honestly. Athletes may not want to answer honestly if they think their coaches might see the results. Also, athletes may not always have sufficient self-knowledge to describe themselves accurately, and they may not have an opportunity to clarify their answers.

Please indicate your level of agreement with each of the following statements by circling the response on the answer sheet that corresponds to your feelings toward each statement. Please respond to each statement as truthfully as you can.

SD	D	MD	N	MA	A	SA
1	2	3	4	5	6	7
Strongly disagree	Disagree	Moderately disagree	Neutral	Moderately agree	Agree	Strongly agree

Question	SD	D	MD	N	MA	A	SA
1. A sport psychology consultant can help athletes improve their mental toughness.	1	2	3	4	5	6	7
2. I respect the opinions of people of my own race more so than those of people of another race.	1	2	3	4	5	6	7
3. I would go to my coach instead of going to a sport psychology consultant.	1	2	3	4	5	6	7

Question	1	2	3	4	5	6	7
4. If a teammate asked my advice about personal feelings of failure related to sport, I might recommend that he/she see a sport psychology consultant.	1	2	3	4	5	6	7
5. I would not go to a sport psychology consultant because my teammates would harass me.	1	2	3	4	5	6	7
6. There are certain problems that should not be discussed outside one's immediate family.	1	2	3	4	5	6	7
7. The people that I associate most with on my team are of the same race as me.	1	2	3	4	5	6	7
8. I would go to a sport psychology consultant if one of my teammates were going to one, too.	1	2	3	4	5	6	7
9. A good idea for avoiding personal worries and concerns is to keep one's mind on a job.	1	2	3	4	5	6	7
10. To help me better understand myself as an athlete, I would like the assistance of a sport psychology consultant.	1	2	3	4	5	6	7
11. I would feel uneasy going to a sport psychology consultant because some people would disapprove.	1	2	3	4	5	6	7
12. I resent anybody who wants to know about my personal difficulties.	1	2	3	4	5	6	7
13. There is something respectable in the attitude of athletes who are willing to cope with their conflicts and fears without resorting to professional help.	1	2	3	4	5	6	7
14. There are great differences between people of different races.	1	2	3	4	5	6	7
15. An athlete with emotional problems during sport performances would feel most secure in receiving assistance from a sport psychology consultant.	1	2	3	4	5	6	7
16. Having seen a sport psychology consultant is bad for an athlete's reputation.	1	2	3	4	5	6	7
17. There are experiences in my life that I would not discuss with anyone.	1	2	3	4	5	6	7
18. If I was worried or upset about my sport performance, I would want to get help from a sport psychology consultant.	1	2	3	4	5	6	7
19. Emotional difficulties tend to work themselves out in time.	1	2	3	4	5	6	7
20. I think a sport psychology consultant would help me perform better under pressure.	1	2	3	4	5	6	7

21. I would not want someone to know about me receiving help from a sport psychology consultant.	1	2	3	4	5	6	7
22. If I went to a sport psychology consultant, I would not want my coach to know about it.	1	2	3	4	5	6	7
23. A sport psychology consultant could help me fine-tune my sport performance.	1	2	3	4	5	6	7
24. If I went to a sport psychology consultant, I would not want my teammates to know about it.	1	2	3	4	5	6	7
25. At times I have felt lost and would have welcomed professional advice for a personal or emotional problem.	1	2	3	4	5	6	7
26. I would have more confidence in a sport psychology consultant if he/she had experience in my sport at a similar competitive level.	1	2	3	4	5	6	7
27. The coach would think less of me if I went to a sport psychology consultant.	1	2	3	4	5	6	7
28. Athletes with a strong character can get over mental conflicts by themselves.	1	2	3	4	5	6	7
29. I would be more comfortable with a sport psychology consultant if he/she were the same race as me.	1	2	3	4	5	6	7

Scoring the Attitudes Toward Seeking Sport Psychology Consultation Questionnaire

Scale scores on the instrument are calculated by summing the responses to the items assigned to each of the four scales and dividing by the number of items. For example, the scale score for 'Stigma Tolerance' can be obtained by summing the responses to items 5, 11, 12, 16, 21, 22, 24, and 27 and dividing by 8.

Four Subscales

Stigma Tolerance:	5, 11, 12, 16, 21, 22, 24, 27	Total Score/8 =
Confidence in Sport Psychology Consultation:	1, 4, 8, 10, 15, 18, 20, 23, 25	Total Score/9 =
Personal Openness:	3, 6, 9, 13, 17, 19, 26, 28	Total Score/8 =
Cultural Preference:	2, 7, 14, 29	Total Score/4 =

Figure 2.2 The Sport Psychology Attitudes – Revised Form questionnaire
Source: Martin et al., 2001

Projective tests

During projective tests, individuals respond to ambiguous stimuli. Psychologists assume that people's responses reveal aspects of their personality including their unconscious material and conflicts (Carducci, 2009). For example, the Thematic Apperception Test (Murray, 1943) consists of a series of cards containing black-and-white illustrations of a person or individuals in ambiguous situations. A blank card also exists. During the test, individuals are presented with each card and asked to create a story about what is happening in the picture. Projective tests are not used commonly in sport and exercise psychology research.

The advantages and disadvantages of projective tests relate to their ambiguity and the freedom individuals have when creating stories (Carducci, 2009). One advantage is the freedom individuals have when responding. It is also difficult for individuals to disguise their responses based on what they believe the test is trying to measure. In addition, psychologists assume that projective tests provide a global and meaningful personality assessment. Responses, however, are difficult to score. Also, results may be influenced by scorers' subjective decisions and biases. It is not always clear what aspects of personality are being assessed.

Behavioural observation

Behaviour observation involves the systematic recording and rating of individuals' behaviours. Psychologists may also record details about the environment (e.g. coach behaviours), the thoughts and feelings of the athletes being watched (e.g. their interpretations of the environment), and the consequences of their actions (e.g. whether they learn new skills) to help understand their behaviours (Carducci, 2009). The Coaching Behaviour Assessment System (CABS; Smith et al., 1977) is an example of a behaviour observation method used in sport, and was designed to guide observations of coaches' behaviours during training and competitions. The behaviours recorded include those that occur in response to athletes' actions, such as how coaches respond to good performances, mistakes and misbehaviour. Scorers also record coaches' spontaneous behaviours relevant to and irrelevant to the training or competition. The CABS has been applied to many sports and has been found to identify different patterns of behaviour among coaches.

Like the other forms of personality assessment, there are advantages and disadvantages to using behavioural observation techniques (Carducci,

2009). Behaviour observation helps to clarify the environmental and personal influences involved in personality and people's actions. Behavioural observation systems also tend to be flexible and easily adapted to different situations. One disadvantage, however, is the ambiguity involved in deciding which behaviours and situational cues are related to the personality dimension being measured. Also, the knowledge that one is being observed may influence people and lead to changes in how they normally behave.

Psychophysiological measures

The assumption underlying psychophysiological measurement techniques is that personality dimensions are related to bodily functions (Carducci, 2009). In recent years, for example, sport and exercise psychologists have become interested in measuring physiological variables, such as hormones and chemicals in the brain, to help them determine if and why physical activity has an influence on mental health (Landers and Arent, 2007).

There are many psychophysiological measures and they can often be used at the same time as other techniques; for example heart rate might be measured as a person is responding to a Thematic Apperception Test card (Carducci, 2009). One limitation, however, is the difficulty in knowing what aspects of personality are related to which bodily response. There is also much variation in the way individuals' bodily functions respond to similar stimuli. These functions change quickly and the reasons are not always clear.

Summary

The various measurement techniques have advantages and disadvantages and are often linked with specific personality theories, for example projective tests are typically associated with psychodynamic approaches. Decisions about which techniques to use are influenced by the personality dimensions psychologists are interested in and the purpose for undertaking the measurement. Generally, however, sport and exercise psychologists have used standardized questionnaires most often. One topic in which sport and exercise psychologists have been interested in studying has been determining if personality factors are related to sporting performance.

👁 Personality and sports performance

Examining the relationship between personality and sports performance is difficult for several reasons. One reason is because there are many different types of sports. Potentially, different personalities suit different sports. A second reason is because personality is broad and consists of various dimensions, and only some characteristics may have relationships with sports performance. Nevertheless, sport and exercise psychologists have conducted a lot of research on the relationship between personality and sports performance, so much so that it is difficult to review the work in its entirety. Instead, the following sections focus on three personality aspects: traits, mood states, and cognitive strategies.

Personality traits

Sport and exercise psychologists have focused on three areas when examining the relationship between traits and performance (Vealey, 2002):

1 They have tried to identify the traits associated with specific groups of athletes, for example the differences between those who play individual or team sports. They have also tried to find differences between athletes and non-athletes.
2 They have tried to assess if traits predict successful performance, such as who will be selected for an Olympic team.
3 They have investigated if participating in sport can lead to changes in personality traits.

Studies focused on personality traits were popular during the 1960s and 70s when researchers often used measures such as the EPQ and 16PF discussed above. In reviewing the research from this time, Morgan (1980) suggested that sport and exercise psychologists could be divided into two camps: those who believed traits could predict performance, and those who thought traits were of little value in predicting performance.

Adherents to either camp can still be identified today. For example, Vealey (2002: 69) concluded that 'no consistent trait personality differences between athletic subgroups have been shown to exist (athletes vs. nonathletes, athletes of one sport type vs. athletes of another sport type, athletes of different abilities or success levels)'. In contrast, Cox (2007) suggested that 'athletes differ from nonathletes in many personality traits' (p. 33), 'differences exist in the personalities of athletes who engage in different sports' (p. 34) and that elite athletes 'differ as a group from less-skilled groups' (p. 37). One reason why sport and exercise psychologists have reached differing conclusions may be because there have been limitations with much of the research, such as the use of unsuitable questionnaires (Vealey, 2002).

There is more agreement among sport and exercise psychologists that personality trait measures are not generally successful enough in predicting behaviour and should not be used to select players for teams, even among those who believe that traits are related to sporting behaviour and performance in some way. In 1980, Morgan suggested that, on their own, traits were of limited value in describing, explaining and predicting behaviour. Instead, he argued a better understanding would emerge when various personality dimensions were measured, such as traits, states and cognitive strategies, along with physiological variables.

Personality mood states

Like traits, much research has examined the relationship between **mood states** and performance. Most research has used the Profile of Mood States (POMS), a questionnaire that measures anger, depression, confusion, fatigue, tension and vigour (Lane, 2007). Based on research during the 1970s, Morgan (1980) proposed that successful sport performance was associated with the 'iceberg profile', so named because of the shape of the graph when successful athletes' scores were compared with those of unsuccessful athletes or the general population (Figure 2.3). When scores from the POMS are transformed so that the averages from a sample of people from the general population equal 50, then successful athletes score lower on anger, confusion, depression, fatigue and tension, but higher on vigour. Morgan also called his iceberg profile the Mental Health Model.

Since Morgan's (1980) proposal, researchers have continued to use the POMS to examine the relationship between mood states and sporting success and it has been a popular area of inquiry. Beedie et al. (2000) reviewed the research to determine if mood states differed between athletes of different ability levels (e.g. novice and elite), and predicted performance. Their results showed that the moods measured by the POMS are not related to ability levels. Athletes of different levels reported similar mood profiles. Results, however, showed that when measured before a competitive event, mood states were somewhat related with performance. Specifically, better performance was associated with vigour, while poorer performance was related to confusion, fatigue and depression. Anger and tension was sometimes associated with better, and sometimes with worse, performance. The relationships were not strong, however, indicating that many other variables influence performance. Also, just because there is a relationship does not imply that positive pre-event mood causes good performance, only that the two variables are related. Similar to the use of trait questionnaires, the POMS questionnaire is not able to predict performance accurately enough to justify using it for athlete selection.

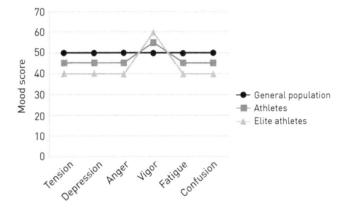

Figure 2.3 Morgan's (1980) iceberg profile

Cognitive strategies

Cognitive strategies refer to the skills and behaviours that athletes use when competing. They are not personality traits or states, but reflect the behavioural components of personality (Weinberg and Gould, 2007). With respect to the three personality levels discussed earlier, cognitive strategies may be placed in the role-related behaviour dimension rather than the psychological core. There has been much research undertaken to examine the cognitive strategies successful athletes use in comparison with their less skilled counterparts.

A number of questionnaires have been developed to measure a variety of cognitive strategies (Krane and Williams, 2010). One example is the Test of Performance Strategies (TOPS; Thomas et al., 1999). The TOPS assesses the frequency athletes use a range of cognitive strategies in training and competition, including goal setting, relaxation, activation, imagery, self-talk, attentional control, negative thinking, emotional control and automaticity. Using the TOPS, Thomas et al. found that older athletes reported less use of imagery and activation strategies, but more automaticity than younger counterparts. Males used less imagery but more automaticity than females. Both male and female international athletes generally used a wider range of psychological strategies than those at lower levels.

It seems possible that athletes might enhance their performances and have more positive sporting experiences by engaging in a number of cognitive strategies, and some of these are presented in Table 2.1 (Krane and Williams, 2010). Based on the research examining cognitive strategies and sport behaviour and performance, some sport and exercise psychologists have developed psychological skills training programmes to teach athletes how to use cognitive strategies like those mentioned in Table 2.1. Evidence is accumulating that athletes find these training programmes helpful, that they are able to better control psychological states, such as anxiety and concentration, and that they experience improved motor skill execution or performance (Weinberg and Williams, 2010).

Goal setting	Self-talk or thought control
Imagery	Arousal regulation
Competition plans	Attention control
Refocusing plans	Refocusing skills
Competition simulation during training	

Table 2.1 Some cognitive strategies used by elite and successful athletes
Source: Krane and Williams, 2010

Summary

To determine if personality is related to sports performance, it is helpful to consider specific dimensions, such as traits, states and cognitive strategies. Although sport and exercise psychologists vary over whether traits have a relationship with performance, most professionals agree that our ability to identify and measure specific characteristics is not sufficient to make accurate predictions about which athletes will be successful. Also, although mood states seem to have a relationship with performance, it is clear that so do many other variables. Some research has suggested that successful athletes use cognitive strategies. There is some evidence that teaching people these cognitive strategies may influence their motor skill execution.

◉ Conclusions

Many people involved in sport believe that certain personality character-istics contribute to success. For example, some individuals believe that being aggressive helps athletes who participate in contact sports. Other people believe that athletes need to be mentally tough to succeed. The research has not generally found substantial evidence to support people's beliefs, and one reason is because personality is a broad concept that encompasses many of the topics discussed in the following chapters. People and their personalities are complex and made up of many different dimensions. Some of these dimensions may contribute to sport and exercise behaviour and performance, whereas others may not. Rather than focus on a broad topic such as personality, greater understanding of sport and exercise behaviour might result from examining specific dimensions such as confidence, anxiety and motivation. These more specific topics are discussed in the following chapters.

◉ Further reading

Lox, C.L., Martin Ginis, K.A. and Petruzzello, S.J. (2006). *The psychology of exercise: Integrating theory and practice* (2nd edn). Scottsdale, AZ: Holcomb Hathaway.

Vealey, R.S. (2002). Personality and sport behaviour. In T.S. Horn (ed.) *Advances in sport psychology* (2nd edn, pp. 43–82). Champaign, IL: Human Kinetics.

Weinberg, R.S. and Gould, D. (2007). *Foundations of sport and exercise psychology* (4th edn). Champaign, IL: Human Kinetics.

◉ Key search terms

Sports performance, cognitive strategies, Eysenck Personality Question-naire (EPQ), 16 Personality Factor Inventory (16PF), mind tools, performance enhancement

Chapter 3

Motivation

The concept of motivation has been defined as: 'The hypothetical construct used to describe the internal and or external forces that produce the initiation, direction, intensity, and persistence of behaviour' (Vallerand and Thill, 1993: 18, translated by the authors). For those of you who participate in sport, the exhilaration felt when your team wins a game or when you have beaten your 'personal best' is indescribable. Not everything about sport, however, is this enjoyable. A lot of hard work and practice is usually behind this success, most of which is not as much fun as the game itself, and matches and training have to continue in various kinds of miserable weather. So what drives us to keep participating? The motivation of athletes to train hard and participate in their given activity is of much interest to sport and exercise psychology researchers. Understanding what drives athletes to perform can provide us with valuable insights about how to improve performance and how coaches can train athletes in ways that tap into their motivation effectively.

In this chapter, we will examine:
- How achievement motivation has contributed to our understanding of motivation through striving for success in sport and competition
- How different motivational orientations influence our task preference, performance and behavioural attributes
- How experiencing different types of motivation can influence behavioural and cognitive outcomes
- How we can manipulate the environment to increase an individual's motivation

◉ Achievement motivation

Achievement motivation is based around the premise that people are generally motivated to achieve success, improve performance, master tasks and be good at desired behaviours. Given that achievement or success within a sporting context is often measured in terms of performance against opponents, the need for achievement is often considered in relation to competitiveness in this setting. Theories in this area focus on individuals' personality traits, which predispose them towards being driven in the need for achievement, as well as how the environment or specific situations influence people's drive for success. Some leading theories in this area will be discussed in the following sections.

Need for Achievement Theory

The Need for Achievement Theory (Figure 3.1) was one of the first models of motivation proposed (Atkinson, 1974; McClelland 1961; McClelland et al., 1953). The basic concept behind this theory is that we each have an inherent desire to achieve success and avoid failure. Whether or not we are motivated to engage in an activity is a balance between our desire to succeed and how likely we think it is that we will fail in our attempt. In a sense:

performance = motivation to achieve success – fear of failure

The theory, however, is specifically focused on describing the different cognitive processes experienced by high and low achievers. The theory comprises five factors which contribute to the likelihood of engaging in achievement behaviour; personality factors, situational factors, resultant tendencies, emotional reactions, and achievement behaviour:

- *Personality factors* relate to the concept discussed above; each of us has the desire to achieve success and avoid failure. The important concept of this factor is whether we are people who strive for success (for the pride and satisfaction) or whether our motive is to avoid failure (to avoid shame and negative feelings). According to the theory, people who are high achievers are more driven by the motive of success, whereas low achievers are more motivated to avoid failure. It may help to think of this in terms of the fact that people who have already achieved success are more likely to want to feel the sense of pride again and strive for more success. On the other hand, low achievers have already experienced the shame of not achieving and as a result are driven to avoid feeling this again in the future.

- *Situational factors* refer to how likely it is that we can achieve success within a particular situation, and this comprises two factors; the probability of success and the incentive value of success:
  - The *probability of success* refers to the likelihood of achieving success in the given situation. For example, this might be influenced by the opponent, how much training has been done, or the weather.
  - The *incentive value of success* relates to how much value is placed on success in the given situation. For example, the probability of success when playing a strong opponent may be low; however, a win against that opponent is of greater value than if success is achieved against a weaker opponent. Relating this back to high and low achievers, the motives of high achievers are to strive for success, and they are likely to be motivated more by situations where they have a realistic opportunity for success. They will, however, also want a degree of value from that success in order to experience those feelings of pride. There is little pride in beating a weak opponent and high achievers are more likely to be motivated to succeed in situations with a moderate probability of success which holds a degree of challenge (e.g. a challenging, but not unbeatable opponent) and, as a result, provides a high degree of value if achieved. The low achiever, on the other hand, is motivated by fear of failure. Their main focus will be to avoid the shame of losing. For this reason, they are most likely to be motivated in situations with a high probability of success, regardless of the value this provides. Situations avoiding risk (high probability of success but low value) against a weaker opponent are their preferred situations. Alternatively, low achievers might also seek out highly unrealistic challenges with a very low probability of success. Although this seems peculiar, it becomes clear when you concentrate on the low achiever's avoidance of shame. There is little shame attached to losing to a much more successful athlete in comparison with an athlete of closer ability to yourself.
- These examples show how both personality and situational factors combine to demonstrate how the person is likely to approach the situation. These are known as *resultant tendencies*. As we said, high achievers will favour situations with a degree of challenge,

whereas low achievers will seek out situations which are easily achieved or incredibly difficult, which no one has any expectancy of them achieving.

- *Emotional reactions* describe the person's emotional focus in relation to success and failure. Does the athlete focus on the pride associated with success or the shame associated with failure? For example, when facing an equally matched opponent, does the athlete mainly consider the pride they would feel should they beat their opponent (focused on achieving success) or are they generally more concerned about the embarrassment that would follow should they lose (focus on avoiding failure)? Based on our discussion, it may come as no surprise that high achievers tend to focus more on achieving success, while low achievers tend to focus on avoiding failure.

- *Achievement behaviour*, the final component of the theory, draws on all the other concepts and relates to the types of behaviour that can be expected of high and low achievers, based on the four previous factors. High achievers are more likely to seek out challenging situations and focus on improving their own performance. For example, if a person has high motives for success and low motives for fear of failure (personality), their achievement behaviour will mean that they will choose to play an opponent who they are equally matched against (moderate probability of success). If they win, this will provide them with a moderate to high incentive value. The result of this combination of personality and situational factors means that their resultant tendency will be to achieve success and the pride involved with this will be the focus of their emotional reactions. This, in turn, will result in high motivation for the challenge (behavioural tendencies).

   Alternatively, in the same situation, a player with low motives for achievement and high motives for avoiding failure would have lower motivation to play the opponent because they would see the equal challenge as a high-risk situation where they run the risk of shame if they lose. This person is more likely to be motivated in situations with a high probability of success (weaker opponent) or a much lower probability of success, where there is less shame in losing; that is, playing against an unbeatable opponent where nobody would expect them to win. As a result, their achievement behaviour tends to avoid risky or challenging situations and they will seek out easy wins or impossible wins. These interactions are summarized in Figure 3.1.

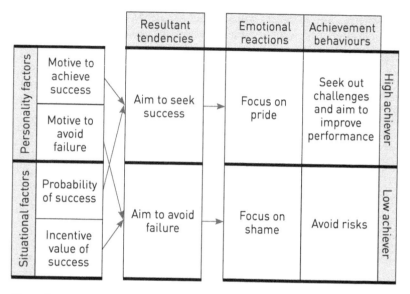

Figure 3.1 **Summary of Need for Achievement Theory**

Achievement Goal Theory

The Achievement Goal Theory (Nicholls, 1984) has been accepted far more within the sport and exercise domain than Need for Achievement Theory. The theory is based around the premise of two stable personality orientations: **task orientation** and **ego orientation**.

Task-oriented people believe that the effort they put into a task is likely to be rewarded with success. Ego-oriented people, on the other hand, are more likely to believe that success is a result of natural ability rather than effort. These different types of athlete are motivated by slightly different values. Task-oriented people are more likely to be motivated to participate in sport for enjoyment and favour tasks which provide the opportunity for self-improvement. For ego-oriented people, their participation is seen as an opportunity to compare themselves with others and demonstrate their superior ability. They prefer tasks which allow them to look good in comparison to others. For example, several players may run onto a football pitch one Saturday afternoon with similar enthusiasm and the same desire to win the game. The task-oriented players are motivated by the fact that they have been practising a particular drill which should help them to improve their game. Although they will want to win, they will measure their success by how well the team has played, win or lose. The ego-oriented players will be motivated by wanting to beat the other team, but they are also likely to want to outshine the other players on their own team. Their measure of success is more likely to be reflected in the outcome of the game.

The popularity of this theory is primarily attributable to the plethora of research that lends support to the distinction between the two orientations. For example, the types of task that task- and ego-oriented people select are very different. Task-oriented people are far more likely to select challenging tasks so that they have an opportunity to assess their development and personal gain that they have achieved from their persistence (Cury et al., 1997). Ego-oriented people, on the other hand, are far more interested in proving that they are good at what they do in comparison to other people. For this reason, they are more likely to select easier tasks in which they can demonstrate their competence (Cury et al., 1997). In mundane tasks, which is often the case with training drills, task-oriented people will show a higher degree of persistence in comparison to their ego-oriented peers (Hanrahan et al., 2003). This is understandable, given that task-oriented people are more likely to value the benefit of their persistence (they believe that effort equals success) than ego-oriented people, who believe that success results primarily from natural ability rather than just from their efforts.

Situation-specific goal achievements

So far, we have discussed the personality traits or dispositions of task or ego orientations. These suggest that, on the whole, people are either task or ego oriented. Research, however, has also explored whether people have different goals in specific situations. This is known as 'goal involvement' and relates strongly to the situational environment. For example, somebody who is primarily ego oriented may display task involvement during aspects of training which focus on personal improvement. Another person who is primarily task oriented might display ego involvement during a competitive match where the emphasis is going to be much more on competition and winning the game.

Clearly, the environment contributes significantly to how task or ego oriented a person might be, and this is known as the **motivational climate**, which can be task or ego supportive:

- A *mastery climate* is one where a coach or parent provides supportive comments when individuals persist in tasks, improve on personal targets, and help others to improve through teamwork. As a result, a mastery climate encourages task involvement.

- A *competitive climate* fosters ego involvement and uses competition and comparison as a basis for evaluation, and high achievers will be more highly rewarded and regarded.

Understanding motivational climate has clear implications for coaches, parents and teachers, who will be trying to encourage the best possible performance from their team, athlete or child. The motivational climate is *key* to facilitating intrinsic motivation, that is, motivation based on enjoyment (Goudas et al., 1995), and wellbeing (Reinboth and Duda, 2006). Research has demonstrated how debilitating a competitive climate can be for less able players. Reinboth and Duda (2004) explored the effects of both types of climate on the **self-esteem** of people with differing abilities. They found that those with high ability had high self-esteem regardless of the motivational climate. The main effect, however, was found in those with low perceived ability, where a competitive climate resulted in much lower levels of self-esteem. As you can imagine, if you are the shining player in a competitive environment, who the coach is comparing with the other players, you will feel confident and will clearly look forward to training each week. Imagine, however, how you would feel as one of the other players in that team, knowing that you are going to be criticized each week even if you have made personal improvements.

Achievement motivation in competition

So far we have discussed the role of achievement motivation in various aspects of sport; however, we also mentioned earlier that, within a sporting context, achievement tends to be assessed via performance in competitive situations. Gill and Deeter (1988) specifically developed the Sport Orientation Questionnaire to measure the concept of achievement motivation within a competitive situation. It measures three types of competitive orientations; competitiveness, win orientation, and goal orientation:

- *Competitiveness* refers to a type of person who enjoys competition and will actively seek out competitive situations because they are motivated to succeed specifically in competition.
- *Win-oriented people* have similar tendencies to the ego-oriented person proposed by Nicholls. They focus on success in competitive

situations, with the aim being to beat others rather than improve their own performance.

- *Goal-oriented people* are more like the task-oriented people proposed by Nicholls. They focus on improving their own performance and measure achievement more by their own standards than others.

Summary

This section has explored some key theories of achievement motivation which have been used to explain performance and competitiveness in a sporting context. Achievement motivation theories have focused on exploring how people with a high versus a low need for achievement vary in terms of their personality dispositions, their motivational drives and focus, task selection, and behavioural tendencies in competitive situations. This information is useful in helping coaches and trainers manipulate the sporting and training environment (motivational climate) in a way that will facilitate athletes to focus on achievement rather than avoiding failure, and facilitate athletes who are task rather than ego oriented so that they are more likely to display the desired behaviours, such as increased persistence, task mastery and enjoyment.

Intrinsic versus extrinsic motivation

So far in this chapter, the concept of motivation has been discussed as a unitary term, where a person is either thought to be motivated or not. The following sections, however, discuss theories which propose that motivation exists on a more complex continuum.

Self-determination Theory

Self-determination Theory (SDT; Deci and Ryan, 1985, 2002) is concerned with the regulation of behaviour and the factors that influence this regulation. The theory proposes that motivation exists on a continuum (see Figure 3.2). Intrinsic motivation forms the far pole of the continuum and is only present with inherently enjoyable behaviours. The further towards the left of the continuum an individual is, the more controlled and the less self-determined their motivation is considered to be.

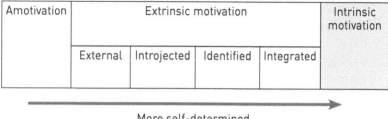

More self-determined

Figure 3.2 Continuum of motivation according to Self-determination Theory

Amotivation describes the absence of any motivation to attempt the behaviour. For example, a sedentary person who does not see the point of, or value the need for, exercise is amotivated. **Extrinsic motivation** refers to participating in an activity to gain some satisfaction of an external demand (Ryan and Deci, 2000), such as exercising to lose weight. Extrinsic motivation can be separated into four types along the continuum, namely, external regulation, introjected regulation, identified regulation and integrated regulation:

- *External regulation* is when the individual's behaviour is controlled by external rewards or the threat of external punishments and these undermine intrinsic motivation (Deci et al., 1999). This is often the case within a medical setting where patients are coerced to take up a healthier lifestyle by a family member or doctor.
- *Introjected regulation* is represented in an individual who accepts the value of a behaviour, but does not truly identify with it or accept it as their own value. For example, an athlete might think that extra training will benefit performance for athletes and as such value the behaviour, however, they may not truly accept that this would benefit them personally. This form of motivation is considered one of the most complex, wherein opposite motives coincide (Koestner and Losier, 2002). The individual may have positive as well as negative feelings towards the behaviour and, as a result, feelings of guilt or shame are felt if they fail to perform (Deci and Ryan, 2000). In the case of the athlete, they may have positive feelings about the benefits of extra training, but they may also have negative feelings about the effort it takes and the benefit they personally would gain. As a result of these conflicting feelings, they might decide not to attend extra training, but would feel guilty about not doing so.

- *Identified regulation* is the process by which people truly accept the value of a behaviour. This often results in individuals adopting the behaviour more readily, as they are able to value the benefit that participating has for them (Deci and Ryan, 2000). For example, a person may be motivated to attend training every day because they value the benefit that it will subsequently have on their performance. This remains a form of extrinsic motivation because the behaviour is still carried out for an external reason, that is, to improve performance, rather than for the sheer pleasure of the behaviour. This form of external regulation is closer to the self-determined end of the scale and is positively correlated with future intentions to continue the behaviour (Chatzisarantis et al., 2005).
- *Integrated regulation* is the most internalized form of extrinsic motivation. Not only are the values of the behaviour considered important, but they are also integrated into other roles enacted in life (Ryan and Deci, 2000). The behaviour is so internalized that it integrates and correlates with other personal values and beliefs and forms part of one's identity (Ryan and Deci, 2000). However, although the behaviour is fully integrated, it is still extrinsically motivated, since the behaviour remains for the purpose of achieving a goal that is 'personally important as a valued outcome' (Deci et al., 1991: 330) and not for the sheer pleasure of taking part.

Finally, **intrinsic motivation** is the motivation to do something for its own sake in the absence of external rewards (Biddle and Mutrie, 2001).

Studies have indicated that the more self-determined an individual's motivation, the more positive the outcomes (Deci and Ryan, 2000) and the better the quality of their sporting experience and sporting attitudes (Pelletier et al., 1995). For example, Pelletier et al. (2001) found that, within a sporting context, self-determined motivation at baseline was associated with higher levels of persistence 10 and 22 months later. Also, a study by Sarrazin et al. (2002) examined the effects of motivation and drop-out in female handballers. Results indicated that dropouts had lower levels of intrinsic motivation but higher levels of amotivation than persistent players.

Motives such as the desire to learn and improve skills, to have fun, and to play for the challenge that the game provides are consistently reported as the main reasons for sport involvement (Frederick and Ryan, 1995; Weiss and Chaumeton, 1992). This suggests that the majority of individuals who participate in sport do so for the sheer pleasure of participation and are intrinsically motivated to do so. As discussed previously, however, not all aspects of sport are as inherently enjoyable as others and an individual may have *identified regulation* for training drills, that is, they value the benefit that the drills have for their performance, yet be *intrinsically motivated* for the sport itself. In addition, the climate in which the sport is played can also have a positive or negative effect on an individual's self-determined motivation, as explained below.

Cognitive Evaluation Theory

Cognitive Evaluation Theory (CET; Deci and Ryan, 1985) is a subtheory within Self-determination Theory concerned with factors that encourage or discourage intrinsic motivation. CET states that intrinsically motivated behaviour is based on striving to satisfy three innate psychological needs. These are the need for competence, autonomy and relatedness. If the social and/or environmental factors in a sport do not satisfy one of these psychological needs, this results in diminished motivation (Deci et al., 1991):

- *Autonomy satisfaction* relates to feeling that the choice to participate in a behaviour is volitional and not controlled by external factors (e.g. parents or coaches).
- *Competence satisfaction* is the perception that you are able to perform the behaviour and achieve the desired outcomes.
- *Relatedness satisfaction* is the need to feel accepted by others (e.g. teammates) and to have supportive relationships (Reis et al., 2000).

Optimal motivation occurs when athletes' needs are met. For example, within the SDT framework, Deci and Ryan (1991) claimed that competence without autonomy results in an individual who is confident they can perform a task but who is participating for external reasons. As a result, when the external reason is removed, the behaviour is no longer performed. This behaviour does not reflect true intrinsic motivation and it appears that for true intrinsic motivation to occur in this athlete, both competence and autonomy must be satisfied.

Summary

In this section, we have discussed how SDT proposes that motivation exists on a continuum and that it is possible to be motivated to participate in an activity for a variety of reasons. In a similar fashion to the way different types of achievement motivation were more adaptive than others (e.g. task orientation), more self-determined forms of motivation are more adaptive in terms of behavioural and affective outcomes. The CET proposes that psychological needs must be satisfied to facilitate intrinsic motivation and as such provides researchers and practitioners with an opportunity to consider how the environment can be manipulated to satisfy these needs and in turn encourage more self-determined motivation.

◉ Developing motivation

The previous sections have discussed different theories of motivation and how different types of orientations and motivation can predict behavioural (e.g. persistence, drop-out), cognitive (e.g. task focus), and affective outcomes (e.g. wellbeing). There is, however, not much use knowing this information if it cannot be used to try to encourage the more adaptive aspects of motivation (e.g. task orientation, self-determined motivation). This section will briefly discuss how the information from the theories can be used to manipulate the environment to encourage these types of motivation in athletes.

A number of key issues emerge that practitioners or coaches should pay attention to when assessing the motivational orientation of their athletes. First, what are their athletes' main foci? That is, do their athletes seem to focus on winning or self-improvement (Achievement Goal Theory)? Do they seek challenges or avoid situations in which they might not achieve (Need for Achievement Theory)? Do they appear to be motivated to satisfy the coach or because they value the benefit of the task (Self-determination Theory)? Once the orientation of the athlete has been determined, then the motivational climate (the environment) can be manipulated to suit the player or to try to encourage the player to develop a more adaptive motivational style.

According to the Need for Goal Achievement Theory, the motivational climate should encourage a more mastery, task-focused environment. Coaches should avoid comparing athletes against each other and should instead focus on individual improvements as measures of success. Feedback should be individualized rather than group based and should provide constructive criticism, emphasizing areas of improvement and acknowledging people's efforts.

According to Self-determination Theory and Cognitive Evaluation Theory, two main types of environment have been identified; an autonomy supportive environment and a controlling environment. An autonomy supportive environment focuses on individuals having choice and opportunities for independent thought and valuing why they are being asked to perform certain behaviours. In an autonomy supportive environment, coaches and leaders listen and acknowledge athletes' feelings, offer positive feedback, and provide relevant information when required. In contrast, controlling environments tend to have coaches or leaders who take charge, use commands and instructions, and motivate through threats and criticisms. Table 3.1 provides an overview of motivational strategies.

Theory	Climate	Strategies
Achievement Goal Theory	Mastery, task-oriented climate	▪ Avoid comparing athletes ▪ Focus on individual improvements ▪ Individualized and constructive feedback recognizing effort and individual improvement
Self-determination Theory, Cognitive Evaluation Theory	Autonomy supportive climate	▪ Provide choice of activities ▪ Listen and acknowledge athletes' feelings, and address any questions ▪ Offer positive feedback, and provide relevant information when required ▪ Avoid using commands and instructions, threats and criticisms

Table 3.1 Summary of motivational strategies

◉ Conclusions

This chapter has discussed four motivation theories; Need for Achievement Theory, Achievement Goal Theory, Self-determination Theory and Cognitive Evaluation Theory. These theories have outlined how different motivational orientations can predict behavioural, cognitive and affective outcomes. In addition, we discussed how understanding the motivational orientation of athletes is important for developing motivational climates which can effectively encourage more adaptive forms of motivation.

◉ Further reading

Deci, E.L. and Ryan, R.M. (2000). The 'what' and 'why' of goal pursuits: Human needs and the self-determination of behavior. *Psychological Inquiry*, 11(4), 227–68.

Hagger, M.S. and Chatzisarantis, N.L. (2007). *Intrinsic motivation and self-determination in exercise and sport*. Leeds: Human Kinetics.

Roberts, G.C. (2001). *Advances in motivation in sport and exercise*. Leeds: Human Kinetics.

◉ Key search terms

Achievement motivation, task orientation, ego orientation, self-determined motivation, intrinsic motivation, psychological need satisfaction

Chapter 4

Aggression

A rugby player punches his opponent after an illegal challenge; an ice hockey player injures a member of the opposition with a body check; a tennis player hurls verbal abuse at the umpire after what they perceive to be a bad line call; a netball player elbows her opposition in the ribs to prevent her from intercepting a pass.

These are examples of aggressive behaviour by athletes similar to those we may have seen in competitive sport, or experienced as perpetrators or victims. As long as competitive sport exists with something meaningful at stake, from millions of pounds in prize money to personal pride, some athletes will act aggressively. Given the high stakes and highly charged environment of sport, it is perhaps surprising that more athletes are not aggressive, although of course rules and boundaries exist to limit their behaviour.

To understand aggressive behaviour in athletes, sport psychologists have drawn mainly on existing theories from other areas of psychology, including instinct-based theories, those using arousal and frustration to explain aggressive behaviour, and theories that consider aggression to be a learned behaviour. Some authors, however, have recently developed more sport-specific frameworks, including the suggestion, which may be somewhat controversial to some, that aggression is an inherent and sought-after element of physical contact sports, such as rugby. This chapter considers these different perspectives on aggression, key factors that are related to athletic aggression, and how we might help athletes to manage aggression.

In this chapter, we will examine:
- Different types of aggression and their definitions
- Theories used to explain why some athletes act aggressively
- When athletes might act aggressively
- Strategies for managing aggression
- Methods of studying aggression in sport

👁 What is aggression?

Consider the examples of aggression which opened this chapter. These examples neatly show how we define **aggression** (Baron and Richardson, 1994). An aggressive act is a *behaviour* (such as punching or verbally abusing someone), not an attitude or emotion (e.g. thinking hostile thoughts about the referee). An aggressive act involves harming or injuring another living thing who does not want to be harmed (e.g. physically by punching them or emotionally by criticizing them in public). Importantly, an aggressive act must involve *intent* on the part of the aggressor (e.g. the netball player purposely elbowing her opponent). Accidentally injuring an opponent is not considered an act of aggression if the key ingredient of intent is missing. The integral element of intent has, understandably, made research into aggression in sport somewhat challenging because it is difficult to determine intent through observing behaviour.

In sport, often aggressive behaviour is confused with *assertive behaviour*. For instance, a badminton player may be described as attacking a shot aggressively. Unless the player is aiming the shot at their opponent in an attempt to injure the person, this is not an aggressive act, because the shuttlecock is not a living thing and so cannot suffer harm or injury as a result of being hit by the player. Instead, this act is described as assertive behaviour.

Types of aggression

Our opening examples also illustrate the two main types of aggression discussed by Coulomb-Cabagno and Rascle (2006): **instrumental aggression** and **hostile aggression**. The netball player provides a good example of instrumental aggression because injuring her opponent is not her primary goal. Her primary goal is competitive, to stop her opponent from winning the ball. To achieve her primary goal, she commits an act of instrumental aggression which involves harming her opponent. The rugby player's primary goal, in comparison, is to injure his opponent and not achieve a competitive advantage, and represents a hostile act of aggression.

Summary

Aggression involves behaviours intended to injure or harm another living thing who does not want to be harmed. These behaviours can be verbal or physical. There are two main types of aggression: hostile aggression, where the primary intent is to injure someone or something, and instrumental aggression, where the primary intent is to achieve a competitive goal by harming or injuring someone.

Theories of aggression

Instinct Theory

Some authors, such as Lorenz (1966), suggest that human beings have basic instincts or drives which they act upon (e.g. because of hunger and thirst, we eat and drink to reduce these drives). These authors view aggression as one of the innate drives or instincts people act upon to reduce. Given that aggression is not socially acceptable in everyday life, people need to find other socially acceptable avenues to release their innate aggression, known as 'catharsis'. Adopting this instinct perspective, we could suggest that sport offers one such socially acceptable context in which we can release aggression. Athletes act aggressively in sport to release their pent-up, innate aggression. Although intuitively appealing, this proposal is difficult to study, and the limited research available offers little support for this theory and the notion that the cathartic release of aggression in sport leads to less aggression in other contexts (Williams and Gill, 2000).

Frustration-Aggression Theory

Dollard et al. (1939) suggested athletes act aggressively when they become frustrated because someone or something is preventing them from achieving their goals. In our example, the tennis player acts aggressively towards the umpire because she is frustrated by not achieving her goal of winning the point and sees the umpire as instrumental in preventing her from doing so. Although this explanation has some validity, not all athletes act aggressively when frustrated and not all acts of aggression stem from frustration (Williams and Gill, 2000). This theory does not provide a full picture of aggressive behaviour in sport.

Social Learning Theory

Social Learning Theory (Bandura, 1986) proposes that much of our behaviour (including aggression) is learned through reward and imitation. People will act aggressively if significant others, such as coaches or parents, reward aggressive behaviour. Rewards may come in various forms, for instance praise or positive feedback or team selection for subsequent matches. People may also be rewarded for aggressive behaviour if it results in scoring a goal, saving the opposition from scoring, or winning a match.

People also act aggressively if they observe their role models, like professional athletes, who they admire acting aggressively and they imitate the modelled behaviour. Bandura (1986) suggests that behaviours are modelled by three main sources: family, media and subculture. A subculture is one that differs from the wider culture of society and many sports have their own subcultures. Many contact sports, for instance, have a subculture where it is expected that players ignore minor injuries and resting is seen as weak. Smith (1980) suggested that sporting subcultures may influence aggression, and in the ice hockey subculture, aggression is valued, reinforced and modelled, serving to increase aggressive behaviour in youth players.

Revised Frustration-Aggression Theory

To account for the limitations of the Frustration-Aggression Theory, Berkowitz (1969) developed the Revised Frustration-Aggression Theory. This revised version suggests that athletes are more likely to be aggressive when frustration increases arousal and anger, and they have learned that aggressive acts are deemed appropriate. In our society, it is seen as more appropriate to act aggressively during sport than in other contexts (e.g. in the supermarket or classroom), and in some sports but not in others (e.g. in rugby but not in snooker). There are also certain situations within sport where it may be seen as more appropriate to act aggressively than others (e.g. when the scores are tied in the final minutes of a game, a player may use instrumental aggression to stop an opponent scoring a try as they are frustrated at the thought of losing the game). The Revised Frustration-Aggression Theory combines elements of the frustration-aggression and social learning theories, and adopts an interactive approach by considering how elements of the situation (e.g. sport versus non-sport setting) combines with elements of the person (e.g. arousal levels) to determine whether or not athletes will act aggressively.

Game Reasoning Theory

The Revised Frustration-Aggression Theory suggests that context plays a role in whether or not athletes act aggressively in sport, and Bredemeier and Shields (1986a; Shields and Bredemeier, 2001) developed this idea in their game reasoning approach to aggression. Their proposals are similar to Kerr's (2004; see below), in that when we play sport, we tend to 'suspend reality' and view aggression differently from how we view it in other areas of life. They propose that our moral reasoning differs between sport and everyday life. Bredemeier and Shields (1986b) asked athletes to reason about hypothetical incidents in sport and non-sport contexts. Their moral reasoning was more egocentric in sport than in everyday life. Their moral judgements focused on making sure they did not lose out in sport, and if acting aggressively was a way of doing this, they thought it was appropriate. They centred their moral reasoning on following rules or a coach's instructions even if this would result in behaviour deemed immoral in everyday life; for instance a football player not admitting to diving in the box if it meant their team was awarded a penalty kick.

Long et al. (2006) offered more support for Game Reasoning Theory. In interviews, 10 elite male athletes discussed their use of cheating, strategic fouls, verbal intimidation, physical violence and intentional rule-breaking. They suggested that they felt under pressure to follow their coach's orders to cheat and adhere to team norms to achieve a win.

Reversal Theory

Reversal Theory (Apter, 2001a) offers a somewhat alternative perspective on aggression, suggesting that for some athletes who play physical contact sports, such as rugby or American football, the physical contact and aggression involved are key reasons why they play the sport (Kerr, 2004). Being aggressive adds to the excitement, enjoyment and positive experience they derive from their involvement. Reversal Theory also proposes, unlike other theories, that athletes display different types of aggression depending on their current frame of mind (or metamotivational state in Reversal Theory terms). There are four pairs of states (briefly described in Table 4.1) and although athletes can only experience one state from each pair at a time, they can experience combinations of states from different pairs. Different combinations give rise to various types of aggression (Kerr, 2004). Reversal theorists use the term 'violence' instead of aggression, but for our purposes we can consider these to be synonymous. There are four types of aggression: anger violence, thrill violence, power violence and play violence:

- **Anger violence** occurs when we experience the *serious* and *rebellious* states. Athletes react to actions against them they deem to be unfair. High arousal is interpreted as anger and they rebel against expectations of them, such as the rugby player who punches their opponent following an illegal challenge.
- **Thrill violence** occurs when we experience the *playful* and *rebellious* states. We enjoy the high arousal, being provocative and rebelling against norms: aggressive behaviour is 'just for kicks'. Athletes who enjoy hurling abuse at officials and get immediate gratification by doing so provide good examples of thrill violence.
- **Power violence** occurs when we experience the *serious* and *mastery* states. Our aim is to dominate our opponent to achieve a competitive goal. Power violence is typically a calculated act, like 'sledging' in cricket. Cricketers may taunt their opposition to intimidate them and negatively affect their performance.
- **Play violence** occurs when we experience the *playful* and *mastery* states: we enjoy the feeling of dominating our opponents, but due to our playful state, we have no intention of causing harm. Sparring with teammates in training is an example of play violence. The teammates are enjoying trying to dominate each other but do not want to cause harm.

Serious state In this state we want to achieve a meaningful goal, prefer low arousal and are concerned with the future consequences of our behaviour Example: a runner training for a major competition	Playful state In this state we enjoy high arousal, want to enjoy the moment, be spontaneous and have no concern for long-term consequences Example: a hockey player enjoying a fun game in training
Mastery state In this state we focus on competition, toughness, strength, being dominant and in control Example: a badminton player smashing a shot to win a match	Sympathy state In this state we focus on cooperation, caring, nurturing and support of either ourselves or others Example: a swimmer helping an injured teammate with rehabilitation
Self state In this state we are focused on meeting our own needs, whether these are for support, comfort or to be competitive and feel in control Example: a tennis player staying away from their family before their first major final	Other state In this state we are focused on meeting others' needs, giving them support, encouragement or instruction, or helping them to achieve Example: a coach developing strategies to help their team win the league

Rebellious state	Conformist state
In this state we want to rebel against rules, norms or expectations and may want to be provocative or unconventional	In this state we want to conform to rules, norms and expectations, to fit in with others and be accepted
Example: a swimmer missing training to socialize with friends instead	Example: a football player sticking to the coach's pre-match rest and nutrition rules

Table 4.1 Metamotivational state definitions

Summary

A number of theories have been proposed to explain aggressive behaviour in sport. The instinct and frustration-aggression theories have insufficient evidence to support their proposals in sport. Other theories, such as the Revised Frustration-Aggression Theory, Social Learning Theory, Game Reasoning Theory and Reversal Theory, offer viable explanations for aggressive behaviour in sport. Key concepts in these theories include reinforcement and modelling of aggressive behaviour, athletes' altered perceptions of morality in sport contexts, and the role of the athletes' motivational states in producing different kinds of aggressive behaviours.

◉ When do athletes act aggressively?

Now that we have some explanations for why, let's consider when athletes might behave aggressively. Researchers have identified a number of factors that may increase the likelihood that an athlete acts aggressively and the key factors are summarized in Table 4.2.

▪ When part of a losing team playing away from home
▪ When less sporting and self-determined in their motivation
▪ When they are older, are male, or participate in contact or collision sports
▪ When competing at higher levels in contact sport or lower levels in non-contact sports
▪ When high in ego orientation
▪ When team norms support aggression
▪ When they perceive their sports environment as one that emphasizes a high performance climate

Table 4.2 Situations when athletes may be more likely to act aggressively or believe aggressive behaviour is acceptable

Jones et al. (2005) observed aggressive behaviours in 21 professional rugby league matches and noted more aggressive behaviours in players of away teams who lost the match. The authors suggested that away teams may be hindered more by their aggressive behaviour than the home team is helped by theirs because officials are more likely to penalize away than home teams.

In male students and athletes, Chantal et al. (2005) found that higher levels of self-reported instrumental aggression were associated with higher self-determined motivation and sportspersonship, whereas higher levels of hostile aggression were associated with less self-determined motivation and lower levels of sportspersonship. Athletes who play sport for more intrinsic reasons (such as pleasure) report more positive sporting attitudes (e.g. respect for the rules and fair play) and are more likely to use instrumental aggression, but are less likely to use hostile aggression. Also, numerous studies have examined the links between goal orientation (task or ego) and aggression in sport, consistently demon-strating that high levels of ego orientation (e.g. valuing winning above all else) are related to aggression and antisocial behaviour (e.g. Kavussanu and Roberts, 2001).

A number of studies have found that, in sport, males are more aggres-sive or report more aggressive tendencies than females (e.g. Bredemeier, 1994; Conroy et al., 2001; Coulomb-Cabagno and Rascle, 2006). This gender difference has been confirmed in child, adolescent and adult athletes. Evidence also suggests that aggression tends to increase with age (Conroy et al., 2001; Romand et al., 2009).

Although some researchers have found that athletes in contact sports perceive aggression as more legitimate than athletes in non-contact sports (e.g. Conroy et al., 2001), others (e.g. Tucker and Parks, 2001) have found that athletes in collision sports (e.g. American football) think aggression is more acceptable than athletes in contact and non-contact sports. Further studies have revealed a more complex relationship. For instance, Maxwell et al. (2009) reported higher levels of aggression at higher levels of competition in rugby (a collision sport) and at lower levels of competition in football and squash (contact and non-contact sports, respectively). Adding to this complexity, Coulomb-Cabagno and Rascle (2006) found that at higher competitive levels, instrumental aggression is more likely and hostile aggression less likely.

As social learning theorists have proposed, the sports environment and athletes' perceptions of this environment can influence levels of aggression and beliefs about whether or not aggression is acceptable. Two key aspects of this environment have been examined: perceived motivational climate and team norms:

- *Perceived motivational climate* of athletes' sports environment is either mastery or performance oriented. In a mastery climate, effort is valued and cooperation and personal development are encouraged. In contrast, in a performance environment, the emphasis is placed on winning; rivalry between team members is encouraged, and players are valued based on their ability. These motivational climates are similar to the individual goal orientations, task and ego. Just as higher levels of ego orientation are associated with more aggressive behaviour, so is a perceived performance climate (Ommundsen et al., 2003). However, a more recent study by Miller et al. (2005) identified that a climate perceived as high in both mastery and performance elements is associated with aggressive tendencies, suggesting that if a coach places an emphasis on winning, regardless of their reinforcement of effort and cooperation, their players are still more likely to act aggressively.

- *Team norms* also appear to relate to athletes' levels of aggression. Chow et al. (2009) showed that players were more likely to report that they would act aggressively if they thought the rest of the team would, that is, if the team had a norm of acting aggressively. This study also revealed that if coaches had greater confidence in their ability to coach during competition and lead the team to success, their athletes reported a greater likelihood of aggressive behaviour. The authors were unable to say with certainty, but based on findings, such as those discussed above, possibly these coaches endorse aggressive behaviour, encourage a performance-oriented motivational climate, or coach teams at a higher level.

Summary

A host of factors may influence whether or not athletes act aggressively: game location, motivation (goal orientation and level of self-determination), type and level of sport, gender, age, team norms and motivational climate.

⊙ How can we manage aggression?

Coaches, athletes and sport psychologists could use the findings of the theories and research discussed above to help to manage aggression. Coaches could help to minimize their athletes' aggressive behaviour by ensuring that they don't foster overly performance-oriented motivational climates and attempt to develop mastery climates. They could do so by praising effort and not just achievement, and encouraging players to focus on improving their mastery of skills rather than trying to outperform others. In turn, this is likely to influence athletes' goal orientations so that they adopt more task than ego orientations, which is known to be related to aggressive behaviour. As well as trying to help athletes develop high task orientation levels, coaches could help to optimize their athletes' self-determined motivation levels. For instance, where appropriate, coaches could give athletes opportunities to influence team decision-making about playing strategies and training.

Significant others, such as parents and coaches, could help to reduce aggression by emphasizing sportspersonship, such as having respect for opponents and match officials. Athletes and coaches can try to establish and reinforce team norms that aggression is not acceptable and recognize the efforts of those athletes who maintain this norm even when the situation might provoke them to act aggressively. Coaches have no control over the athlete's gender, the competition venue (home or away), competitive level or type of sport (e.g. contact or non-contact). Nevertheless, if coaches are aware of the links between these factors and aggressive behaviour, they can be vigilant of the need to focus on other more modifiable factors, such as motivational climate, to try to minimize aggression in these athletes and contexts.

Many of the following suggestions combine proposals from the revised frustration–aggression and social learning theories. Parents, coaches and older athletes can act as role models by responding to potentially aggressive encounters in non-aggressive ways and can positively reinforce non-aggressive responses they observe in others. Developing team norms that aggressive behaviour is unacceptable employs the Revised Frustration-Aggression Theory principle that athletes will only act aggressively if it is deemed to be appropriate in that event or context. Coaches and sport psychologists could also help athletes to develop strategies, such as controlled breathing, as a way of dealing with arousal and anger in place of being aggressive.

Summary

Aggression can be managed by establishing a team norm that aggressive behaviour is not acceptable and emphasizing a high mastery motivational climate. Modelling and reinforcing non-aggressive behaviour and encouraging a task orientation in athletes may also help athletes to manage their aggression.

◉ Methods used to study aggression in sport

Researchers who have studied aggression in sport have used a range of different methods and approaches. Each of these methods offers advantages, but also has limitations which stem from the methods themselves and the topic under investigation. Here we consider the advantages, limitations and key elements of these different approaches.

Observational studies

Some authors have used observational methods to study aggression in sport (e.g. Coulomb-Cabagno and Rascle, 2006). Typically, these studies involve recording competitive games and rating the number and kinds of aggressive behaviours that occur. Researchers need to have clear definitions of the behaviours they are interested in, for instance to distinguish between hostile and instrumental aggression, and need to make multiple observations. Clear definitions ensure that investigators observe behaviours that are representative of the norm; for example if teams were only observed at away venues, this would not represent a true and complete representation of aggressive behaviour.

Researchers also need to make sure that their observations are reliable and demonstrate intra-rater and inter-rater reliability:

- **Inter-rater reliability** means that two different observers agree on the behaviours that were observed after independently observing the same competitive action.
- **Intra-rater reliability** means that one observer makes consistent observations, measured by the person observing the same event twice, with sufficient time between the two observations to rule out simply remembering the initial ratings.

The main advantage of observational approaches is that researchers can record and analyse athletes' actual aggressive and non-aggressive behaviours and responses as they occur in real-life competitive sport. The main limitation is that, as mentioned at the outset of the chapter, we cannot infer intent by observing someone's behaviour, and this is a critical element of the definition of aggression.

Self-report studies

A second well-established method involves administering measures to athletes that ask them to report on their likelihood of using aggression, their beliefs about the acceptability of using aggression, and their moral judgements in sporting situations. Conroy et al.'s (2001) study illustrates an example of a self-report method. There are two main types of measures that are used to assess these different variables: questionnaires and hypothetical scenarios.

There is a range of questionnaires which researchers can use, but whichever they select they need to ensure that the questionnaire has good levels of **reliability** and **validity**; in other words, unless they are state responses that change over time, people's responses to the questionnaire are consistent, or reliable, and the questionnaire does measure what it is supposed to, or is a valid measure.

The key advantage of using questionnaires to measure aggression is that researchers can gain opinions and responses from a large number of athletes in a short space of time and can ensure that they all respond to the same questions. A key limitation is that some athletes may not respond honestly about their aggressive behaviour and so their self-reported behaviour may not match their actual behaviour during competition.

Hypothetical scenarios present athletes with an example situation from their sport and they are asked to indicate how they would probably respond if they found themselves in this situation (e.g. Chow et al., 2009). The main advantage of using scenarios, similar to questionnaires, is that responses to exactly the same situation can be obtained from a large sample of athletes. Again, the main limitation is that athletes may not necessarily report exactly how they have behaved in the past or would do in the future. Instead, some may respond how they think others would expect them to, in what is termed a 'socially desirable' manner.

Interview studies

Some authors (e.g. Grange and Kerr, 2010, in their study of physical aggression in Australian rules football) have used interviews to explore athletes' views on and use of aggression. Typically, authors use semi-structured interviews which include some predetermined questions, but also allow athletes freedom to discuss additional issues that are important to them and which the researcher may not have identified beforehand. It is helpful if the interviews are conducted by the same interviewer as the dynamics of the interview can be affected by a range of factors such as the gender, age and sporting experience of the interviewer.

Interviews generate qualitative data in the form of people's comments about their experiences and opinions, and these data are usually grouped into themes that represent common experiences and opinions across participants. Such analysis relies on researchers' interpretations of athletes' comments. A secondary analysis of a sample of the data conducted independently by another researcher may help to test and confirm these interpretations. As these interpretations are intended to represent athletes' experiences and opinions, asking athletes themselves to confirm the themes and interpretations also enhances credibility.

A key advantage of using interviews is that the researcher can obtain in-depth information from respondents and has the opportunity to follow up on any of the respondent's comments. A limitation of this method is that because interview studies involve small numbers of participants (partly through necessity as one interview generates pages and pages of transcribed conversation), the findings cannot easily be generalized to other samples.

◁◉▷ Conclusions

Athletes' aggressive behaviours in sport appear to be influenced by various personal, social and environmental factors. It may be possible to manipulate some of these factors, for instance through modelling non-aggressive behaviour, to help athletes to manage their aggression. Managing aggression seems to be particularly important when the results of a recent study in ice hockey are considered. Gee and Leith (2007) identified that, contrary to the popularly held belief, aggressive behaviour did not relate to greater performance success.

⊙ Further reading

Gill, D.L. and Williams, L. (2008). *Psychological dynamics of sport and exercise* (3rd edn, Chapter 13). Champaign, IL: Human Kinetics.
Kerr, J.H. (2004). *Rethinking aggression in sport.* Abingdon: Routledge.

⊙ Key search terms

Hostile aggression, instrumental aggression, Game Reasoning Theory, Social Learning Theory, Reversal Theory, Revised Frustration-Aggression Theory, contact sports, collision sports

Chapter 5

Arousal

As you have no doubt experienced, participating in sport can be highly arousing. Think back to the last time you played sport, when you may have felt both physical and mental symptoms of arousal, such as increased heart rate or mental alertness. You may have felt your arousal level had a positive effect on you and your performance. Conversely, you may have felt the arousal you experienced was detrimental for your performance. Because arousal is such a pervasive and almost inevitable consequence of competing in sport, sport psychologists have devoted a great deal of time to trying to understand this phenomenon and how athletes can manage their arousal to make it work for, and not against, them. In this chapter we discuss the relationship between arousal and sport performance.

In this chapter, we will examine:
- The definition and dimensions of arousal
- Theories used to understand the effects of arousal on sport performance
- Factors affecting arousal and its influence on sports performance
- Strategies athletes can use to manage arousal and its effects on performance

Defining arousal

Landers and Boutcher (1998) suggest that Sage's (1984) definition of arousal is best used to understand arousal in sport. Sage views **arousal** as an energizing mechanism that allows us to recruit the resources needed to engage in intense and vigorous activity. It also helps to consider Malmo's (1959) definition; he identifies arousal as a continuum of excitation, ranging from a comatose state to one of intense excitement. When we are relaxing in front of the TV, our arousal level is much lower on this continuum than on the day of an important competition when we're excited about the prospect of taking part.

High levels of arousal manifest in three different ways: mentally, physically and behaviourally:

- Mentally, we might worry about how well we will perform in the competition, leading to negative emotions such as anxiety.
- Physical changes due to increased arousal might include increased heart and respiration rates or increased muscle tension.
- High levels of arousal might be associated with changes in behaviour, such as a rugby player passing the ball to the opposition because they have made an incorrect decision, or fumbling a pass from a teammate.

It's easy to see how these mental, physical and behavioural elements of arousal are related. Our rugby player, in a state of heightened arousal, experiences worries about the size and reputation of the opposition and is concerned with avoiding their tackles. She starts to experience increased heart rate and tension in her shoulder muscles as a result. When passed the ball by a teammate, her preoccupation with the size of the opposition player bearing down on her, coupled with her unwanted muscle tension, causes her to lose focus on the ball and, less coordinated than normal due to her muscle tension, she drops the pass.

Summary

Arousal ranges on a continuum from deep coma to extreme excitation and is our body's way of preparing us for an upcoming challenge. Arousal may, however, have detrimental effects on athletes' mental and physical states and on their behaviour. Mentally, athletes may worry about their performance, physically they may experience muscle tension, and their behaviour may be affected.

Theories of arousal and performance

Drive Theory

Initially, sport psychologists used theories from other areas of psychology to explain the relationship between arousal and sports performance. One such theory is Drive Theory (Hull, 1943). Its key proposal is that when drive (or arousal) is increased, athletes most probably display well-learned or practised behaviours, known as the dominant response. In her summary, Gill (2000) states that essentially Drive Theory proposes a linear relationship between arousal and performance such that increases in arousal will lead to increases in performance (see Figure 5.1). If we consider Drive Theory's proposal that increases in arousal result in increased likelihood of the athlete's dominant response occurring, then the relationship between arousal and sports performance is not quite this simple. For expert performers, the dominant response is most likely the correct one, resulting in a skilled and superior performance. In comparison, for novice performers, the dominant response is not yet likely to be the correct skilled response required. For novice performers increased arousal is likely to lead to poorer performance.

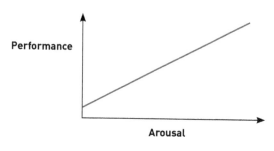

Figure 5.1 Drive Theory

Task complexity is also likely to play a part in this relationship. For simple tasks, and tasks considered simple by experts may not be viewed as such by novices, increases in arousal will result in increases in performance. For complex tasks, which again are defined in somewhat relative terms, increases in arousal will be associated with decreases in performance.

Although sport psychologists initially adopted Drive Theory to help understand the relationship between arousal and performance, empirical tests were inconclusive (Gill, 2000). Sport psychologists have looked for an alternative model to explain this relationship and once again identified a theory outside sport psychology as a potential explanation: the inverted-U hypothesis (Yerkes and Dodson, 1908).

Inverted-U hypothesis

The inverted-U hypothesis was developed by Yerkes and Dodson (1908), who suggested that optimal performance occurs when we experience a moderate level of arousal, and performance is poor when arousal is either high or low (Figure 5.2). As arousal increases from low to moderate levels, corresponding gradual increases in performance occur, while performance decreases gradually as arousal increases from moderate to high levels.

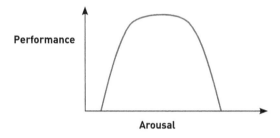

Figure 5.2 Inverted-U hypothesis

Factors affecting the inverted-U relationship

Landers and Boutcher (1998) discuss two factors that influence the arousal–performance relationship: task complexity and individual differences:

1 *Task complexity:* Although the inverted-U relationship applies to both complex and simple tasks, the optimal or moderate arousal level differs in relation to task complexity (see Figure 5.3). For complex tasks, such as putting in golf, the optimal level of arousal is lower than with simple tasks, such as a deadlift in weightlifting. As another example, during basketball, athletes' optimal arousal levels in general play are probably higher than when they attempt free throws.

2 *Individual differences:* Landers and Boutcher (1998) outline three key individual differences: trait anxiety, level of extroversion/ introversion and skill level:

   ▪ *Trait anxiety:* This reflects a general tendency to perceive specific situations as anxiety provoking. Athletes with high competitive trait anxiety will probably become anxious during most of the competitions in which they participate.

- *Level of extroversion/introversion:* Athletes with high levels of extroversion like to be the centre of attention, prefer to be in social situations, and tend to focus less on themselves and more on external events and stimuli. Highly introverted athletes, in comparison, are less outgoing, focus more on their own thoughts and feelings, and prefer smaller social groups. Given these definitions, it is not surprising that introverted and highly trait anxious athletes' optimal levels of arousal are lower than that of extroverts and low trait anxious individuals (see Figure 5.3).
- *Skill level:* Similarly, highly skilled athletes, who are able to cope better with high levels of arousal than less skilled athletes, perform optimally at higher absolute levels of arousal.

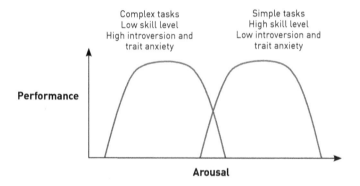

Figure 5.3 Factors affecting optimal arousal in the inverted-U hypothesis

Research evidence: inverted-U hypothesis

Landers and Boutcher (1998) have identified that while some studies have not found support for an inverted-U relationship between arousal and sports performance, other studies have found support. Some of these studies were laboratory based, using performance measures such as motor steadiness and reaction time, as did Arent and Landers (2003), whose study is considered in more detail below. Other studies used real-world sports skills, such as jumping efficiency in sports parachutists or pistol shooting performance.

In Arent and Landers' (2003) study, 104 male and female students performed a reaction time task while cycling on a cycle ergometer at one of the following percentages of heart rate reserve: 20, 30, 40, 50, 60, 70,

80, or 90%. The researchers asked participants to cycle while performing the reaction time task to determine the effects of different arousal levels (relative to the individual) on reaction time task performance. Participants were informed that cash prizes were available for the three fastest individuals to develop a sense of competition and to increase the cognitive demands of the simple reaction time task (responding as quickly as possible by pressing a response key when a red light stimulus was presented). Participants also completed two measures of anxiety about the upcoming task (one of these, the CSAI-2, is described in Chapter 6) and then completed 12 reaction time trials. This is known as an experimental study, as discussed in the box below.

Contrary to the inverted-U hypothesis, the researchers found a linear relationship between arousal and movement time (MT: the time taken to complete the full movement). However, an inverted-U relationship was identified between arousal and reaction time (RT: the time taken to react to the light and initiate the movement) and response time (RT plus MT). As the inverted-U hypothesis predicts, performance was poorest at the lowest and highest levels of arousal (20 and 90% of heart rate reserve) and best at moderate levels of arousal (60 and 70% of heart rate reserve). Arent and Landers (2003) concluded that the inverted-U hypothesis does offer a worthwhile model for understanding the arousal–performance relationship and should not be completely rejected in favour of more recent models.

Thinking scientifically →
spotlight on experimental research

We have already discussed the details of Arent and Landers' (2003) findings, but a closer look at the methods they used to obtain their results provides a useful insight into some key concepts involved in experimental research. Here we consider different types of variables used in experimental research, what we mean by randomization, manipulation and control, and why they are important aspects of experimental research:

- *Independent and dependent variables:* Arent and Landers (2003) wanted to determine if arousal influences performance on a reaction time task. Arousal is termed the *independent variable* because researchers manipulate this variable and it is hypothesized to influence the *dependent variable*, in this case, reaction time performance.

- *Randomization:* Participants were randomly allocated to one of eight arousal (or experimental) conditions: cycling at 20, 30, 40, 50, 60, 70, 80, or 90% of heart rate reserve. Randomization means that there is an equal chance of each participant being allocated to any of the experimental conditions. Randomization is important in experimental research to ensure that any effects of the independent variable (in this case, arousal level) on the dependent variable (reaction time performance in this example) cannot be attributed to allocating all the participants with a particular characteristic to one of the experimental conditions. In this study, for instance, randomization ensured that all the participants who were cyclists were not allocated to only one condition.
- *Manipulation:* In experimental studies, researchers manipulate one variable (arousal in this study) to determine its effects on another variable (reaction time performance). It is important that the manipulation is standardized, or carried out in the same way, across all participants. In this study, arousal was manipulated by asking participants to cycle at a specific percentage of heart rate reserve which was calculated using the same method for each participant.

   Manipulation often includes different *levels* of the independent variable, and Arent and Landers' (2003) study provides a clear illustration. The different levels of arousal induced in the participants (20–90% of heart rate reserve) represent different levels of the independent variable. Although the level of the independent variable differs between different conditions, within each condition the manipulation was held constant. Arent and Landers did this in their study by ensuring that participants didn't begin the reaction time trials until they had cycled for 60 seconds at the required arousal, and if their arousal level deviated from this target level, participants repeated the trial when the required arousal level was re-established.
- *Control:* In experimental research, investigators try to control, or eliminate, any variables that might affect the results. For instance, Arent and Landers (2003) excluded any individuals who were taking medications that might affect heart rate. Another variable controlled was participants' characteristics; all the participants were healthy, college-aged adults. The measures and protocol used in the study were standardized for all participants so that the results could not be affected by any differences in the measures or protocol used with different

participants. Participants were also familiarized with the experimental protocol and performance test to control for any effects on performance of learning or a lack of understanding of what is required.

Arent and Landers' (2003) support notwithstanding, some of the key criticisms levelled at the use of the inverted-U hypothesis to describe the relationship between arousal and sports performance include:

1 Moderate levels of arousal are not beneficial for performance in all sports.
2 Arousal is multidimensional, including behavioural, physical and cognitive dimensions, and this model does not account for this multidimensionality, instead considering arousal only as a unidimensional construct.
3 The inverted-U hypothesis describes the relationship between arousal and performance, but does not provide an explanation. Models such as the Multidimensional Anxiety Theory (Martens et al., 1990b) and the Catastrophe Model (Fazey and Hardy, 1988) do attempt to provide explanations for this relationship and not just descriptions, as we will see in Chapter 6.
4 It is unlikely that performance increases and decreases occur in a gradual, incremental fashion as arousal level increases to, or decreases from, a moderate level. Consider how arousal has affected you in the past when your arousal level has increased beyond an optimal level. Did your performance gradually worsen, as the inverted-U hypothesis suggests, or did you experience a sudden drop in performance? Fazey and Hardy (1988) addressed this criticism in their Catastrophe Model and we examine its proposals in Chapter 6.

The second of these criticisms was tackled by Hanin (1989) in his individualized zones of optimal functioning hypothesis to which we turn our attention in the next section.

Individualized zones of optimal functioning (IZOF) hypothesis

As the name of this hypothesis suggests, Hanin (1989) proposed that each athlete has an individualized zone of optimal functioning, or range of arousal in which they produce their best sporting performances. Arousal levels outside this zone will be associated with suboptimal performance (Figure 5.4). There are important differences between the inverted-U and the IZOF hypotheses:

- the inverted-U hypothesis suggests that we perform at our best at a single, moderate level of arousal; in comparison, the IZOF hypothesis suggests that we have a zone, or range, of arousal in which we perform optimally
- the inverted-U hypothesis suggests that all athletes perform optimally at a universally defined moderate level of arousal (although this is influenced by some general athlete and task characteristics discussed above) and arousal levels above and below this point result in suboptimal performance. In contrast, the IZOF hypothesis suggests that not all athletes will produce their best performances when moderately aroused. One athlete's IZOF may be represented by objectively high levels of arousal and another's by objectively low levels of arousal. The IZOF hypothesis accounts for individual differences in levels of arousal that are associated with optimal sports performance.

Arousal too low	Optimal arousal	Arousal too high
Suboptimal performance	Best performance	Suboptimal performance
Below zone	In zone	Above zone

Figure 5.4 Individualized zones of optimal functioning (IZOF) hypothesis

Research evidence: individualized zones of optimal functioning

Raglin and Morris' (1994) research lent support for Hanin's (1989) proposal that different athletes will perform optimally at different levels of arousal with nine female volleyball players. Similar to most studies that have examined the IZOF hypothesis, the athletes' anxiety was measured rather than arousal. We discuss pre–competition anxiety and a commonly used measure of this response in Chapter 6. Based on the athletes' anxiety levels one hour prior to both an easy and a difficult match, Raglin and Morris identified that in comparison with normative levels of anxiety, that is, the average level of anxiety experienced by large samples of similar athletes, two athletes' optimal level of anxiety could be classified as low, four athletes' optimal anxiety was classified as moderate, and optimal anxiety was classified as high for the remaining three athletes. As the IZOF hypothesis predicts, optimal levels of anxiety differed between athletes. Based on this hypothesis, we would also expect that the athletes' performances would be better when their anxiety was within their own IZOF, although findings were not supportive. Nonetheless, an interesting finding was that prior to the easy match, only two athletes reported anxiety levels within their IZOF, whereas prior to the difficult match, seven of the athletes' anxiety levels were within their IZOFs.

Raglin and Morris's (1994) results provide some support for the idea of IZOF and that athletes may be more likely to experience anxiety within this zone prior to difficult competitions, suggesting a link between optimal anxiety and performance demands. However, results did not support the IZOF hypothesis proposal that performance would be superior in players who experience pre-competition anxiety within their IZOF compared with those whose anxiety was above or below this zone. The authors suggest that their lack of support was due to their inadequate measure of performance – percentage of total playing time that each player was on court.

Subsequent research using more robust performance measures, usually with individual athletes, has, however, bolstered support for the link between IZOF and performance. One such study was conducted by Robazzo et al. (2004) and involved 10 elite karate athletes. These authors extended the IZOF hypothesis to examine the relationship between performance and in and out of zone emotions, bodily symptoms and task-specific qualities. The athletes reported the level of positive and negative emotions they experienced (e.g. tense, aggressive), bodily symptoms (e.g. headache, energetic) and task-specific qualities (e.g. anticipation, strength) prior to 10 competitive events. After each competition, they provided a rating of their performance in their first-round match. Each athlete's own IZOF was calculated and, overall, results of the study supported the proposal that performance is better when emotions and bodily symptoms, but not task-specific qualities, were within the athlete's own IZOF.

Although the IZOF hypothesis can be seen as a development of earlier models (Drive Theory, inverted-U hypothesis), it too has its critics. In its original form, just like the inverted-U hypothesis, this hypothesis does not take into account the multidimensional nature of arousal. Since its conception, however, researchers have adapted the model to do so, as we have seen in the study by Robazzo et al. (2004) discussed above. Also, similar to the inverted-U hypothesis, the IZOF hypothesis provides us with a description of how, but not an explanation of why, arousal (or anxiety and other pre-competition emotional and physical symptoms) is related to sports performance. One theory that offers some insight into why arousal may affect performance in different ways is Reversal Theory.

Reversal Theory

Reversal Theory (Apter, 2001b) is a broad theory of motivation, emotion and personality, but here we will only examine its use by sport psychologists for understanding the arousal–performance relationship. Although Drive Theory and the inverted-U hypothesis proposed only one way in which arousal affects performance, Reversal Theory suggests that the effect of arousal on performance depends on how athletes *interpret* their current level of arousal. In turn, their interpretation depends on their current mental state, or in Reversal Theory terms, their metamotivational state. Specifically, the metamotivational states that influence arousal interpretations are known as the telic and paratelic metamotivational states. In Chapter 4, the more simple terms the serious and playful states were used; let's briefly recap on their meaning:

- When in the **telic (serious) state**, we are motivated to achieve something meaningful, we are looking ahead to the future, and we want our current behaviour to contribute towards longer term goals. Often, we also prefer to experience low levels of arousal.
- When in the **paratelic (playful) state**, we are motivated to be spontaneous and to engage with and enjoy what we are doing. We do not concern ourselves with any future consequences of our behaviour and do not need it to have any long-term purpose. Often, we also prefer high levels of arousal.

These states are seen as polar opposites, meaning that if we are in one state we cannot be in the other. Although we may have a preferred level of arousal in each state, we don't always experience our preferred levels of arousal. Figure 5.5 illustrates the emotional responses proposed to occur with different levels of arousal in these two states. In the telic state, with a typical preference for low arousal, we experience low arousal as pleasant relaxation but high arousal as unpleasant anxiety. Our preference for high arousal in the paratelic state leads us to interpret high arousal as pleasant excitement and low arousal as unpleasant boredom.

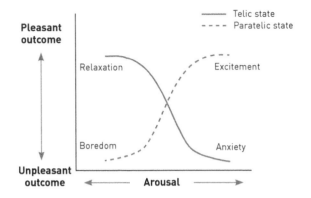

Figure 5.5 Reversal Theory states and arousal
Source: Reprinted with kind permission from Potocky and Murgatroyd, 1993

In applying the above ideas to sports performance, the optimal level of arousal for performance is not simply dependent on arousal level, but on how individuals interpret their arousal levels, which is determined by their metamotivational states. In the telic state, performance should be optimal when arousal is low, and in the paratelic state, performance should be optimal when arousal is high. Overall, performance should be better when there is no discrepancy between the arousal level the athlete is experiencing and the level they would prefer, and worse when there is a discrepancy between preferred and felt arousal levels (see Kerr, 1985).

Reversal Theory, arousal and performance: research evidence

Males and Kerr (1996) conducted a study with nine elite male slalom canoeists who were currently ranked in the top 10 in their country. Among other measures, the athletes reported their felt and preferred arousal levels prior to a number of competitions. Overall, as Reversal Theory predicts, performances were better when there was no discrepancy between felt and preferred arousal levels and worse when a discrepancy was reported. Results from two of the athletes provide a good illustration of these findings. Athlete one performed his best in front of his home crowd just after his selection for the national team and athlete two performed his best at the World Championships. In both cases, preferred and felt arousal levels were perfectly matched. Athlete one performed his worst at the World Championships and athlete two at a less important local event. In both cases, the athletes' levels of felt arousal were lower than the level they would have preferred to experience.

In a second study, Kerr et al. (1997) asked a group of novice and experienced archers to perform an archery task in four different conditions:

- telic state with high arousal
- telic state with low arousal
- paratelic state with high arousal
- paratelic state with low arousal.

They manipulated metamotivational state via the task instructions and arousal via physical activity and relaxation. No effects were found for the group as a whole, but when the experienced archers were considered independently, a marginal effect was found in support of Reversal Theory predictions. The discrepancy between preferred and felt arousal was greater, as expected, when participants performed the task in the telic state with high arousal and the paratelic state with low arousal. In addition, performance was superior when felt and preferred arousal levels were matched, that is, with low arousal in the telic state and high arousal in the paratelic state.

Perkins et al. (2001) conducted a further study which examined grip strength in a group of 28 elite athletes from explosive sports. Participants performed the task under six conditions: in the telic state with high or low arousal; in the paratelic state with high or low arousal, and with no state manipulation and high or low arousal. The athlete's metamotivational state was manipulated using imagery and their arousal was manipulated via different breathing rates. The study found mixed support for Reversal Theory proposals. There was no interactive effect of felt arousal and metamotivational state on performance as Reversal Theory would predict; that is, we would expect performance to be better under conditions of high arousal in the paratelic state and low arousal in the telic state. In partial support of Reversal Theory predictions, the athletes preferred a higher level of arousal when in the paratelic state and reported more anxiety and excitement in the telic and paratelic states, respectively. Nevertheless, regardless of arousal level, athletes performed better when in the paratelic state.

Summary

Sport psychologists have examined the use of Drive Theory, the inverted-U hypothesis, the individualized zones of optimal functioning (IZOF) hypothesis and Reversal Theory for understanding the relationship between arousal and sports performance. Drive Theory and the inverted-U hypothesis have been subject to a great deal of criticism. However, research support does exist for the inverted-U hypothesis, and factors affecting the level of optimal arousal have been identified including skill level, personality and task complexity. Research support for the IZOF hypothesis is mixed and recent extensions of this approach that consider arousal and other pre-competition responses, such as emotions and bodily symptoms, have supported its wider use. The use of Reversal Theory within sport psychology is less widespread, but is increasing and initial results suggest that it may offer insight into how athletes' states of mind influence their arousal interpretation and its subsequent effect on performance.

◉ Managing arousal

As discussed in this chapter, if athletes' pre-competition arousal levels are not optimal, whether high, low, or moderate in absolute terms, their performance may suffer. Athletes may use psychological strategies to help manage their arousal, with the aim of either increasing or decreasing arousal until the optimal level is reached.

Some of the strategies used to manage arousal are also used to manage anxiety (e.g. relaxation, imagery and self-talk). We may also use physical relaxation strategies to combat the increased heart rate, respiration rate and muscle tension that can result from increased arousal. An athlete might use imagery (see Chapter 7) to increase or decrease arousal. To increase arousal, a footballer may image himself scoring goals in a previous match, or to decrease arousal, a figure skater may imagine herself performing moves confidently in her familiar training environment. We could also use self-talk (self-generated statements directed at ourselves) to manage arousal level. A weightlifter may use self-talk to increase arousal (e.g. 'Come on, power!') before she attempts a lift and you may have seen weightlifters in the Olympics using self-talk out loud. Alternatively, to lower arousal after making a mistake, a tennis player may use self-talk, such as 'Stay calm, relax, stay calm'. These strategies are discussed in more detail in Chapters 6 and 7, so here we focus on one specific strategy to manage arousal: pre-performance routines.

Pre-performance routines

A **pre-performance routine** is an established and practised set of thought processes and behaviours athletes carry out before they perform a self-paced skill, like a penalty kick in football, a gymnastics routine or a shot put. Importantly, a self-paced skill does not depend on other people to determine when the athlete initiates their perform-ance of the skill and is not affected by others during its performance. Examples of pre-performance routines that you may have observed include the tennis player who bounces the ball and turns their racket a certain number of times before they serve, or the rugby player who takes a consistent number of steps back from the ball and images it flying through the posts before kicking for a conversion. Some elements of athletes' pre-performance routines are clearly visible to others (e.g. bouncing the tennis ball), whereas only athletes are aware of others (e.g. imaging a successful kick). Singer (2002: 367) lists the following as elements of a pre-performance routine, with a brief explanation of the role of each element (the italics emphasize key aspects of each element):

- *self-regulation of thoughts and emotions* so that they are compatible with what needs to be done
- narrow, deep and sustained *concentration*
- *ideal self-efficacy* and high but attainable performance expectancies
- optimal distribution in level and type of cortical activation in certain locations of the brain, indicating *a quiet mind*
- optimal visual orientation to the target (frequency and duration of fixations), indicative of *direction of attention*
- consistency in generating a routine in *attaining pre- and during performance states that facilitate performance*
- *automaticity* in activating those processes that enable one *to perform effortlessly, effectively and successfully*.

A pre-performance routine is a useful strategy for managing arousal, possibly because, as Singer (2002) suggests, it increases athletes' percep-tions of control over their performance, reducing the cognitive effects of arousal, and the physical and behavioural elements which are likely to follow. Singer also suggests that ideally the routine should be *automatic* so that the athlete doesn't have to consciously think about what to do and when. As a result, athletes then carry out the skill (e.g. shooting an arrow in archery or potting a ball in snooker) with little conscious input to disrupt their skilled performance.

Summary

Athletes can use various strategies to either increase or decrease pre-competition arousal to their preferred optimal level. These strategies include relaxation, imagery and self-talk (discussed in more detail in Chapters 6 and 7). A strategy we considered in more detail was pre-performance routines when the skill is self-paced (such as pistol shooting). Pre-performance routines may help athletes manage their arousal through a combination of strategies that can provide them with increased perceptions of control over their performance by executing a consistent and familiar routine prior to each performance attempt.

⊙ Conclusions

Athletes' pre-competition arousal levels seem to influence subsequent performance. Based on theory and research, we may suggest that optimal arousal differs among athletes and may depend on their personalities, their skill levels, their current motivational states, and the task they will perform. As is often the case, the different theoretical approaches discussed above have not always received consistent support from research. However, with the exception of Drive Theory, each perspective appears to offer worthwhile proposals to further understanding of the arousal–performance relationship. Useful strategies for increasing or decreasing pre-competition arousal include imagery, self-talk, relaxation and pre-performance routines.

⊙ Further reading

Kerr, J.H. (1997). *Motivation and emotion in sport: Reversal theory* (pp. 89–114). Hove: Taylor & Francis.

Landers, D.M. and Arent, S. M. (2010). Arousal-performance relationships. In J.M. Williams (ed.) *Applied sport psychology: Personal growth to peak performance* (6th edn, pp. 221–46). Boston: McGraw-Hill.

Williams, J.M. (2010). Relaxation and energizing techniques for regulation of arousal. In J.M. Williams (ed.) *Applied sport psychology: Personal growth to peak performance* (6th edn, pp. 246–66). Boston: McGraw-Hill.

Key search terms

Arousal and sport, inverted-U hypothesis, Drive Theory, individualized zones of optimal functioning (IZOF) hypothesis, Reversal Theory, telic state, paratelic state, pre-performance routines

Anxiety

In the previous chapter we considered arousal and how it might affect sporting performance. A concept closely related to arousal is anxiety which, similar to arousal, has attracted considerable attention from sport psychologists. Also similar to arousal, it is unlikely that any sports performer, at whatever level of competition, has never been anxious about sports competition. In this chapter we consider how anxiety influences sports performance.

In this chapter, we will examine:
- Different forms of anxiety and their definitions
- Models used to understand the relationship between anxiety and performance
- A self-presentation explanation for why athletes become anxious
- Strategies that athletes can use to manage their anxiety

Defining anxiety

Most of us find particular situations anxiety provoking, for instance sitting an exam or competing in sport. This tendency reflects our **trait anxiety**. Competitive trait anxiety represents our predisposition to see sports competition as anxiety provoking and this is likely to influence our **state anxiety**. State anxiety reflects our current anxiety in a specific situation and varies from one situation to another (e.g. increasing from less to more important sports competitions). State anxiety is influenced by trait anxiety: higher trait anxiety probably results in higher state anxiety because the athlete perceives an increased threat of being negatively evaluated (Martens, 1977). Competitive trait anxiety has been defined as:

> a tendency to perceive competitive situations as threatening and to respond to these situations with feelings of apprehension or tension (Martens, 1977: 23)

and state anxiety as:

> subjective, consciously perceived feelings of apprehension and tension, accompanied by or associated with activation or arousal of the autonomic nervous system (Spielberger, 1966: 17).

As we saw previously, arousal is multidimensional and so too is anxiety, with both cognitive and somatic dimensions. **Cognitive anxiety** represents the mental aspects of anxiety: the worries, doubts and concerns we have about our performance. **Somatic anxiety** represents our perceptions of the physiological symptoms of arousal, such as increased respiration rate or sweaty palms. Cognitive anxiety is defined as 'fear of failure and negative expectations about performance' and somatic anxiety as 'the individual's perceptions of their physiological state' (Hardy et al., 1996: 142).

Summary

Some athletes have a tendency to experience anxiety during competition and this is known as competitive trait anxiety. State anxiety is the anxiety experienced by athletes at a particular event. Both trait and state anxiety come in two separate forms: cognitive and somatic. Cognitive anxiety reflects the athlete's worries, concerns and doubts about performance, and somatic anxiety their perceptions of the symptoms of physiological arousal.

⊙ Theories and models describing the anxiety–performance relationship

Multidimensional Anxiety Theory

Martens et al. (1990b) proposed relationships between competitive state anxiety and sports performance in their Multidimensional Anxiety Theory. In line with their different composition, sources of derivation and pre-competition temporal patterning, Martens et al. proposed that cognitive anxiety, somatic anxiety and self-confidence demonstrate different relationships with performance. Self-confidence is discussed in more detail in Chapter 7, but in Multidimensional Anxiety Theory it is defined as the positive component of cognitive anxiety. The relationships predicted by Multidimensional Anxiety Theory are shown in Figure 6.1, illustrating that performance is predicted to decrease with increases in cognitive anxiety (a negative linear relationship), to share an inverted-U relationship with somatic anxiety, and to increase with increases in self-confidence (a positive linear relationship).

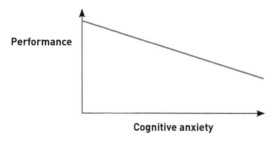

(a) Relationship between cognitive state anxiety and performance

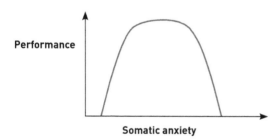

(b) Relationship between somatic state anxiety and performance

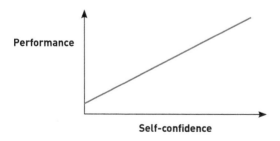

(c) Relationship between self-confidence and performance

Figure 6.1 Multidimensional Anxiety Theory

Research into Multidimensional Anxiety Theory

Craft et al. (2003) conducted a meta-analysis to determine whether or not the relationships predicted in Multidimensional Anxiety Theory have been supported by research. The aim of a **meta-analysis** is to use statistical analysis to provide an overview of the results of not just one study, but of all the studies which have examined a specific research question. By doing so, we can identify a consensus of the research findings in that area.

Craft et al.'s (2003) meta-analysis was based on 29 published and unpublished studies which examined the relationship between anxiety and performance and used the Competitive State Anxiety Inventory-2 (CSAI-2; Martens et al. 1990a) to measure pre-competition state anxiety. This is a commonly used measure of athletes' cognitive and somatic anxiety and self-confidence in relation to a competition in which they are about to participate. Each psychological variable is measured by nine questions. The scale used to respond to these questions and some example questions are provided in Table 6.1.

	Not at all	Somewhat	Moderately so	Very much so
I am concerned about losing *(cognitive anxiety question)*	1	2	3	4
My body feels tense *(somatic anxiety question)*	1	2	3	4
I feel self-confident *(self-confidence question)*	1	2	3	4

Table 6.1 Example items from the CSAI-2

Craft et al.'s (2003) results did not support the predicted negative linear relationship between cognitive anxiety and performance and their results concerning the relationship between somatic anxiety and performance were inconclusive. Only a few studies used the appropriate statistical analyses to allow the researchers to determine whether or not somatic anxiety and performance shared an inverted-U relationship as the theory predicts, but these studies did reveal an inverted-U relationship. As predicted, results supported a positive, albeit weak, relationship between self-confidence and performance. Craft et al. (2003) suggested that this mixed support for the theory's predictions may indicate one of two things:

1 The theory's predictions are incorrect.
2 The CSAI-2 is not a suitable measure of cognitive and somatic anxiety and self-confidence, meaning that the predicted relationships between these variables and performance are unlikely to be demonstrated.

They favoured the second of these two explanations because the CSAI-2 has been previously criticized as a measure of anxiety and self-confidence (Lane et al., 1999). It remains to be seen whether or not Multidimensional Anxiety Theory offers a viable model of understanding the relationship between pre-competition anxiety and athletic performance.

One of the key criticisms of Multidimensional Anxiety Theory is that although it adopts a multidimensional perspective of anxiety, it does not consider possible interactions between different dimensions of anxiety. As mentioned previously, cognitive and somatic anxiety, although separate constructs, are nevertheless related. A model that considers the interactive effects of different dimensions of anxiety could increase understanding of this complex response to competition, and its relationship with performance. This was one of the reasons why Fazey and Hardy (1988) developed their Catastrophe Model.

Catastrophe Model

In Chapter 5 we noted that one criticism of the inverted-U hypothesis was its proposal that once arousal increases above an optimal, moderate level, performance gradually declines, with incremental increases in arousal. Fazey and Hardy (1988) felt that this does not reflect athletes' real-life experiences. To account for this and the potential interactive effects of different dimensions of anxiety on performance, they developed the Catastrophe Model, as depicted in Figure 6.2. The model predicts interactive relationships between cognitive anxiety, physiological arousal and performance and is best understood by examining each of its surfaces individually:

- Beginning with the back of the performance surface (Figure 6.3a) when *cognitive anxiety is low*, physiological arousal and performance demonstrate what has been described as a 'gentle inverted-U' relationship. Increases and decreases in physiological arousal are associated with corresponding increases and decreases in performance, as proposed in Multidimensional Anxiety Theory for somatic anxiety and in the inverted-U hypothesis for arousal, but in a less dramatic fashion.

- Moving to the right-hand surface of the model (Figure 6.3b) where *physiological arousal is high*, cognitive anxiety and performance are negatively related with increases in cognitive anxiety resulting in gradual decreases in performance, matching proposals made in Multidimensional Anxiety Theory.
- Next, in the left-hand side of the model (Figure 6.3c) when *physiological arousal is low*, the model predicts a positive relationship between cognitive anxiety and performance, with increases in anxiety mirrored by increases in performance. This proposed relationship does not match Multidimensional Anxiety Theory proposals.
- Possibly the most important, and certainly the most dramatic, predicted relationship between these three variables occurs when *cognitive anxiety is high*, as depicted on the top, flat surface of the model (Figure 6.3d). The athlete's already high cognitive anxiety is associated with a high level of performance, and as physiological arousal increases, so does performance. This continues until physiological arousal increases beyond the individual's threshold level and, because cognitive anxiety is already elevated, results in a sudden, dramatic and catastrophic decrease in performance to a level far below that prior to the experienced catastrophe. Fazey and

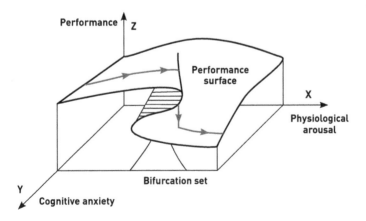

Figure 6.2 Catastrophe Model
Source: Reprinted from Hardy, 1993 with kind permission of John Wiley & Sons Ltd

Hardy (1988) suggested that when such a catastrophic decline in performance has occurred, simply restoring physiological arousal to pre-catastrophe levels will not help the athlete to regain high levels of performance. Instead, large decreases in physiological arousal are needed if the athlete has any chance of achieving their previously high level of performance.

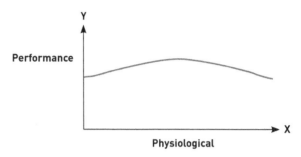

(a) Low cognitive anxiety

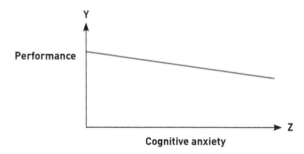

(b) High physiological arousal

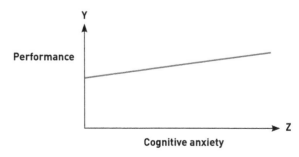

(c) Low physiological arousal

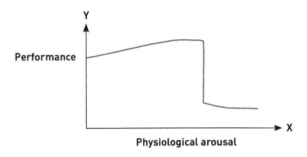

(d) High cognitive anxiety

Figure 6.3 Relationships between anxiety, arousal and performance in the Catastrophe Model

The Catastrophe Model makes two additional predictions concerning performance:

1 When physiological arousal and cognitive anxiety are both high, performance will be either catastrophic or excellent, but not mediocre; in other words, all or nothing with nothing in between.
2 When cognitive anxiety is high, the same level of physiological arousal will have a different effect on performance depending on whether arousal is increasing towards, or decreasing from, its maximum level. When arousal is increasing, performance will increase, and when arousal is decreasing, performance will decrease. This effect is called 'hysteresis'.

Only a few studies have used the Catastrophe Model to examine the relationship between anxiety and performance, probably because its complexity makes it difficult to investigate. Hardy and Parfitt (1991) tested the model's predictions with eight female basketball players who completed free throws one day prior to an important competition, to produce a condition of high cognitive anxiety, and one day after, to produce a condition of low cognitive anxiety. Physiological arousal was manipulated by asking them to complete shuttle runs prior to performing the free throws. The researchers confirmed that their anxiety manipulation had worked as the athletes were more anxious on the day prior to than following competition. Their results indicated support for the hysteresis hypothesis and for the proposal that at high, but not low, levels of cognitive anxiety, performance has the potential to be either catastrophic or exceptional.

Edwards et al. (2002) offered further support for the Catastrophe Model in an interpretative study involving interviews with eight elite male athletes from different sports. The athletes discussed competitions where they had experienced a catastrophic drop in performance, as described by one gymnast (p. 7):

> It went from this steady performance, that I was doing throughout the day, nothing was going wrong, confidence was just the same ... and then all of a sudden I got on one piece [of equipment] and the performance went from a good start or an unexpected good start to this unexpected, 'I'm on the floor!' ... and it was like just from one extreme to the next.

These performance catastrophes were experienced alongside a substantial decrease in self-confidence and an increase in cognitive anxiety, and, to a lesser extent, an increase in somatic anxiety.

This support for the Catastrophe Model notwithstanding, Cohen et al. (2003) did not find support for either performance catastrophes or hysteresis. However, we need to consider these results with caution because participants' cognitive anxiety was only increased to moderate and not extreme levels and the athletes performed a darts-throwing task in the laboratory, not a task from their own sport, which limits how meaningful their performance on this task was to them.

Directional perception hypothesis

When we examined the relationship between arousal and performance, we noted that one approach, Reversal Theory, emphasized the importance of individuals' interpretation of their arousal. Jones and his colleagues have suggested that this is an important factor when considering the effects of anxiety on performance, leading them to propose the directional perception hypothesis (Swain and Jones, 1993).

They suggested that to understand the relationship between anxiety and performance, we need to consider both the level (or intensity) of the athlete's anxiety and the athlete's interpretation of their anxiety. In other words, does the athlete interpret their anxiety as facilitative (helpful) for performance or as debilitative (unhelpful) for performance? They propose that although different athletes may experience the same level of anxiety, they may interpret its effects on performance differently and it is this interpretation, and not level, of anxiety that is most influential for performance.

There is support for the idea that not all athletes interpret pre-competition anxiety as debilitative for performance, and further evidence that athletes' interpretations of anxiety differ in relation to a range of factors, including competitive orientation, type of sport and level of competition. In a study by Jones et al. (1993), female gymnasts performed in a beam competition before which they reported their intensity and interpretation of anxiety. Based on their performances, they were divided into two groups: good and poor performers. As the authors predicted, and as we would expect, the good performers reported more facilitative interpretations of anxiety, and these were related to higher levels of self-confidence.

Some researchers have found support for Swain and Jones' (1993) proposal that anxiety interpretation will be more strongly related to performance than anxiety intensity (e.g. Butt et al., 2003). In contrast, other studies' results do not support this proposal (e.g. Jerome and Williams, 2000). More research is needed to determine which is more influential for performance – the athlete's intensity of anxiety prior to competition or their interpretation of this anxiety.

Evidence concerning individual differences in athletes' interpretations of anxiety is more conclusive. For instance, Jones and Swain (1992) found that, compared with less competitive athletes, those who were more competitive reported higher levels of self-confidence and more facilitative interpretations of cognitive and somatic anxiety prior to competition. Athletes from different sports also reported different interpretations of anxiety in a study by Hanton et al. (2000). Rugby players interpreted pre-competition somatic anxiety as facilitative for performance, whereas rifle shooters interpreted their pre-competition somatic anxiety as debilitative for performance. This is not surprising when we consider that rugby is a gross motor sport with a high degree of contact and where physiological arousal may help players to face these demands, while rifle shooters need a steady hand and so their perception that somatic anxiety will be detrimental for performance also makes sense. When Perry and Williams (1998) compared interpretations of anxiety between novice, intermediate and advanced tennis players, they found that, as expected, advanced tennis players reported more facilitative interpretations of anxiety and higher levels of self-confidence, like the good performers in Jones et al.'s (1993) study. In addition, males reported more facilitative interpretations of cognitive and somatic anxiety than did females.

Summary

A number of theories and models are used to understand the relationship between anxiety and athletic performance. Based on research conducted to date, we cannot fully reject or accept any of these theories/models. There is evidence to support and evidence to contradict each theory/model. Further research is needed before we can fully understand the relationship between anxiety and sports performance.

⊙ Why do athletes get anxious? Anxiety and self-presentation

The models and theories of anxiety and performance that we have considered make predictions about how anxiety might influence sports performance, but they tell us little about why athletes get anxious. One explanation that has received recent research attention is based on Impression Management Theory (Leary and Kowalski, 1990). Consider the following quote from Leary (1992: 347):

> Whenever people compete, they run the risk of conveying negative images of themselves – that they are unskilled, incompetent, unfit, unable to handle pressure, or whatever – to observers, teammates, coaches, opposing team members, and, often, the world at large.

As a result, athletes may try to monitor and control the images they convey to others and these processes are known as **impression management**, or self-presentation (Schlenker, 1980). According to Leary and Kowalski (1990), we are motivated to engage in self-presentation for three main reasons:

1 *Social and material gain:* an athlete may use self-presentation to show that they are like other team members to help them fit in and gain social status, or a professional athlete may want to present an image of a hard-working, good role model for children to help secure sponsorship contracts.

2 *Development of self:* our self-image is reinforced and influenced by how others see us. We may use self-presentation to influence others' perceptions of us, for instance as a worthwhile team member, which reinforces this image we hold of ourselves.

3 *Emotion regulation:* we may use self-presentation to present an image of being calm and in control which not only helps us to convey this image to others, but helps us to convince ourselves that this is how we feel.

There are a number of factors that increase our motivation to impression manage: goal relevance of impressions, value of desired outcomes, and discrepancies between desired and current image. Table 6.2 summarizes each of these factors and provides examples of when these may be relevant in competitive sport.

Factor	Explanation	Sporting examples
Goal relevance of impressions	Impression management is more relevant when our behaviour is public, when others exert an influence over outcomes we want to achieve, and when future interactions are likely with people in the current situation	■ Competing in front of spectators, friends and family or the media ■ Team selection based on the coach's decisions about us as an athlete ■ Future interactions with teammates, the coach and the opposition
Value of desired outcomes	Impression motivation is increased when the goals we want to achieve are not attainable by everyone, and when significant others who have status or power can influence their attainment	■ Gaining team selection from a squad of players ■ Training or playing in front of a national team selector
Discrepancies between desired and current image	Our impression motivation increases when we believe that the image we convey to others is not the image we want to convey	■ A substitute player who wants to be seen as competent and talented but their current role prevents them from doing so

Table 6.2 Factors that increase motivation to impression manage and some sporting examples

Self-presentation and anxiety: research evidence

As Leary (1992) predicted, athletes' **self-presentation concerns**, such as concerns about appearing fatigued or incompetent, do predict competitive trait anxiety (Hudson and Williams, 2001; Wilson and Eklund, 1998). Hudson and Williams (2001) also asked their study participants (male and female runners) who they most wanted to impress; 34% most wanted to impress their opponents and 29% most wanted to impress their coach. McGowan et al. (2008) also revealed that athletes' self-presentation concerns predict state anxiety. Based on a large sample of athletes across a range of sports and competitive levels, their results showed that cognitive state anxiety was predicted by athletes' self-presentation concerns about appearing athletically untalented and lacking mental composure and somatic state anxiety was predicted by self-presentation concerns about physical appearance.

Summary

A growing body of evidence is emerging that one of the primary reasons why athletes experience competitive anxiety is their self-presentation concerns. In our interactions with others, we aim to present positive images of ourselves to achieve social and material gain, to develop our self-identity, and to regulate emotions. Our motivation to impression manage is increased when others' impressions of us influence the achievement of goals which are not attainable by all and when we feel that a discrepancy exists between the image we want to convey and the image others have of us.

◉ Managing anxiety

A number of strategies, or interventions, have been proposed to help athletes to manage their anxiety and here we consider five key strategies: imagery, cognitive restructuring, relaxation, goal setting, and self-talk.

Possibly, different interventions are more suitable for managing the different anxiety types that we have encountered (cognitive and somatic anxiety), a suggestion labelled the **relaxation matching hypothesis** (Davidson and Schwartz, 1976). According to the relaxation matching hypothesis, cognitive anxiety is best managed using mental, or cognitively based, strategies, such as imagery, and somatic anxiety is best managed using bodily or physical-based strategies such as physical relaxation.

Studies conducted by Maynard and colleagues have demonstrated some support for the relaxation matching hypothesis with male, semi-professional footballers. In their first study, Maynard et al. (1995a) used a positive thought control intervention, a cognitively based strategy (Suinn, 1987), which involves training the athlete in the use of positive thoughts and controlling and using negative thoughts positively. In the second study, Maynard et al. (1995b) used a somatically based physical relaxation strategy to target somatic anxiety. Overall, results of these studies presented support for the relaxation matching hypothesis, with stronger support coming from the second of the two studies.

We now look in more detail at the five strategies:

- *Imagery:* Imagery was briefly introduced in Chapter 5. Because it is often promoted as a way to build self-confidence, it is discussed in more depth in Chapter 7. According to the relaxation matching hypothesis, imagery might be more suitable for managing cognitive anxiety, although it may also assist with the control of somatic symptoms.

- *Self-talk:* **Self-talk** refers to intentional statements that we say to ourselves either covertly (in our head) or overtly (out loud). An athlete experiencing anxiety might use self-talk to convince himself that he can cope against a difficult opponent, for instance 'Stay calm and focus on playing your game', as did elite female hockey players in Thomas et al.'s study (2007a) described below. Self-talk is generally categorized in one of two ways: cognitive or motivational (Hardy et al., 2001):
  - *Cognitive self-talk* focuses on the technical aspects of the sport or the athlete's goals and strategies, such as a tennis player about to serve who might use the following self-talk: 'High ball toss, clean contact'.
  - *Motivational self-talk* includes phrases or words intended to motivate the athlete, increase confidence and manage anxiety, for instance a runner might use the following self-talk coming up to the bell: 'You can do this, stay strong'.

- *Cognitive restructuring:* Cognitive restructuring involves reinterpreting negative thoughts and emotions to perceive them positively. For example, a footballer who is experiencing anxiety about bad weather could restructure their negative thoughts: 'This wind is terrible, I'll never keep the ball under control today', to 'Everyone has to play in this wind, you've done it in training and today's no different'. Thomas et al. (2007b) showed the efficacy of cognitive restructuring which involved athletes identifying, disputing and replacing negative symptoms of anxiety with positive interpretations of their anxiety.

- *Goal setting:* A goal is a target that we aim to achieve and three types of goals have been identified: outcome, performance, and process goals (Hardy and Jones, 1994):

- *Outcome goals* focus on an objectively defined social standard that we aim to achieve (e.g. placing in the top five in a triathlon).
- *Performance goals* focus on achieving a personal standard (e.g. a high jumper aiming to jump 5 cm above her personal best).
- *Process goals* focus on the processes involved in the sport (e.g. a javelin thrower focusing on his technique during the release of the javelin). Kingston and Hardy (1997) demonstrated in their study with golfers that process goals in particular were useful in helping athletes to control their cognitive anxiety.
- *Relaxation:* Physical relaxation can take a variety of forms but here we focus on just two: progressive muscular relaxation and centring:
  - *Progressive muscular relaxation* (PMR) is a whole-body relaxation strategy, which involves the athlete alternately tensing and relaxing each muscle, working progressively through the body's muscles. The main goal of PMR is to help the athlete to recognize unwanted muscle tension and then relax the muscle to remove this tension. Complete physical relaxation prior to a sporting event is unlikely to be particularly helpful as the athlete is more likely to want to fall asleep than compete when in such a physically relaxed state. PMR could, however, be a useful strategy to promote relaxation and sleep the night before an important competition. Alternatively, an athlete may use this technique with isolated muscle groups prior to competition, for instance a rifle shooter who experiences unwanted muscle tension in the shoulder muscles. Jones (2003) discusses the use of PMR as a method of managing not just arousal but other unwanted emotions experienced by the athlete.
  - *Centring,* as advocated by Gill (1986), to reduce arousal, focuses on regulating breathing and is more applicable for use prior to and during competition. Using this technique, the athlete focuses on taking deep, slow breaths, centres their attention on a specific area of the body (usually the navel) and may covertly repeat a calming word, e.g. 'Relax, relax ...'. Often when we become anxious, our breathing rate increases and negative thoughts race through our mind, and centring is a way of countering these effects. This brief technique can be useful during actual competition, and, anecdotally, has been used during particularly hairy moments when rock climbing. Savoy (1993) used centring as part of an intervention package with a female basketball player

and noted decreases in the athlete's cognitive and, more so, her somatic anxiety.

You may have noted that these strategies are not mutually exclusive, for instance cognitive restructuring and centring may include an element of self-talk. Although researchers often focus on just one strategy to enable them to isolate its effects on anxiety, in reality, athletes may use a combination of strategies. Indeed, Thomas et al. (2007a) found that the athletes in their study used a combination of strategies to deal with the anxiety they experienced in the seven-day competition period that was examined. On the day of competition, athletes who tended to view their anxiety as facilitative for performance (facilitators) used cognitive restructuring, imagery, positive self-talk, relaxation, performance and process goals. Two to one days prior to competition, facilitators used imagery, performance goals, cognitive restructuring and rationalization. In the two to three days following competition, they used imagery and rationalizing negative thoughts to review and reinterpret negative competition experiences. Athletes who tended to view their anxiety as debilitative for performance (debilitators) tried to use these strategies to manage their anxiety but their attempts were unsuccessful. On the day of competition, however, they did report that physical warm-up routines and support from others were useful strategies for managing their anxiety.

Thomas et al. (2007b) followed up this study with three of the hockey players who consistently experienced debilitative anxiety. They taught the athletes to use imagery, relaxation, restructuring, rationalization, self-talk and goal setting. They noted little effect on cognitive and somatic anxiety intensity, with the latter only decreasing in one athlete; in contrast, self-confidence increased in all three athletes. Importantly though, interpretation of cognitive and somatic anxiety changed from debilitative to facilitative and self-confidence interpretation became more facilitative as a result of the intervention. Performance was also seen to improve in all three players.

Summary

Different strategies can be used by athletes to manage their competition anxiety including relaxation, imagery, cognitive restructuring, self-talk and goal setting. Evidence exists to support the relaxation matching hypothesis that cognitively based strategies are more appropriate for managing cognitive anxiety and physically based strategies for managing somatic anxiety.

Facilitators may make better use of anxiety management strategies than debilitators, but research suggests that debilitators can be taught to use these strategies effectively to manage anxiety and improve performance.

Conclusions

Prior to competition, athletes may experience cognitive and somatic anxiety and a number of models and theories have been proposed to understand the relationship between anxiety and performance, for which evidence is mixed. A more conclusive finding is that one source of athletes' competition anxiety is their self-presentation concern, that is, concern about presenting an image of a talented, composed athlete to significant others. Not all athletes interpret their anxiety as debilitative for performance, instead, some perceive their anxiety as facilitative for performance and this seems to be related to higher levels of self-confidence and performance accomplishment. Facilitators seem to make better use of strategies such as imagery and relaxation to manage their anxiety, but training programmes can also help debilitators to make effective use of such strategies.

Further reading

Cox, R.H. (2006). *Sport psychology: Concepts and applications* (6th edn). London: McGraw-Hill.
Lavallee, D., Kremer, J., Moran, A.P. and Williams, M. (2004). *Sport psychology: Contemporary themes*. Basingstoke: Palgrave Macmillan.
Moran, A.P. (2004). *Sport and exercise psychology: A critical introduction*. Hove: Routledge.

Key search terms

Cognitive anxiety, somatic anxiety, trait anxiety, state anxiety, Multidimensional Anxiety Theory, directional perception hypothesis, Catastrophe Model, managing anxiety, anxiety strategies

Chapter 7

Self-confidence

In his study of elite athletes from various sports, Hemery (1986) found most had high levels of **confidence** and thought their self-beliefs contributed to success. Similarly, many non-elite coaches and athletes think self-confidence influences performance. Given that many individuals proclaim the benefits of self-confidence, it is understandable that sport psychologists have investigated the topic, along with how it is developed and influences performance. Although Hemery found most elite athletes had high levels of confidence, he also observed that many sometimes experienced self-doubt. Despite experiencing some self-doubt, however, these individuals still believed that they could perform well at the highest competitive levels (Hardy et al., 1996).

In this chapter, we will examine:
- How confidence is defined
- Theories sport psychologists use to understand confidence
- The relationship confidence has with performance, behaviour, emotions and thoughts
- Ways to enhance confidence, with a focus on imagery

Self-confidence definition and theory

Although sport psychologists have proposed many self-confidence definitions, a common theme among them is a focus on athletes' perceptions about their abilities to achieve success (Hardy et al., 1996). Vealey and Chase (2008: 66) recently defined self-confidence as 'the belief that one has the internal resources, particularly abilities, to achieve success'. A tennis player with high levels of confidence, for example, believes she has the skills, strength, stamina and tactical sense to beat her opponent in an upcoming game. Sport psychologists have drawn mainly on two self-confidence theories when conducting research and working with athletes: Bandura's (1997) Self-efficacy Theory and Vealey's (2001) Model of Sport Confidence.

Bandura's Self-efficacy Theory

Bandura's (1997) Self-efficacy Theory has underpinned most research examining sport confidence (Vealey and Chase, 2008). **Self-efficacy** refers to athletes' beliefs that they can execute the behaviours required to produce desired outcomes (Bandura, 1977b). Bandura differentiates self-efficacy from outcome expectations, which involve beliefs that certain behaviours will lead to given outcomes. For example, a high jumper might believe he is able to execute the correct technique and attain a certain height to win an upcoming competition (self-efficacy). His outcome expectation is that winning the competition will result in him being selected to represent his country at the Olympics. Both outcome expectations and self-efficacy influence behaviour and performance. Athletes who do not think a specific behaviour will result in desired outcomes (low outcome expectancy) may be less motivated to try those actions. In addition, athletes who think a specific behaviour will result in a desired outcome, but who doubt their ability to perform that behaviour, may also be less motivated.

In addition to self-efficacy, motivation and ability influence behaviour and performance. According to Bandura (1977b), when athletes have the skills and the desire, their self-efficacy is a major predictor of performance. Bandura suggested self-efficacy influences people's behaviours, thoughts and emotions. For example, swimmers with high self-efficacy will probably choose to attend training more regularly, expend more effort, and persist longer than those with low self-beliefs. These confident individuals will set higher goals and have more helpful thoughts and emotions. As a result of their efforts, they may have better chances of success. Later we will examine research supporting Bandura's suggestions.

People's self-efficacy beliefs are constructed from four major sources: mastery experiences, vicarious experiences, verbal persuasion, and physiological and emotional states (Bandura, 1997). These four sources enhance or deflate self-efficacy. In cricket, for example, batters observing teammates performing well against fast bowlers may experience enhanced self-efficacy. Alternatively, these individuals' batting self-efficacy may drop if they observe teammates struggling. The presence of these sources, however, does not automatically change self-efficacy. Any source changes self-efficacy only when performers interpret the information associated with that source. Cricket batters' self-efficacies may not improve, for example, when they observe teammates performing well against fast bowling if they think their teammates are much more skilled than themselves.

The four information sources are briefly described:

- **Mastery experiences** have the most influence on self-efficacy. Having completed the task previously provides the most authentic evidence that an individual can be successful (Bandura, 1997). Previous success may enhance self-efficacy, whereas past failures may reduce self-belief. Previous successes and failures do not necessarily influence self-efficacy. Most individuals acknowledge that sports performance is influenced by various factors, such as opponents' abilities, circumstances surrounding the events, and officials' decisions. Athletes' interpretations of these variables influence whether previous performances influence self-efficacy. A sprinter who achieved a personal best in a recent competition, for instance, may not have enhanced self-efficacy in an upcoming race if she believed her time was assisted by a strong wind.

- **Vicarious experiences** refer to watching models undertake an activity (Bandura, 1997). The model might be a person performing the task in front of the athlete, such as in the cricketing example above. Symbolic modelling occurs when people watch individuals perform on video monitors or other visual media, such as when watching athletes on television. Self-modelling occurs when individuals watch themselves perform, such as when coaches film their athletes for instructional purposes. Self-modelling also includes imagery. The affect that observing a model has on self-efficacy is influenced by how individuals interpret the demonstration. The change in self-efficacy from observing a demonstration is also influenced by factors associated with the model; for example demonstrations may be more influential when the model is similar to the athlete in ability and other personal attributes. Demonstrations may also be more influential when athletes observe multiple models rather than a single person.

- **Verbal persuasion** involves other people expressing their faith in an individual's capabilities, such as when coaches tell their athletes they have improved. Bandura (1997) suggested that verbal persuasion alone may be limited in its ability to produce lasting self-efficacy increases, but can lead to improvements if realistic. Verbal persuasion might improve self-efficacy enough so that individuals persist until they succeed. Mastery experiences may then enhance self-efficacy further. Verbal efforts to increase self-efficacy are influenced by athletes' perceptions of persuaders' credibility and knowledge of the activity. Athletes may believe the words of highly respected, experienced coaches, for example, more than those of individuals who have not played or taught the sport.
- *Physiological and emotional states* provide clues as to athletes' abilities to meet task demands. People who get tired walking, for example, may have low beliefs that they can run marathons. As another illustration, football players who notice they are tense and have butterflies racing around their stomachs prior to a game may believe they are not capable of performing well. Similar to other information sources, actual physiological and emotional states do not influence self-efficacy. Instead, athletes' interpretations of their physiological and emotional states influence their self-efficacy.

Information sources do not operate in isolation. In any situation, athletes may be exposed to multiple sources and the effect of each may be different. In addition, athletes may differ in their responses to the sources and interpret them according to various criteria (Bandura, 1997). Coaches might find their attempts to build self-efficacy more successful if they consider how athletes will probably react to their interventions.

Vealey's Model of Sport Confidence

Building on Self-efficacy Theory, Vealey (1986) proposed a model that has underpinned much research on sport confidence. Vealey (2001: 556) defined **sport confidence** as the 'degree of certainty that individuals possess about their ability to be successful in sport'. For example, cricketers with high levels of sport confidence believe they are able to score 100 runs in an upcoming game. Sport confidence may be considered as either state-like or trait-like, depending on the time reference of interest (Vealey, 2001). Sport psychologists interested in athletes' self-beliefs at a specific moment in time are interested in state sport confidence. Sport psychologists who ask athletes how certain they typically are in their abilities are interested in trait sport confidence. Vealey proposed three types of sport confidence, as illustrated in Figure 7.1 (Vealey and Chase, 2008):

- *Resilience* refers to athletes' beliefs they can regain focus, recover from poor performances, resolve doubts, and overcome setbacks.
- *Physical skills and training* refers to athletes' beliefs in their abilities to execute the physical skills and movements needed for successful performance.
- *Cognitive efficiency* refers to how certain athletes are that they can focus, maintain concentration, and make suitable decisions.

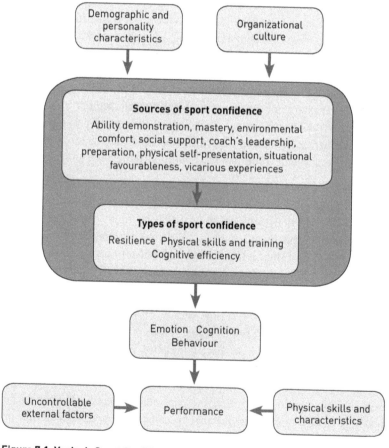

Figure 7.1 Vealey's Sport Confidence Model
Sources: Adapted from Vealey, 2001; Vealey and Chase, 2008

Athletes' self-confidence is influenced by nine information sources, listed in Table 7.1 (Vealey et al., 1998). The sources of sport confidence have similarities with Bandura's (1997) sources of self-efficacy. Both theories, for example, include mastery and vicarious experiences. Understanding the information sources provides athletes and coaches with ideas about how to build confidence and perhaps enhance performance.

Source	Confidence improves when athletes
Mastery	Think their skill levels have improved
Ability demonstration	Demonstrate greater ability than others
Vicarious experiences	Watch others perform well
Social support	Believe others are supportive and encouraging
Coach leadership	Have faith in their coach's leadership abilities
Preparation	Feel physically and mentally prepared
Physical self-presentation	Think they appear well to others
Situational favourableness	Believe the situation is favourable towards them
Environmental comfort	Feel comfortable in the environment

Table 7.1 Sources of sport confidence
Source: Adapted from Vealey et al., 1998

Vealey (2001) argued that the sporting organizational culture influences the ways in which athletes' confidence is developed and manifested. For example, Olympic athletes have suggested that their confidence can be fragile and unstable as a result of the pressures and distractions associated with international competitive events, such as the Olympics Games (Gould et al., 1999). Vealey (2001) also argued that differences among individuals, in terms of their demographics (e.g. age and gender) and personality characteristics, influence the display and development of self-confidence. For example, research has suggested that females report lower levels of confidence than males when involved in activities perceived to be more masculine (Lirgg et al., 1996). Males report lower levels of confidence compared with females in sports considered to be more feminine (Clifton and Gill, 1994).

Like Bandura (1997), Vealey (2001) described sport confidence as a 'mental modifier' that influences how athletes feel, think and behave (and perform). Similarly, Vealey (2001) also acknowledged that uncontrollable external factors, such as the weather, luck or opponents, may influence performance. Another influence on performance includes athletes' actual physical skills and capabilities. Although confidence may lead to more helpful emotions, behaviours and thoughts, sometimes athletes' performances are hindered or enhanced by factors outside their control, or they do not have the necessary resources to complete a task successfully.

Summary

Self-confidence refers to athletes' beliefs that they have the skills and abilities to achieve success. Sport psychologists have used Bandura's (1997) and Vealey's (2001) theories most often to understand athletes' self-confidence. Both Bandura and Vealey hypothesized that athletes' beliefs in their abilities to succeed influence their motivation, behaviours, thoughts and emotions in ways that enhance the likelihood they will be successful. In the following section we examine the research that supports Bandura's and Vealey's hypotheses.

Self-confidence, performance, behaviour, thoughts and emotions

Performance

Sport psychologists have focused a lot of attention on the relationship that self-confidence has with performance (Vealey and Chase, 2008). In this section the major research findings are examined with respect to design – descriptive or experimental.

One major finding from the descriptive research is that athletes and coaches believe self-confidence contributes to sporting success. For example, in Durand-Bush et al.'s (2001) survey of 335 athletes from 35 sports, including elite and non-elite individuals, participants identified self-confidence as one of the most important or useful mental skills (along with goal setting, commitment and focusing). As a second example, Olympic athletes and coaches have identified self-confidence as an influence on performance at the elite level (Gould et al., 1999, 2002). Although athletes' and coaches' perceptions do not provide evidence that confidence influences performance, research suggests they are likely to be open to strategies designed to increase self-beliefs.

A second major finding is that self-confidence differs between successful and unsuccessful athletes. In Durand-Bush et al.'s (2001) survey, self-confidence was higher in elite athletes than in their non-elite colleagues. In other studies, gymnasts and divers who qualified for the Olympic Games had higher self-confidence than non-qualifiers, with self-confidence data being collected before the qualification trials (Highlen and Bennett, 1983; Mahoney and Avener, 1977).

A third major theme is that self-confidence, when measured prior to an event, is related to sport performance (Craft et al., 2003; Moritz et al., 2000; Woodman and Hardy, 2003). The relationship is not strong, however, and there are two possible reasons:

1 Maybe the relationship is strong, but scientists have not been able to measure performance, confidence or both accurately enough.
2 It is likely that confidence is not the only influence on performance. Athletes' performances are probably influenced by a number of other factors, such as the weather or luck.

Sport psychologists have found that the confidence–performance relationship is influenced by other factors. For example, the relationship appears stronger when athletes are performing familiar rather than novel tasks (Moritz et al., 2000). According to Bandura (1997), people need to understand the demands of a task before they can make accurate self-efficacy judgements. With novel tasks, people may not understand the skills and abilities needed for successful completion and may be less capable of predicting their performances than with familiar activities. As a second example, the confidence–performance relationship seems to be stronger at higher (e.g. elite) than lower (e.g. club) levels of competition (Woodman and Hardy, 2003). At higher levels of competition, performance variation might be lower because athletes are performing well-learned tasks, whereas individuals operating at lower levels of competition may be less proficient. Also, athletes at higher levels of competition may have greater self-awareness of their abilities than those at lower levels. Individuals competing at higher levels may be able to make more accurate self-efficacy judgements compared with people playing at lower levels of competition.

It is generally not possible to conclude from descriptive research that self-confidence influences performance. Even when measured prior to a competition, it is still not clear that self-confidence influenced performance, only that the two variables were related. Experimental research does exist, however, indicating that self-confidence may be a causal factor in motor skill execution (Vealey and Chase, 2008). In a classic study, Nelson and Furst (1972) had 12 pairs of participants arm wrestle each other when both contestants believed the weaker individual to be the stronger person. In 10 of the 12 pairs, the winner was the person who was objectively weaker, but thought to be stronger by both participants. These results suggest that a person's expectations may have an influence on performance. Other researchers, since Nelson and Furst, have also found that participants manipulated to have high levels of self-efficacy perform better than those with low levels of self-belief (Weinberg et al., 1981; Wells et al., 1993).

Behaviours, cognitions and emotions

Evidence supports the hypothesis that athletes with higher levels of confidence or self-efficacy may exert more effort and persist longer when performing compared to individuals with lower self-beliefs (Cox and Whaley, 2004; George, 1994; Weinberg et al., 1981). In addition, confident athletes may have stronger intentions to continue participating in their sports and select more difficult tasks when given the opportunity compared with people with less self-belief (Chase, 2001; Escarti and Guzman, 1999). It seems reasonable to suggest that individuals who select difficult tasks, expend lots of effort, and persist in their attempts may improve their skill levels more and attain higher levels of sporting success than individuals who choose easy activities and who do not persevere.

As might be expected, self-confidence is related to various self-perceptions such as perceived ability, self-esteem, perceived success and sport identity (Cox and Whaley, 2004; Hall and Kerr, 1997; Vealey, 1986). In addition, confidence has been related with **problem-focused coping** (as opposed to **emotion-focused coping**), competitiveness, goal commitment and a task mastery goal orientation (Grove and Heard, 1997; Hall and Kerr, 1997; Lerner and Locke, 1995; Swain and Jones, 1992). Self-confidence may also be related to concentration and effective decision-making (Smith et al., 1995). Based on these findings, it might be expected that confident individuals, compared with those who doubt their abilities, may have the positive self-perceptions and adaptive achievement-related beliefs that contribute to enhanced performance (Vealey and Chase, 2008).

Self-confidence is positively related to positive mood and emotion, and negatively related to negative mood and emotion (Prapavessis and Grove, 1994; Treasure et al., 1996). In addition, it appears that self-confidence helps buffer the influence of anxiety on performance (Vealey and Chase, 2008). For example, high levels of self-confidence are associated with positive or facilitative interpretations of anxiety symptoms. In contrast, low levels of self-belief are associated with negative or debilitative interpretations of anxiety symptoms (Edwards and Hardy, 1996; Thomas et al., 2004).

Summary

Research supports Bandura's (1997) and Vealey's (1986) hypotheses that self-confidence leads to better performance through influencing people's behaviours, thoughts and emotions. They predicted that, for example, confident individuals would try harder and for longer when engaged in an activity and, as a result, they are more likely to be successful.

Enhancing self-confidence

Table 7.2 presents Short and Ross-Stewart's (2009) suggestions for improving self-efficacy based on Bandura's (1997) four information sources. Any attempt to increase self-efficacy or confidence will probably be more successful when drawing on more than one information source. For example, coaches might set realistic goals focused on skill improvement (mastery experiences), encourage athletes to use positive self-talk (verbal encouragement), and film the individuals doing well in competition (vicarious experience). Sport psychologists often suggest imagery improves confidence, and this method is now discussed.

Mastery experiences
■ Structure environment to ensure success
■ Focus on progressive skill development
■ Make use of simulation training
■ Modify equipment so it is suitable for athlete
■ Make use of realistic goal setting
■ Focus goals on skill learning rather than outcome (winning)
■ Reset goals when needed to keep them realistic
Vicarious experiences
■ Use models similar to the athlete
■ Have models express high levels of self-efficacy
■ Make use of self-modelling via video
■ Teach athletes to use imagery

Verbal persuasion
▪ Use verbal persuasion that is believable ▪ Focus on athletes' capabilities rather than deficiencies ▪ Focus on learning progress made rather than just competitive results ▪ Encourage the use of positive self-talk
Physiological and emotional states
▪ Teach athletes to interpret emotional and physiological states as signs of readiness ▪ Teach athletes coping strategies so they can regulate their emotional and physiological states

Table 7.2 Suggestions for enhancing self-efficacy
Source: Short and Ross-Stewart, 2009

What is imagery and does it work?

Imagery is a mental process involving multisensory experiences in the absence of actual perception (Callow and Hardy, 2005). For example, athletes might see themselves lying on their backs holding a barbell above their heads even though they are not in the training environment or have access to equipment. They may also feel the weight pushing down on their hands, the tension in their bodies as they perform bench press repetitions, and their laboured breathing.

Research reveals that imagery may lead to increased motor skill execution, learning and confidence (Driskell et al., 1994; Short and Ross-Stewart, 2009). For example, Driskell et al. provided evidence that imagery improved motor skill execution for both cognitive and physical tasks, as well as being helpful for both novice and experienced participants.

Making the most of imagery

Holmes and Collins' (2001) PETTLEP (physical, environment, task, timing, learning, emotion and perspective) model identifies seven aspects assisting the production of effective images. Each of the seven aspects is detailed below:

- *Physical:* Athletes may find their imagery more effective if they manipulate the physical component to resemble, as much as possible, physical preparation, execution and outcome. For example, athletes might replicate the movement rather than just stand, sit or lie still. They can also hold equipment and wear sports clothing. In addition, athletes can imagine coping with the fatigue and discomfort associated with their sports.

- *Environment:* Individuals can mimic the training and performance environments. They might even undertake imagery at the actual location. If unable to physically recreate the environment, athletes might make use of videos, photographs and descriptions from others who have performed at the location.
- *Task:* Individuals will probably find their imagery more effective if they focus on the same things they attend to during training and competition. To help them, athletes may use the same types of self-talk cues during imagery that they employ when training and performing.
- *Timing:* Generally, athletes will probably obtain benefit when they keep the timing of their imagery similar to that of actual movement. There may be occasions, however, when slowing down the images may be beneficial (Callow and Hardy, 2005). Slower images might, for example, help individuals to identify and address aspects of poor technique, or help with skills they typically rush under pressure.
- *Learning:* As learning takes place, there are changes in the sensations individuals experience with movement. For example, the sensations individuals have when first learning free weight exercises is different to those they have when they have developed efficient technique. Athletes may find their imagery most helpful when they focus on the sensations they experience when physically performing tasks.
- *Emotion:* Effective imagery includes the emotions people have when physically performing the task. A recommendation sometimes made is that athletes can combine imagery with relaxation techniques. Many participants, however, prefer to be highly aroused for training and performance. On the basis of current evidence, individuals are advised to imagine the activation levels and emotions they desire when actually performing (Holmes and Collins, 2001).
- *Perspective:* People can image a movement from two perspectives: internal or external. During **internal imagery**, individuals perceive the task as they would if actually performing the movement ('through their own eyes'). During **external imagery**, individuals perceive the task from the third person perspective, as if they were watching a video of themselves performing. Over the years, sport psychologists have differed regarding the perspective advocated. According to Callow and Hardy (2005), one consideration is the type of task being imagined. If form is important, then individuals might be best to adopt an external visual perspective (e.g. during

gymnastics). If the task relies on perceptual information, athletes may benefit from an internal visual perspective.

Summary

Drawing on Bandura's (1997) and Vealey's (2001) information sources can help coaches and athletes identify specific strategies to enhance self-confidence, as illustrated in Table 7.2 above. Imagery is one strategy that has been found to enhance confidence and Holmes and Collins' (2001) PETTLEP model can assist in making imagery most effective.

Conclusions

Many coaches and athletes believe that self-confidence is a key ingredient to successful performance. Sport psychologists have provided supporting evidence that self-belief leads to the behaviours, thoughts and emotions that underpin optimal performance. Bandura's (1997) and Vealey's (2001) models have provided a solid theoretical base to the research and have great applied value. Both models allow sport psychologists to identify strategies to help athletes in their specific situations and illustrate how research and practice in sport psychology benefit from a good theoretical understanding of the issues with which athletes and coaches grapple.

Further reading

Bandura, A. (1997). *Self-efficacy: The exercise of control*. New York: Freeman.

Short, S. and Ross-Stewart, L. (2009). A review of self-efficacy based interventions. In S.D. Mellalieu and S. Hanton (eds) *Advances in applied sport psychology: A review* (pp. 221–80). London: Routledge.

Vealey, R.S. (2001). Understanding and enhancing self-confidence in athletes. In R.N. Singer, H.A. Hausenblas and C.M. Janelle (eds) *Handbook of sport psychology* (2nd edn, pp. 550–65). New York: Wiley.

Key search terms

Self-confidence, self-efficacy, imagery, psychological skills training

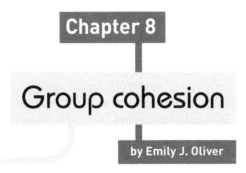

Chapter 8

Group cohesion

by Emily J. Oliver

Examining the dynamics and processes within groups is important in any context where individuals need to work efficiently together. Researchers have studied group dynamics in a number of domains including the military, businesses, schools and, more recently, sport. This chapter will focus specifically on one aspect of group dynamics, namely group cohesion.

Cohesion has been described as a prerequisite to athletic success (Straub, 1975), and the term is frequently employed by sports commentators when describing a seemingly close-knit and efficient sports team. For example, the 'invincible' Arsenal soccer team of 2004–05, who remained unbeaten throughout the season, were described as highly cohesive both as a playing unit and off the field. Conversely, other teams appear divided, with publicity about locker-room disagreements and players arguing on the pitch – in some infamous cases, leading to physical assaults. This poor cohesion is often linked with disappointing performances, despite the obvious potential and talent of the team, for example the 2004 US Olympic basketball 'dream team'. Given the perceived importance of cohesion within teams, it is unsurprising that this topic has received a great deal of research focus. This chapter will consider the evidence examining the effects of cohesion on performance and both group and individual factors. In addition, we will discuss some of the proposed antecedents (causes) of cohesion, and evaluate the effectiveness of interventions designed to increase the cohesion of a team.

In this chapter, we will examine:
- How cohesion is defined and conceptualized in sport
- Ways in which cohesion has been measured and studied
- The effects of cohesion on performance, team and individual outcomes
- How to improve the cohesion of a team

⊙ What are groups?

Given that cohesion occurs within groups, it is important to consider what is meant by this term. What makes a number of individual athletes or players a 'group', or a 'team'? Researchers have composed and argued over many definitions of a group (for a thorough discussion, see Carron et al., 2005). There are common elements, however, to most of the definitions. A **group** is held to contain two or more individuals that interact with each other (Shaw, 1981), typically with a common goal. Other characteristics of a group may include shared values or norms (e.g. Sherif and Sherif, 1956), and the presence of formal or informal roles. Sports teams can be considered groups because there is a common goal (e.g. winning), individuals define themselves as belonging to that group, and typically within the team there is a structured organization and defined roles (e.g. captains).

Within sport, there are several different groups of athletes that may be considered or referred to as a team. For example, at the Olympics, we refer to 'the British archery team', and in 2008 the British cycling team won 'Team of the year' in the BBC Sports Personality Awards. In the competition arena, however, most members of these 'teams' compete as individuals. Carron (1988) suggested that sports teams can be classified according to the type of the interactions between their members:

- *independent teams:* in which individuals compete separately (e.g. Ryder Cup golfers)
- *reactive teams:* occur in sports in which individuals have to respond to the actions of their teammates, but not necessarily work at the same time (e.g. bowler and wicketkeeper/fielder in cricket)
- *coactive teams:* in which individuals compete side by side but with limited interaction (e.g. members of a rowing boat)
- *interactive teams:* these occur in sports in which there is ongoing interaction between team members (e.g. football, volleyball).

How does a group form?

Tuckman (1965) developed a widely used group development model to explain the processes that occur when a group develops and becomes more cohesive as a unit. His model comprises four main stages, referred to by the mnemonic 'forming', 'storming', 'norming', and 'performing'.

A fifth stage, known as 'adjourning', was added in later model development (Tuckman and Jensen, 1977):

1   During *forming*, the group begins to establish its task and purpose, and group members familiarize themselves which each other.
2   *Storming* is so called due to the disagreements or conflicts that arise. The newly formed team may disagree regarding decisions made or the strategy they are pursuing to reach the group goal.
3   Once this conflict has been resolved, *norming* occurs, during which common effects of group membership can be observed. During this stage, group norms and standards of behaviour become evident, and the group cooperates to move towards the goal. Individuals are now more likely to engage in **groupthink**; that is, when groups strive for normality instead of appraising and considering a range of options (Janis, 1972), and to make sacrifices for the benefit of the group as a whole.
4   *Performing* refers to the functioning of a stabilized group, which is operating effectively in pursuit of its goal.
5   *Adjourning* refers to the period following task accomplishment, in which contact between members and their dependency on the group is reduced.

Summary

Groups are typically defined as two or more individuals who interact with each other, working towards a common goal (e.g. Shaw, 1981). Tuckman's (1965) group development theory has been applied to examine the processes involved in group formation, known as 'forming', 'storming', 'norming' and 'performing'. Within sport, teams and groups may vary in their composition and intradependency.

What is cohesion?

Defining cohesion

One of the classic definitions of **cohesion** suggests that it is the total field of forces causing individuals to remain in a group (Festinger et al., 1950). Other early definitions of cohesion focus on how strongly members are attracted to the group (Festinger et al., 1963), or how resistant the group is to outside disruption (Gross and Martin, 1952). Alternative definitions focus on the similarity of group beliefs, opinions or goals (e.g. Paskevich, 1995). This could include beliefs about the purpose of the group, what goals it should be pursuing and how, or more generic cultural beliefs. A widely used definition specific to sport describes cohesion as the tendency for a group 'to stick together to pursue goals and achieve member satisfaction' (Carron et al., 1997: 3). This definition is useful as it highlights not only goal pursuit, but also member satisfaction as one of the desired outcomes of group functioning.

A conceptual model of cohesion

In 1985, Carron et al. published a paper which presented a new conceptual model of cohesion (Figure 8.1), which divides cohesion into four main constructs. Two of these focus on the integration of the group as a whole, and two focus on individuals' attraction to the group. In each of these subcategories, social and task elements are included. Cohesion is comprised of four facets:

1 group integration for the task (GI–T)
2 group integration for social factors (GI–S)
3 an individual's attraction to the group task (ATG–T)
4 an individual's attraction to the group socially (ATG–S).

Cohesion is highest when each element is high:

- High GI–T occurs when a group is united and efficiently integrated in pursuing its performance- or task-related goals.
- High GI–S occurs when a group is socially close, enjoys spending time together and may socialize often.
- ATG–T is high when an individual is strongly concerned with and desires the task outcome being pursued by the group.
- ATG–S is high when an individual is closely affiliated with the group and desires its company.

Carron et al.'s (1985) model has two major strengths:

1 It looks at individuals' perceptions of their own feelings towards the group, as well as the group's feelings as a whole. This gives us a more accurate idea of the cohesion of a group, because it may be possible for individuals to be highly attracted towards the group, but the group to be poorly integrated, with many divisions and conflicting goals.

2 It distinguishes between task and social concerns of group members; that is, it differentiates between how an individual may feel about the group as a unit to achieve a specific goal (task focused) versus how they may feel about the group as a social unit.

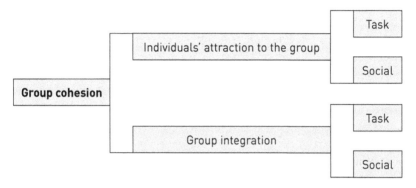

Figure 8.1 A conceptual model of cohesion
Source: Adapted from Carron et al., 1985

Summary

Cohesion in sport has been defined as the tendency for a group 'to stick together to pursue goals and achieve member satisfaction' (Carron et al., 1997: 3). Carron et al.'s (1985) model of cohesion suggests that it is comprised of four main elements; group integration for the task (GI-T), group integration for social factors (GI-S), an individual's attraction to the group task (ATG-T), and an individual's attraction to the group socially (ATG-S).

◉ Measuring cohesion

The Group Environment Questionnaire

The most widely used measure of cohesion within sports research is the Group Environment Questionnaire (GEQ; Carron et al., 1985). The GEQ contains items measuring the four elements of cohesion; individuals' attraction to the group task, individuals' attraction to the group socially, the group's integration for the task, and the group's integration socially. It is designed to be completed by athletes or group members.

Issues to consider when measuring cohesion

It is important to consider when determining the cohesion of a group that there may be subgroups or units within a team that could have differing levels of cohesion (e.g. offensive versus defensive units in American football teams). Accurately predicting behaviour or perform-ance may be dependent on selecting the most appropriate unit to measure cohesion; that is, the team versus functional subgroups. In some cases, it may be useful to measure extra-group perceptions of cohesion; that is, how cohesive a group is perceived to be by individuals who are not part of the group. This may give a more accurate rating if a group has become too insular or defensive, and is unable to accurately perceive its own state.

Cohesion: a note on cause versus effects

The vast majority of cohesion-focused research has been cross-sectional in nature. Alternatively, scientists measure cohesion at one time point (e.g. start of the season), and the outcome variable at a later point (e.g. performance halfway through the season). A problem with these approaches is that it can be difficult to ascertain the direction of causality. This is important to keep in mind when reading through the research findings below. Although the studies are presented as 'antecedents' and 'effects', the majority are merely correlates. Their classification is predominantly based on theory, or the original authors' classifications.

Summary

Based on Carron et al.'s (1985) conceptual model, the Group Environment Questionnaire (GEQ) is the most widely used measure of cohesion in sport. A number of important issues to consider when measuring cohesion were discussed, including how to obtain the most relevant and accurate rating of a group's cohesion level.

👁 Factors affecting team cohesion

Group characteristics

Widmeyer et al. (1990) conducted a well-known experiment which examined the links between different team sizes and cohesion. Participants were divided into basketball teams with either three, six or nine players, and asked to play a number of matches with three players on each team. They found that task cohesion was highest in teams of three players, and it was suggested that this enabled the teams to have a goal that all team members had to be involved in pursuing. Both **task cohesion** and **social cohesion** were lowest when teams had nine players. It is possible that in this case players were surplus to the task requirements (only three needed at any one time), resulting in low task cohesion. In addition, social cohesion may have been low due to divisions or cliques within the team, or there may have been too many players for individuals to get to know. Social cohesion was highest in teams with six players. It was assumed that this occurred because teams were small enough for all players to know each other, and large enough so that there was a mix of personalities within the team. Interestingly, the most successful teams had six players. These teams were able to use the skills and resources of all players, without having any detrimental effects of inefficient group coordination.

Leader characteristics

Gardner et al. (1996) examined associations between coaching behaviours and team cohesion. They found small but significant positive correlations between task cohesion and social support, use of positive feedback, a democratic leadership style, and the use of training and instruction-related feedback and comments. An autocratic (or dominating) leadership style was negatively correlated with task cohesion. Furthermore, social cohesion was positively associated with the use of training and instruction, and social support. Leadership behaviours, such as 'promoting teamwork', or 'fostering acceptance of group goals', have also been associated with higher task and social cohesion (Callow et al., 2009). Although not experimental studies, these findings suggest that there may be a link between the way a coach behaves and the cohesiveness of their teams.

Additional possible antecedents

Research has suggested a number of additional antecedents of cohesion. For example, environmental factors such as achievement climates have been differentially related to cohesion. Heuzé et al. (2006) reported that climates that were high in ego involvement and low in task involvement were related to low levels of task cohesion. Conversely, climates that were high in task involvement and low in ego involvement were associated with higher task cohesion, as well as higher levels of collective efficacy. Lastly, climates that were low in ego involvement and moderate in task involvement were associated with high levels of social cohesion. It has also been shown that collective efficacy, or the group's shared belief in its capability, is an antecedent of cohesion (Heuzé et al., 2007). In other words, a group which is more confident in its ability to achieve its objectives is likely to be more cohesive. In addition, the actions of individuals within the team, such as sacrificing time or personal goals, can influence the development of cohesion (e.g. Prapavessis and Carron, 1997).

Summary

Research has suggested that group size, the behaviour of the leader or coach, and the motivational climate created are all associated with group cohesion. Additional factors that might influence cohesion include collective efficacy, member sacrifices, and communication within the group. Some of these factors have been targeted in interventions designed to increase group cohesion (see later section).

◉ Why is cohesion important?

Performance

Many studies have also explored the relationship between winning and losing, and group cohesion. Carron et al. (2002) examined associations between cohesion and winning percentage in a sample of college and club basketball and soccer teams, finding a strong positive association between task cohesion and success. Ruder and Gill (1982) found that winning was associated with an increase in cohesion, and that losing was associated with decreases in three of the four cohesion facets (namely ATG-T, GI-T and GI-S). Furthermore, pre-match cohesion predicted post-match feelings of teamwork, sense of belonging and overall cohesion.

In an attempt to better understand the direction of causality between cohesion and performance, Mullen and Cooper (1994) completed a meta-analysis (that is, a quantitative summary) of seven studies. The studies included in their review examined early season cohesion and performance, and later season cohesion and performance. They concluded that there was stronger evidence supporting the influence of time one performance on time two cohesion, than the other way around. They also found a small, but still significant, effect from cohesion to performance. A team that is successful is likely to become more cohesive, and equally a team that is less successful can improve performance by increasing their cohesion. More recently, in an experimental study, Grieve et al. (2000) provided further support for the performance to cohesion relationship, by showing that winning teams reported higher levels of cohesion, and success predicted cohesion scores.

It is worth noting that the type of team may influence the link between cohesion and performance. Carron (1988) suggested that independent, coactive and reactive sport tasks (see descriptions above) do not require high levels of cohesion to achieve successful performance; that is, in these types of team, the relationship between cohesion and performance is weak. When considering interactive sports (e.g. hockey, rugby), however, performance is strongly associated with both task and social cohesion. In these sports, functioning as a cohesive unit is more closely linked to an ability to successfully perform, as performance is highly dependent on efficient interaction.

Cohesion and performance: additional mechanisms?

Further study has attempted to tease out other factors that may be involved in the team cohesion: performance relationship. Patterson et al. (2005) found that higher norms for social interactions and high team social cohesion (GI-S) were associated with the best performances. Conversely, higher norms for social interactions and low social cohesion were associated with poor performances. In this study, task cohesion was unrelated to performance. Collective efficacy may also mediate the cohesion–performance relationship, with Paskevich (1995) providing evidence that greater task cohesion results in greater collective efficacy, which in turn is related to improved performance levels.

Individual-level effects

Affective states

Using the Profile of Mood States (POMS; see Chapter 2), Terry et al. (2000) found that social cohesion was related to reduced levels of tension and depression, and higher levels of vigour. Furthermore, higher task cohesion was linked to lower levels of tension, depression and anger. Cohesion has also been negatively correlated with jealousy within teams (Kamphoff et al., 2005), and high task cohesion is associated with decreased cognitive state anxiety before games (Prapavessis and Carron, 1996).

Social loafing

Social loafing is said to occur when individuals reduce or invest less effort when involved in a group task, when compared to an individual task (Latané et al., 1979). It may occur for a number of reasons, including being able to gain reward from minimum effort, or saving effort for individual tasks. A number of studies have examined links between social loafing and cohesion, because it might be expected that in a more cohesive team, individuals may be motivated by the team goal and feel more of a responsibility to their teammates. Naylor and Brawley (1992) compared social loafing in different types of team, and found that social loafing was high in coactive teams with low social cohesion. Conversely, social loafing was low in interactive teams with high task cohesion. McKnight et al. (1991) found that identifiability (such as whether an individual's performance or effort is measurable and/or made public) was also an important factor. When identifiability was high, loafing was low. When indentifiability was low, performance was high if task cohesion was high, but when task cohesion was low, loafing occurred. Lastly, in an experimental study with football teams, it has been shown that increasing cohesion decreases social loafing (Hoigaard et al., 2006).

Return to team

Cohesion has been associated with increasing the likelihood that a team will stay together over time. Canadian researchers (Spink et al., 2010) measured the team cohesion reported by ice hockey players at the end of season one, and used this to predict whether these players would return to their team the following season. They found that 'returners' (players who came back to their original teams) reported significantly higher levels of task cohesion than those who chose not to return.

Group-level effects

A number of beneficial outcomes have been associated with group cohesion. Higher task cohesion is linked with greater resistance to disruption, and increased conformity to group norms (Brawley et al., 1988). Task cohesion is also positively associated with role clarity and role acceptance (e.g. Dawe and Carron, 1990), in that in teams with high task cohesion, athletes are likely to report a greater understanding of their role requirements, and a greater acceptance of the scope and need to fulfil these roles. Cohesion is also related to increased levels of the group's confidence in itself, or collective efficacy (e.g. Paskevich, 1995; see earlier comment regarding possible antecedents of cohesion).

Interestingly, cohesion has also been associated with a number of less desirable consequences. For example, increased cohesion can contribute to greater pressure to conform, the increased incidence of groupthink, and self-deception among group members (Buys, 1978). Research has identified some of these negative effects occurring in sports teams (see box).

Thinking scientifically → **negative effects of cohesion?**

Several researchers have considered that increased cohesion may not always lead to positive effects. In their early theorizing, models of cohesion described potential negative effects such as an increased pressure not to let down your teammates (Prapavessis and Carron, 1996). In an elite sporting environment, increasing the pressure on athletes through their perceived responsibility to their teammates may have a detrimental outcome, such as impaired performance (see Chapter 6).

More recent work with athletes has supported the idea that sometimes cohesion can have negative effects. In interviews with athletes from a range of sports, researchers found that 56% of individuals thought there were disadvantages associated with high levels of social cohesion, and 31% felt there were disadvantages associated with high levels of task cohesion (Hardy et al., 2005). Some of the disadvantages are shown in Table 8.1.

Focusing on the effects of cohesion in one team, a qualitative study with junior ice hockey players found that performance decreased as the team became more cohesive (Rovio et al., 2009). When players were asked why they thought this occurred, they suggested that there was less need for them to evaluate their individual performance and strategies, because the pressure to conform was so high. This may have resulted in team members agreeing with certain goals or decisions when privately they felt that these were not a good idea. Players said that the team tended to engage in groupthink, where debates and contrasting ideas diminished. This may have led to a decrease in creative strategies and game plays being used. Finally, the more cohesive group also felt more polarized.

	Task cohesion	Social cohesion
Personal level	Negative affect Incompatible attitude Perceived pressures Lower member contribution	Decreased focus Reduced task commitment Social isolation Social attachment problems
Group level	Reduced social relations Communication problems	Time wasting Goal-related problems Communication problems

Table 8.1 Negative consequences of cohesion
Source: Adapted from Hardy et al., 2005

Summary

A body of research suggests that cohesion has a small positive effect on subsequent performance. In turn, performance has been shown to result in increased levels of cohesion. Other factors associated with higher cohesion include decreased social loafing, more positive affective states and an increased likelihood of players remaining with a team. Group-level effects include enhanced efficacy, role understanding and conformity.

⊙ How can we develop team cohesion?

From examining the research above, it can be seen that there are a number of factors that could be targeted to increase the cohesion of a group. For example, interventions focusing on altering the behaviour of a coach to use more social support and a democratic style of leadership may result in increased team cohesion. Prapavessis et al. (1996) presented a conceptual framework to be used as a basis for implementing team-building programmes in sport. This suggested that if the structure or the environment of a group are altered to affect processes such as cooperation, sacrifice and team goals, then group cohesion will increase. They provide an excellent overview of specific techniques and strategies that can be used, such as increasing identity and distinctiveness through having a group kit, or enhancing structure through weekly meetings and elected captains. Table 8.2 summarizes some of the studies and techniques that have been associated with group cohesion in sports teams.

Study	Activity/intervention	Effect on cohesion
Dunn and Holt (2004)	Personal disclosure and mutual sharing	Increased
Senécal et al. (2008)	Team goal setting	Increased
Martin and Davids (1995)	Five-day group development training course	Increased
Van Raalte and Cornelius (2007)	Hazing (e.g. initiation tasks)	Decreased
McClure and Foster (1991)	Fifteen-week team-building programme	Increased
Cogan and Petrie (1995)	Team-building programme	No effect

Table 8.2 Examples of interventions or activities linked to team cohesion

Conclusion

Research examining cohesion in sport seems to indicate that there are a number of positive outcomes of fostering a more cohesive team. Although the effect of cohesion on performance may be small, research does suggest that cohesion is a modifiable factor which may contribute to performance enhancement. It is important to remember, however, that the vast majority of research has not established causal relationships, and further research is required to determine the most effective way of enhancing group cohesion.

Further reading

Beauchamp, M.R. and Eys, M.A. (2007). *Group dynamics in exercise and sport psychology: Contemporary themes.* New York: Routledge.

Carron, A.V., Hausenblas, H.A. and Eys, M.A. (2005). *Group dynamics in sport* (3rd edn). Morgantown, WV: Fitness Information Technology.

Evans, C.R. and Dion, K.L. (1991). Group cohesion and performance: A meta-analysis. *Small Group Research*, 22(2), 175–86.

👁 Key search terms

Group cohesion, group effectiveness/efficiency, group productivity, collective efficacy, social loafing, Group Environment Questionnaire (GEQ), coactive teams

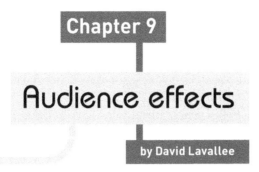

Chapter 9

Audience effects

by David Lavallee

I went to England, practiced for a week on grass, and then played the qualifying matches for the tournament at Queen's Club in West London, the most important of the Wimbledon tune-ups. My opponent in the first round was Pat DuPre, from Stanford ... I won the first set handily, 6–1. I thought, this is pretty easy. Then all of a sudden, a woman in the crowd started yelling at me, really heckling me. I thought, what's going on here? It turned out to be DuPre's wife. She was all over me during the last couple of sets, and I lost the match, 7–5, 7–6. I don't know whether she was doing it with other players as well and I'm not going to say it's the reason I lost, but it definitely threw me off. Here was another lesson: as you play better people in different circumstances, more and more things will start to happen that you have never experienced before. You learn to adjust. At the time I was just flabbergasted.
(McEnroe, with Kaplan, 2002: 60–1)

I had to put my fingers in my ears ... the noise, I'd never heard anything like it in my life. When her race started, I thought I either wait or I go for it. I didn't really know the rules, whether I was allowed to stop or not so I thought I'd better get going before she came round, otherwise I'd have been racing her down the back straight. I just used the energy she was producing. I said to myself, they're cheering for me, they're cheering for me.
(Phillips Idowu talking about his best jump in the triple jump final while Cathy Freeman, an Australian athlete, was running in the final of the 400 metres in the 2000 Sydney Olympics, during which she won a gold medal, *Independent on Sunday*, 1 October 2000)

Sport is normally played in the presence of an **audience**. For example:

- a total of 13.5 million people attended Premier League football matches in England in the 2008–09 season, with an estimated average attendance of 35,599 per game (English Premier League Attendance: 2008/2009, n.d.)
- an average of 40,080 people attended the Union of European Football Association Champions League matches in 2008–2009 (Attendances: Champions League 2008–2009, n.d.)
- the Indianapolis Motor Speedway in America hosts an annual 500-mile car race with more than 250,000 people estimated to be in attendance (Take a seat: Study puts Indy's capacity at 257,325, 27 May 2004)
- over 9 million people will attend sporting events at the 2012 Olympic and Paralympic Games in London (Ticketing, n.d.).

Although not all sporting competitions attract such large audiences, sport provides a good context in which to learn about the effects of audiences in a real-world setting. As illustrated in the above quotes from John McEnroe and Phillips Idowu, athletes can be affected in different ways when performing in front of an audience.

> **In this chapter, we will examine:**
> - Theories explaining how the presence of an audience can have an effect on performance
> - Research studies examining the impact of audiences on performance
> - The home advantage in sport

Theories of audience effects

Sport performance rarely occurs in isolation because athletes compete against opponents, with teammates, or in front of others in an audience. In this chapter we focus specifically on the effects audiences may have on performance in sport, and define an audience as 'the presence of others who are attending to, and evaluating, task performance' (Jones et al., 2007: 105). Theories and research in the area will be reviewed, followed by a discussion of the home advantage phenomenon in sport. First, however, we examine some of the earlier research in social psychology which has informed our understanding of **audience effects** in sport.

Social facilitation

Some of the first documented data in the fields of social psychology and sport psychology were published in a journal article in 1898 by psychologist Norman Triplett (Green and Benjamin, 2009). A keen cyclist, Triplett (1898) reported in his article interesting trends he noticed when reading through the official archives of the Racing Board of the League of American Wheelmen. These data included the times of the following three types of professional races: actual race times against other competitors, either paced or timed; paced races against time; and unpaced races. Triplett consistently noted in this archival research that, on average, racing cyclists with a pacemaker were five seconds faster than without. Rather than suggesting a cyclist gained an advantage due to the aerodynamics of racing behind another person at times during a race, Triplett's theory was more psychological and related to racing in the presence of other people. To test his theory, Triplett designed a follow-up experiment in which children were instructed to wind a thread on a fishing reel as quickly as possible, either with another child doing the same thing, or alone. This research, as also reported in his classic journal article, found that children in the study spun the reel faster when in competition with other participants than when alone. The findings demonstrated the co-action effect: a phenomenon whereby enhanced performance comes about by the presence of others simultaneously and independently engaging in the same activity.

Floyd Henry Allport (1924) followed up on Triplett's (1898) work by removing the competitive element and examined the effects of the mere presence of others on performance. In his research, Allport found that performance increased when passive observers were present in experiments, compared with conditions when participants performed alone. Allport (1924: 262) coined the term **social facilitation** in his work and originally defined it as an 'increase in response merely from the sight or sound of others making the same movement'. Subsequent research over several decades using different cognitive and motor tasks, and both human and animal participants, supported the notion of social facilitation, but many studies also found conflicting results. The critical factor for determining if performance was facilitated or inhibited was later identified by Robert Zajonc (1965), and focused on whether the task the individual was performing was well learned or novel.

Drive Theory

In the 1960s, the research of Zajonc (1965) helped to clarify the inconsistent findings in social facilitation. Zajonc proposed that the presence of others could bring about facilitated or impaired performance depending on the type of task being performed. He noted a pattern in previous research: the presence of an audience tended to enhance performance when individuals performed simple tasks that they knew well; whereas performance decreased when individuals performed difficult or complex tasks that were not well learned. Zajonc explained these results based upon Drive Theory (Hull, 1943), which suggests that increases in arousal lead to elicitation of the person's predominant behaviour associated with any particular task (also see Chapter 5). According to Zajonc (1965), when an individual first learns a complex task, the incorrect response is dominant and the presence of an audience will, via increased arousal, produce poorer performance. Likewise, with familiar or easy tasks, individuals will perform better in the presence of an audience than they would on their own.

Zajonc et al. (1969) demonstrated support for Drive Theory in what has come to be a landmark study in social psychology research. Instead of studying sports participants, Zajonc et al. (1969) elected to study cockroaches running through an easy or difficult maze, either alone or in pairs. The researchers also manipulated whether the cockroaches ran the maze with an audience of other cockroaches (who were in clear boxes adjacent to the maze), or without an audience. Why did they choose to study cockroaches? The researchers argued that humans' conscious processes, which cockroaches do not have, were not an important component of audience effects, but rather arousal itself. In other words, the use of cockroaches allowed the researchers to remove the conscious processing elements and focus just on arousal. Zajonc et al. (1969) found that the presence of others in both conditions (pairs or with observers) increased performance (that is, faster times) in the easy maze, but decreased performance in the difficult maze when compared to the alone condition. Zajonc et al. (1969) interpreted these findings as support for the Drive Theory of social facilitation and, specifically, that the presence of others increased arousal states and led to the elicitation of dominant behaviours. During this state of arousal, Zajonc et al. (1969) argued that performance increases when the task is easy or familiar, whereas performance decreases when a task is difficult or unknown. As such, social facilitation effects came to be understood as based on two components: the presence of others; and the ease of the task for the individual.

At the same time, some researchers questioned why the mere presence of an audience itself could have a social influence. For example, Cottrell et al. (1968) proposed the evaluation-apprehension theory for social facilitation, which suggests that it is the fear associated with being judged that affects performance. These researchers suggested that people learn throughout their lives that social rewards and punishments are strongly linked to evaluations made by others. They also hypothesized that when we find ourselves with a social presence, we will experience an acquired arousal based on evaluation apprehension. Cottrell et al. (1968) found support for their theory in research with three audience conditions: blindfolded, and therefore unable to evaluate the performance; merely present – passive and uninterested; and attentive. Results showed that social facilitation only occurred in the third condition when the audience was perceived to be evaluative.

Zajonc's (1965) research on Drive Theory has informed the study of audience effects since its publication and has led to social facilitation being defined as an improvement in the performance of well-learned/ easy tasks and a deterioration in the performance of poorly learned/diffi-cult tasks in the mere presence of the same species (Hogg and Vaughan, 2005: 278). Within the field of sport psychology, the early research by Martens and Landers (1969, 1972) provided support for the theory that the presence of others is a source of arousal. Another interesting study of audience effects and social facilitation was conducted by Micheals et al. (1982). These researchers initially (secretly) watched pool players at a university union bar and rated them as either above or below average. The above-average players, who made an average of 71% of their shots when playing alone, increased performance to 80% when an audience of four began watching them. The below-average players, who made 36% of their shots when playing alone, decreased performance to 25% when an audience of four started watching them.

Summary

Research from over 100 years has found that the presence of an audience can have both positive and negative effects on performance in sport settings. As a way to integrate and summarize the conflicting findings, Bond and Titus (1983) examined all the studies conducted in the area simultaneously through a method called a meta-analysis. After reviewing over 200 studies comprising over 20,000 participants, they found that the presence of others facilitated performance to a greater extent with familiar or easy tasks, but there was less evidence that performance decreased in the presence of others with unfamiliar or difficult tasks. An interesting application within the area of audience effects is whether there is a home advantage in sport.

◉ Home advantage

If you have ever seen the 1939 film, *The Wizard of Oz*, you may recall the main character Dorothy repeatedly saying 'There's no place like home.' Although she was not referring to sports, this statement has become well established in the world of sport through what is known as the **home advantage** phenomenon. This refers to the observation that teams playing on their home fields or areas generally have an advantage towards a win in sports. Home advantage has been shown to exist in several team, and some individual, sports, and for countries organizing major tournaments (e.g. Olympics, Paralympics and the football World Cup). The phenomenon has been defined as the performance advantage of an athlete, team or country when they compete at a home ground compared to their performance under similar conditions at an away ground (Koning, 2005). Wallace et al. (2005: 429) state that 'home advantage effects are more apparent in some sports than in others, but in no sport that we are aware of do athletes typically perform worse at home'.

The first study of the home advantage in sport was carried out by Schwartz and Barsky (1977). They focused on the North American sports of professional baseball, basketball, football and ice hockey, and in each case showed evidence supporting an advantage when playing at home. Subsequent research has focused predominantly on team sports and has found the home advantage phenomenon to be robust. The magnitude of the home advantage, however, varies significantly across sports (Courneya and Carron, 1992; Nevill et al., 2005; Nevill and Holder, 1999). Using longitudinal data across a range of different team sports, Stefani (2007) recently found a home field advantage – calculated as a fraction or percentage of (home wins – home losses)/total games – in the following professional sports: rugby union (25.1%); football (21.7%); basketball (21.0%); Australian rules football (18.8%); American football

(17.5%); ice hockey (9.7%) and baseball (7.5%). These results suggest that, for example, rugby union teams have a 25% greater chance of winning at home than away.

Although most of the published data on home advantage comes from research in team sports, the medal count of the country organizing the Olympic Games tends to be higher than expected (Balmer et al., 2001, 2003). Ten out of the 13 countries who have hosted postwar Olympic Games (excluding 1984 and 1988 when some countries boycotted the games) have a higher percentage of gold medals as part of their overall haul when at home compared to when away (Koning, 2005). Because most of the medals given at the Olympics are for athletes competing alone, this finding suggests that home advantage exists in individual sports as well. Recently, UK Sport commissioned a research project to examine the effect of home advantage in single-sport international championships (UK Sport, 2009). A total of 94 World and European Championships, and nearly 10,000 individual results, were examined across 14 sports on the 2012 Olympic programme. Hosting World and European Championships were found to have a significant influence on performance. On average, the host country achieved a 25% increase in their results in comparison to when they were not at home. In 73% of the events studied, the host's performance was higher than their average performance at events that they were not hosting (excluding 'non-competitive hosts').

According to Stefani (2007), there are three contributing factors implicit in the home advantage:

- the home team's familiarity of the home venue (a tactical factor)
- the travel fatigue of a visiting team (a physiological factor)
- the effect of the home crowd on the home and visiting teams by cheering or booing (a psychological factors).

Although a combination of these factors is usually present during sport competition, the influence of the crowd is generally accepted as the most consistent and powerful factor contributing to home team performance (Nevill and Holder, 1999). For the purpose of this chapter we focus predominantly on audience effects and the home advantage.

Home advantage and audience effects

The effects of the home crowd on athletes' psychological states have been one focus of research attention in the area. Basketball players, for example, have reported to have higher levels of confidence and motivation when playing at home compared to away (Bray and Widmeyer, 2000; Jurkovac, 1985). State anxiety and mood states have also been found to be more positive among home players prior to matches (e.g. Terry et al., 1998; Thuot et al., 1998), although in some studies, researchers found no differences in psychological states between home and away competitions (e.g. Duffy and Hinwood, 1997; Kerr and Vanschaik, 1995). In each of the studies where no differences were found, however, the mood measures were taken prior to the start of the competitive events, and so the influence of the audience on psychological states of the competitors during the event may not have been fully realized (Jones et al., 2007).

The specific characteristics of audiences, such as size, density and behaviours, have also been the focus of research examining the relationship between audience effects and home team performance (Jones et al., 2007). With regard to the size of an audience, Dowie (1982) and Agnew and Carron (1994) assessed the absolute size of the crowd, that is, the number of fans attending a match, in the sports of football and ice hockey, respectively, but, contrary to their hypotheses, found no relationship between home advantage and crowd size. A study by Jones et al. (2001) in English club cricket also provides indirect evidence against the influence of crowd size, as the researchers identified a significant home advantage of 57%, although there were seldom audiences greater than 50 in attendance at matches. Nevill et al. (1996), however, found that crowd size was positively related to the home advantage in English and Scottish football. Their results showed that in leagues where crowd sizes were generally large (Premier and Division 1), teams had better home winning percentages than in two leagues (G.M. Vauxhall League and Scottish Second Division) where crowd sizes were generally small. In terms of crowd density, that is, the number of people in an audience relative to the facility's capacity, Pollard (1986) found no association with the home advantage in soccer. Schwartz and Barsky (1977) found the opposite in professional baseball, because home team winning percentages increased significantly when crowd density was lower, that is, density of less than 20%, compared to when crowd density was higher, that is, larger than 40%. Agnew and Carron's (1994) study found that as crowd density increased, so too did the extent of the home advantage in ice hockey.

Researchers have also investigated audience behaviours and have generally found that spectator support has a positive effect on home team performance – when cheering was directed at the home team. Researchers who have studied basketball, for example, found that when crowds behaved normally, that is, cheering for the home team and booing the visiting team, home teams won more games (Greer, 1983), while visiting teams committed more rule violations and were penalized to a greater extent (Thirer and Rampey, 1979).

A home disadvantage?

Although numerous studies support a performance advantage of an athlete, team or country when they compete at a home, the home advantage phenomenon has been questioned under special circumstances. Probably the best-known contradictory evidence was provided by Baumeister and Steinhilber (1984), who found in an archival study that the home advantage was overturned in high-pressure, championship situations where teams that hosted the decisive game of the series had a better chance of losing the game (and the championship title) than winning it. For example, professional baseball results in North America showed home teams won only 39% of their decisive championship games, compared with an average home winning percentage of 60% earlier in the season. Professional basketball home players in the same study had lower foul shooting percentages compared to previous games, and in baseball, home players committed more fielding errors. Similar findings supporting a home disadvantage have also been reported from archival studies of golf (Wright et al., 1991) and ice hockey (Wright et al., 1995).

A rare opportunity to study audience effects on sport performance in a natural setting occurred when a measles epidemic resulted in a quarantine preventing any fans from attending 11 games played by two university basketball teams (one male and one female) in the US (Moore and Brylinksy, 1993). The researchers used this opportunity to compare the performance – total points scored, field goal percentages and free throw percentages – of the two teams in the presence and in the absence of spectators over the season. The results indicated that the performances of both teams actually improved in the absence of spectators. Given sport events are seldom contested when the same teams play with and without spectators in attendance, the results do raise a question as to whether audiences do actually facilitate sport performance and provide a home advantage or disadvantage (Jones et al., 2007).

Summary

The home advantage phenomenon can be considered a psychological phenomenon, especially when performers are closely matched in terms of ability (Hagger and Chatzisarantis, 2005). Home advantage effects are more apparent in some sports than in others, and supportive audiences generally lead to better performances than unsupportive audiences. The same supportive audiences that can help enhance performance in most situations can also lead to performance decrements in championship situations.

Conclusions

The utility and application of theory and research on audience effects are relevant to sport psychology. Although audiences will vary in size, density and behaviour, there is almost always an audience present during sport competitions. Audience effects in sport should be interpreted as a social exchange that in many ways depends on the athlete's subjective interpretation of the social situation (Wankel, 1984).

Further reading

Jones, M.V., Bray, S.R. and Lavallee, D. (2007). All the world's a stage: The impact of an audience on sport performers. In S. Jowett and D. Lavallee (eds) *Social psychology in sport* (pp. 103–13). Champaign, IL: Human Kinetics.

Nevill, A., Balmer, N. and Wolfson, W. (eds) (2005). The extent and causes of home advantage: Some recent insights (Special issue). *Journal of Sports Sciences*, 23(4).

Strauss, B. (2002). Social facilitation in motor tasks: A review of research and theory. *Psychology of Sport and Exercise*, 3, 237–56.

Key search terms

Arousal, audience, Drive Theory, home advantage, social facilitation, social presence

Chapter 10

Leadership

Most of you will have no difficulty in identifying some great sporting leaders, such as Sir Alex Ferguson, manager of Manchester United Football Club, Sir Clive Woodward, coach of the England rugby team, or Sir Bobby Moore, arguably England's finest football captain. According to Simonton (2008: 248) a leader is someone 'whose influence over group cohesion, decision making or productivity exceeds the average member of the group'. A leader is considered to be someone who decides the direction or goals that a team or player is aiming for and helps them to get there effectively. In a sporting context, the leader tends to be a team or individual's coach, teacher or captain. Just because we can easily recognize great leadership, however, does not make the task of identifying what makes good leaders easier. Sport psychologists have attempted to address this question in numerous ways.

According to Behling and Schriesheim (1976), leadership theories have tended to focus on leaders' traits and behaviours, and whether they are universal or situation specific. Trait theorists propose that good leaders have certain personality characteristics. On the other hand, behaviour theorists focus on the behaviours great leaders display. According to Behling and Schriesheim, these traits and behaviours can be universal and common to all great leaders, or specific to certain situations, but not necessarily applicable to others.

In this chapter, we will examine:
- Whether leadership is a quality that one is born with or can be developed
- Whether good leadership is common across all situations or is situation specific
- Whether leadership is a result of a type of personality or the display of specific behaviours

- How coaching behaviour is assessed using the Coaching Behaviour Assessment System
- How understanding leadership behaviour can be used to train coaches to be effective leaders

Theories of leadership

Universal trait theories of leadership

Universal trait leadership theories propose that good **leaders** are born and not made, and all key leaders will share common personality traits predisposing them to being naturally talented leaders. For example, the Great Man Theory of leadership proposes that all good leaders possess certain traits or characteristics which make them great leaders. This theory gained popularity with the introduction of personality tests in the 1920s. The ability to determine people's personality traits lead to interest in whether these tests could identify prospective leaders.

For the theory to be supported, however, research must be able to identify characteristics which are common to all leaders. Two research reviews, however, failed to identify traits that were universal to all great leaders (Sage, 1975; Stogdill, 1948). Few researchers have explored this type of research since Sage's 1975 review.

Situational trait theories

Situational trait theories also maintain the idea that a set of personality traits or characteristics underpin good leadership; however, contrary to universal trait leadership theories, situational trait theories propose that specific traits will only be successful in some situations, whereas in other situations, a different set of personality traits will be more sought after.

One such situational trait theory is Fiedler's (1967) Contingency Theory. This was originally designed to explain leadership within a work-related context, however, it has since been applied to examine leadership in other contexts such as sport. Fiedler proposed that the success of leadership depends on two things; the personality of the leader, and to what extent the situation allows the leader the freedom and power to have an effect on the situation. As such, there is an interaction between the personality of the leader and the situation. For this reason, this type of theory is often referred to as adopting an 'interactionist approach'.

According to Contingency Theory, leaders fall into two broad categories; relationship motivated or task motivated:

- *Relationship-motivated leaders* are primarily concerned with the relationship between themselves and their followers, and in most sporting contexts this would be the team. Their main interest is to develop positive relationships with the team members and a successful competitive outcome is considered to be secondary to this.
- *Task-motivated leaders* have a primary concern for achieving the task in question and the relationships with the team members are secondary to a successful sporting outcome.

The second aspect to Fiedler's (1967) Contingency Theory is the situation in which the leader is trying to achieve results. This relates to how much the leader is able to exert their influence in a given situation. According to Fiedler, 'situational favourableness' is dependent on three factors; the relationship between leaders and their teams, that is, how well liked they are, the difficulty of the task, and how powerful they are as leaders.

The theory proposes that the different types of leadership (relationship and task motivated) will deliver better performances in different types of situational favourableness. When the situational favourableness is low, the task-oriented leader is likely to deliver higher performance results. This is also the case when the situational favourableness is high. The relationship-oriented leader tends to deliver the best results when the situational favourableness is at a moderate level.

Universal behaviour theories

Having identified that universal trait theories were unsupported, researchers turned their interests to whether there were universal behaviours that make a good leader. Universal behaviour theories proposed that certain types of behaviour could be observed in all leaders. If supported, these theories have the benefit of meaning that leaders can be taught to be good by learning the behaviours in question.

Two key factors form the basis of universal leadership behaviour research. These are consideration and initiating structure:

- *Consideration* refers to a positive relationship between the leader and the team based on trust and friendship. Leaders exhibiting **consideration behaviours** tend to use a democratic style, where members of the team contribute ideas and are made to feel part of the decision-making process.
- *The initiating structure* refers to leadership behaviour that forms clear boundaries between the leader and the followers, that is, the team. Leaders exhibiting this form of behaviour tend to be autocratic in their leadership, where they make the decisions and the followers take orders, with the aim of achieving increased performance.

Although these behaviours appear to be polar opposites of each other, it is possible for a leader to exhibit high levels of both consideration and initiating structure. The important aspect of the theory is how people exhibit a balance of these two types of behaviour to lead their team effectively. For example, a leader demonstrating a high degree of initiating structure behaviour might be effective in managing a young team of inexperienced players. As these players grow in confidence, however, the leader may need to adapt that style to acknowledge the athletes' development and will need to demonstrate higher degrees of consideration behaviour. It is this ability to effectively alter and balance behaviour that is considered to be what makes a great leader.

Trying to teach an individual, however, to develop both consideration and initiating structure behaviour is not easy. For this reason, Behling and Schreisheim (1976) proposed their functional model of leadership, which proposed that more than one individual with complementary talents be appointed to leadership roles. For example, a team that has a manager with a high level of initiating structure behaviour would be recommended to appoint a coach with a high level of consideration behaviour. In this way, where one leader is lacking, a different leader can compensate, providing the best possible combination for the team's success. Loughead and Hardy (2005) examined the leadership behaviours of coaches and peer leaders, that is, team captains and members of the team. They identified that these positions tended to be associated with different leadership behaviours, lending support to Behling and Schreisheim's (1976) proposal of complementary roles. Loughead and Hardy (2005) identified that coaches tended to use more **initiating behaviours**, focusing on training and autocratic behaviour, whereas the peer leaders demonstrated more use of consideration behaviours focused towards social support and democratic behaviour.

Situational behaviour theories

The interaction between the leader and the situation was discussed in the previous section where we referred to the Contingency Theory by Fiedler (1967). As discussed, however, Fiedler focused on the interaction between the relatively stable personality traits of the leader and the environmental situation. Situational behaviour theories also propose an interaction between the leader and the situational environment; however, these theories focus on leaders' behaviours rather than their personality. These types of theories probably have the most support, with numerous researchers proposing different forms of the theory (e.g. Chelladurai, 1978; Smoll and Smith, 1989). Some of the key theories in this area will be outlined here.

The Multidimensional Model of Leadership

The Multidimensional Model of Leadership was proposed by Chelladurai (1978, 1993) and suggests that three antecedents influence a leader's behaviour; situational factors, leader characteristics and member characteristics:

- *Situational factors* refer to situation-specific factors, such as what sport is being played, the weather influencing play, or the opponents' characteristics.
- *Leader characteristics* relate to the characteristics of the leader, such as their gender, personality, and how much experience they have in the leader role and so on.
- *Member characteristics* relate to the characteristics of the team or followers, such as their gender, their experience of playing/ coaching, and their personalities.

These three antecedents are believed to influence different aspects of a leader's behaviour:

1 *Required behaviour* refers to whether the leader is required to behave in a certain way to achieve success in a given situation (Chelladurai, 1993). For example, when playing against a technically superior team, a coach may need to behave in a instructive and authoritarian manner to direct the team through the challenge.

2 *Actual behaviour* is where the leader will have their preferred style of leadership behaviour.
3 *Preferred behaviour* relates to the way in which the team members would prefer the leader to behave. For example, one team may prefer strong leadership and an authoritarian coach, whereas others might prefer a coach who socializes with them to build a relationship and rapport with the players.

It is perhaps unsurprising that the key antecedent influencing a leader's actual behaviour is the leader's characteristics. The personality and gender of the leader are naturally going to influence the way in which they behave. In a similar way, the characteristics of the members or players are likely to affect the preferred behaviour they expect of their leader. For example, a young inexperienced team may prefer a strong authoritarian leader, whereas a more experienced player or team might prefer a leader with a more democratic style, which takes their own experiences into account. Crust and Azadi (2009) found that mentally tough athletes (identified by a questionnaire) had a preference for leaders who focused on instructive behaviours and they preferred not to have leaders who focused on social support.

According to the theory, the situational characteristics will most probably influence the required behaviour of the leader, that is, how they are expected to behave, and preferred behaviour – how the team would like them to behave. For example, in a game against a tough opponent, the club might expect the leader to behave with confidence in their players and direct them in a strong and powerful manner (required behaviour); equally, the team may also be looking to the coach to provide them with strong leadership and, as such, would expect a more authoritarian leader (preferred behaviour).

The theory further proposes that the different types of behaviour exhibited by the leader will influence the players' performance and satisfaction. The required and actual behaviours of the leader are likely to influence the performance of the player or team. The actual and preferred behaviours are most likely to contribute to players' or team's satisfaction. The relationships between leadership behaviour and performance and satisfaction are based on how much the different types of behaviour (required, actual and preferred) match and are summarized in Figure 10.1. To summarize these relationships, Chellaudurai made five proposals:

1 If all three behaviours are in agreement, the behaviours are said to be congruent. This should lead to high satisfaction and good performance.

2 If all three behaviours are in disagreement, the behaviours are said to be incongruent. This is likely to lead to poor performance and low satisfaction.

3 When the behaviour is congruent with what is required, but incongruent with the players' preferences, there is likely to be good performance but low satisfaction.

4 Where the behaviour is incongruent with what is required, but is congruent with the players' preferences, this is likely to result in poor performance; however, the players are likely to be satisfied with the coach.

5 Finally, where the required behaviour and the preferred behaviour are congruent, yet the actual behaviour of the coach is incongruent, this is likely to result in a situation where the coach loses their position (low performance and low satisfaction).

Research in the area has supported the Multidimensional Model of Leadership and the proposal that leadership behaviour can affect athlete satisfaction and performance. For example, Chelladurai (1984) and Weiss and Friedrichs (1986) demonstrated that coaching behaviours associated with positive feedback, social support, and training and instruction have been positively related to athlete satisfaction. In addition, Fox et al. (2000) explored the relationship between instructor leadership behaviour and satisfaction among exercise participants. Exercise leaders were asked to demonstrate either:

- behaviours that encouraged social engagement and support
- or a leadership style that focused on correcting errors with little attention to social interaction.

Results demonstrated that exercise participants reported more enjoyment and satisfaction with the supportive leadership than the instructional leadership.

In perhaps a more comprehensive test of the multidimensional model, Myers et al. (2005) demonstrated that coaches' self-efficacy, or their confidence that they could affect the team or player effectively, had a positive influence on their behaviour, team satisfaction and team performance. Coaching self-efficacy is considered one antecedent leader

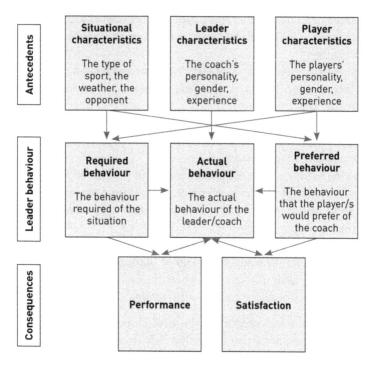

Figure 10.1 Multidimensional Model of Leadership

characteristic. Interestingly, the study also demonstrated that a coach's gender could influence the relationship between their behaviour and team satisfaction and performance in female teams. In male coaches, for example, their character-building efficacy, or confidence that they could develop players' characters, was negatively related to team satisfaction; that is, higher levels of character-building efficacy were associated with lower team satisfaction. In female coaches, their motivation efficacy, or beliefs that they could influence team motivation, was positively related to team satisfaction – higher motivation efficacy was associated with increased team satisfaction.

Leadership Behaviour Model

The Leadership Behaviour Model (Smoll and Smith, 1989) is also considered a situation-specific behavioural theory. The main premise of the theory is that the coach's behaviour will influence the players' perceptions of the coach, and this, in turn, will affect the players' response. For example, if a coach shouts a direct insult at a player during a match, the athlete may perceive this to be reflective of the coach's frustration at their performance and as a result will increase their effort in the game. In addition, Smoll and Smith also acknowledge other variables which could potentially influence coaching effectiveness (see Figure 10.2), such as the coach's characteristics and perceptions of players, the situation, and athletes' characteristics.

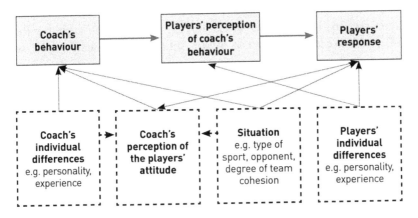

Figure 10.2 **Leadership Behaviour Model**

In a similar fashion to Chelladurai's multidimensional model, the Leadership Behaviour Model accounts for the effect of individual differences (e.g. personality, experience) and the specific situation (e.g. type of sport, opponent) on the coach's and players' attitudes and behaviour. In addition, Smoll and Smith (1989) propose that how the player chooses to respond to the coach's behaviour will contribute to the coach's perception of the player's attitude. These variables will then feed back and influence subsequent behaviour. Taking our example, where a coach shouts a direct insult at a player during a match, this may be the result of the coach having an aggressive type of personality (an individual difference). If the coach sees the player shaking their head in response (player response), the coach might perceive this as a reflection of the player's negative attitude and, as such, this perception will feed back into future behaviour. The coach might, for example, demonstrate increased frustration towards the player in question. The ability of coaches to accurately identify the attitudes of players has been shown to be better in coaches of individual players as opposed to team players (Lorimer and Jowett, 2008). This is perhaps unsurprising, given that the coach only has one player to understand with individual sports, whereas team coaches have several players' attitudes to take into consideration.

The accuracy of the coach in identifying a player's perceptions is important in determining how they will react towards that player. As a result, Lorimer and Jowett (2010) investigated whether badminton coaches' perceptions of players' attitudes, thoughts and feelings (known as 'empathic accuracy') could be improved by providing feedback. Coaches were asked to view videos of players during matches and at intervals were asked to make an assessment of players' attitudes and intentions. These were then compared, for accuracy, to players' perceptions of their own attitudes and intentions at the time. One group of coaches received no feedback, whereas the other group were provided with feedback regarding their empathic accuracy. The accuracy of both groups of coaches improved with the more videos they watched, demonstrating the importance of experience in player perception accuracy. The group receiving feedback, however, improved significantly more than the control group, demonstrating that this skill could be further improved with feedback.

Summary

This section has introduced four key types of leadership theory. These are summarized in Figure 10.3 and below:

1 Universal trait theories, such as the Great Man Theory, propose that leaders are born and not made and that leaders share common personality traits which predispose them towards being great leaders. There is not much research support for this type of theory, with little evidence of common traits being identified.

2 Situational trait theories, such as Fiedler's (1967) Contingency Theory, propose that leaders do possess specific traits. Whether or not these traits make leaders successful, however, will vary in different situations. Traits that make a great leader for one team or athlete, for example, may not necessarily make a great leader for another. Attention was then turned to behavioural attributes of leaders.

3 Universal behaviour theories suggest that good leaders will display specific behavioural attributes which contribute to their success. This means that people can be taught to display these behaviours and as a result good leaders can be trained.

4 Situational behavioural theories were explored, specifically the Multidimensional Model of Leadership (Chelladurai, 1978, 1993) and the Leadership Behaviour Model (Smoll and Smith, 1989). The situational behavioural theories are the most widely accepted type of theories, proposing that there is an interaction between the environmental context and the behaviour of the leader. Different aspects of the environment are believed to contribute to the way the leader chooses to behave and vice versa. The success of the interaction is what determines whether or not a leader's style is considered successful.

Universal	Trait	Leaders are born	Great Man Theory
Universal	Behaviour	Leaders are made	Considerations and initiating structure
Situational	Trait	Interaction between personality traits and the environment	Contingency Theory
Situational	Behaviour	Interaction between leader behaviour in specific situations	Multidimensional Model of Leadership, Leadership Behaviour Model

Figure 10.3 Summary of leadership types

Coaching

So far, we have discussed a number of theories of leadership which have been used within sporting contexts to assess leadership qualities. In most sporting contexts, the leader in question tends to be the coach. You may have noticed that a number of the different theories refer to the effects of the coach's behaviour. For this reason, research has also focused on coaching behaviour and how this can be manipulated or changed to enhance the leadership qualities of coaches.

Assessing coaching behaviour

As briefly discussed in Chapter 2, the Coaching Behaviour Assessment System (CBAS; Smith and Smoll, 1997) is an observation method by which the behaviour of coaches can be assessed or measured. Behaviours are divided into reactive and spontaneous behaviours:

1 *Reactive behaviours* refer to how coaches relate or react to the behaviours of the team. For instance, as in our previous example, a coach might shout abuse at a player who has fouled a member of the opposite team, resulting in a penalty. Reactive behaviours are divided into responses to desirable performance, responses to mistakes, and responses to misbehaviour:

   - *Responses to desirable performance* include either reinforcement or non-reinforcement. Reinforcement refers to positive reward for the behaviour, while non-reinforcement refers to a lack of response for the desirable behaviour. For example, if a player makes a clean tackle and wins possession of the ball, the coach might shout an encouraging comment (reinforcement) or might not comment at all (non-reinforcement).
   - *Responses to mistakes* refer to mistake-contingent encouragement (providing encouragement following the mistake), mistake-contingent technical instruction (instruction on how to correct the mistake), punishment (reprimanding the mistake), punitive technical instruction (instruction to the mistake given in a hostile way), and ignoring mistakes (lack of any response towards the mistake).
   - Finally, there is only one *response to misbehaviour*, which is keeping control. This refers to reactions that are intended to control the behaviour of the team.

2 *Spontaneous behaviours* refer to behaviours that are initiated by the coach, but not in direct response to team behaviours. For example, the coach might shout a tactical instruction at the team, but this is not in response to anything that the team has already done. Spontaneous behaviours are divided into game-related and game-irrelevant behaviours:

   - *Game-related behaviours* refer to general technical instructions (instruction on technique), general encouragement, and organization (e.g. assigning roles to players). Remember that none of these are in response to a mistake by the team, but are spontaneous behaviours.
   - *Game-irrelevant behaviours* relate to general communication which is not related to the state of play.

These different types of behaviour are summarized in Figure 10.4.

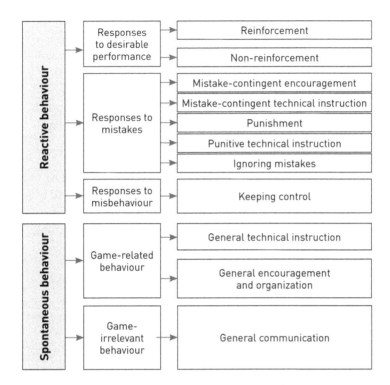

Figure 10.4 Coaching Behavioural Assessment System (CBAS)

Coaching behaviour

Having addressed the different types of behavioural responses exhibited by coaches, research needs to address whether or not coaches can be trained to use the appropriate responses to making them better leaders. The Coach Effectiveness Training programme is one such scheme which uses research from the Coaching Behaviour Assessment System (CBAS) to train youth coaches. The programme aims to teach coaches how to develop effective cohesion within their team through team-building strategies. The strategies used are based on five principles of coaching identified by Smith and Smoll (1997):

1   The first principle is that coaches should try to develop a mastery environment (see Chapter 4), where the focus is on learning new skills and developing confidence rather than a competitive environment where the focus is on winning.

2   The second principle addresses how the coach interacts with players and suggests that coaches should try to maintain a positive attitude such that they provide positive reinforcement, constructive criticism delivered in a positive and friendly way and encouragement.

3   The third principle relates to how the team members interact with each other. Coaches should try to develop support and cohesion among the team members and should develop a sense of commitment to the team.

4   The fourth principle suggests that the team members should be involved in developing the rules, roles and responsibilities held by the team members. The concept behind this principle is that if players have had the opportunity to be involved in these decisions, they are more likely to engage and comply with the rules.

5   The fifth principle is that coaches should reflect on their own coaching behaviour to monitor their effectiveness and improve as coaches. A central aspect of this point is for coaches to use the CBAS to determine how often they are exhibiting the desirable and less desirable behaviours. Research has demonstrated that Coach Effectiveness Training has been effective in increasing the desirable behaviour seen in coaches (e.g. positive reinforcement; Smoll et al., 1993) as well as youth team player's self-esteem (Coatsworth and Conroy, 2006).

Summary

This section has explored how the behaviour of coaches is assessed using the CBAS. The CBAS identifies a range of behaviours which coaches display in different situations and in response to different types of player behaviour. This assessment method provides a useful tool for researchers and trainers to use when helping to develop an effective coaching style. One such training programme is the Coach Effectiveness Training programme, which helps to train effective youth coaches. This programme focuses on developing coaches who are supportive of young players and build mastery environments to promote skill improvement, effort and team cohesion. The use of the CBAS is a central feature of the programme, helping inexperienced coaches to reflect on the balance of adaptive and maladaptive behaviours in their coaching style which can then be moderated to become more effective.

◉ Conclusions

This chapter has explored the different types of leadership theories. Theories in this area vary with regards to whether or not they consider traits or behaviours to be common among all great leaders, and whether or not traits and behaviours are common across all situations or are specific to certain contexts. The most widely accepted of these theories appears to be those which propose an interaction between the environment (situation) and the behaviour of the leader. These types of theory have led researchers to be interested in developing good leaders by helping them to display effective behaviours in different contexts. Developing instruments to measure the behaviour of coaches or leaders in the form of the CBAS has helped researchers to identify the behaviours of coaches and to implement training programmes to produce effective youth coaches. Whether training programmes such as these, however, help to produce the next 'great' coach, as opposed to an effective coach, is to be determined.

◉ Further reading

Coatsworth, J.D. and Conroy, D.E. (2006). Enhancing the self-esteem of youth swimmers through coach training: Gender and age effects. *Psychology of Sport and Exercise*, 7, 173–92.

Fox, L.D., Rejeski, W.J. and Gauvin, L. (2000). Effects of leadership style and group dynamics on enjoyment of physical activity. *American Journal of Health Promotion*, 14, 277–83.

Lorimer, R. and Jowett, S. (2010). Feedback of information in the empathic accuracy of sport coaches. *Psychology of Sport and Exercise*, 11, 12–17.

◉ Key search terms

Coaching behaviour in sport, leadership in sport, Multidimensional Model of Leadership, Contingency Theory, coach–athlete relationship

Chapter 11

Mental health

For centuries, many people have argued that physical activity is related to mental health. These individuals have suggested that healthy minds reside in healthy bodies. Scientific study of the link has been more recent, and only in the last few years has a clearer understanding of the exercise and mental health relationship emerged (Biddle and Mutrie, 2008). The results have been encouraging, and recently the UK's chief medical officer suggested that:

> physical activity can be considered both for its therapeutic effects on mental illness, and also for its impact on mental health ... effects are consistent and plausible across a range of mental health outcomes. **(Department of Health, DH, 2004: 58–9)**

Sometimes, people participating in sporting and exercise activities can experience negative psychological issues; for example overtraining, eating disorders and drug abuse (addressed in Chapter 13). In this chapter, however, we focus on the positive influence exercise may have on various mental health dimensions.

In this chapter, we will examine:
- Definitions of mental health, mental illness, mental health problems and mental disorders
- The influence of exercise on mood, depression and anxiety
- Possible reasons why exercise might influence mental health

◉ Mental health and mental illness

Mental health and mental illness lie along a continuum (United States Department of Health and Human Services, USDHHS, 1999). At one end, **mental health** refers to successful mental functioning, leading to productive activities, fulfilling relationships, and the ability to cope with adversity (USDHHS, 1999). Good mental health allows individuals to live satisfying, meaningful and fulfilling lives. At the other end of the continuum, **mental illness** refers to diagnosable mental disorders. Mental disorders are characterized by changes in thinking, mood and/ or behaviour; and distress and/or unsuccessful functioning (USDHHS, 1999). Depression is an example of a mental disorder with changes in thinking (e.g. inability to concentrate), mood (e.g. people feel depressed) and behaviour (e.g. individuals lack the energy to carry out normal tasks). Throughout life, our place on the continuum varies depending on many factors, such as genetics and the social environment. Sometimes people move down the continuum and have mental health problems, but do not have mental disorders. **Mental health problems** refer to 'signs and symptoms of insufficient intensity or duration to meet the criteria for any mental disorder' (USDHHS, 1999: 5). Some individuals, for example, might become so unhappy about their appearance that they change their eating patterns enough to be diagnosed with an eating disorder (a mental health illness). For other people, however, their unhappiness about their appearance may be the basis of a mental health problem rather than an illness, because their change in eating patterns is not enough to be given an eating disorder diagnosis. Physical activity seems to help people to move up the continuum, and is one reason why sport and exercise psychologists (and others) recommend we undertake regular exercise.

◉ Exercise and mood

Morgan's Mental Health Model

In Chapter 2 we examined Morgan's (1985) Mental Health Model (or iceberg profile) with respect to sport performance. Morgan suggested that his model also applies to regular exercise. When regular exercisers are compared with the general population, they have lower tension, depression, anger, fatigue and confusion. Exercisers, however, have higher vigour (you may like to review Chapter 2). The Mental Health Model, or iceberg profile, provides a description of the way physical activity is related to post-exercise mood. A different relationship emerges when mood is examined during exercise.

Mood during exercise

Broadly, during exercise, as the intensity of effort increases, there is a decrease in positive, and an increase in negative, mood states, although people differ in how they react (Biddle and Mutrie, 2008). Table 11.1 presents a model explaining how exercise intensity influences mood (Ekkekakis et al., 2005). At moderate exercise intensities, below the lactate threshold – the lowest work rate at which blood lactate appearance begins to exceed removal – most people experience a positive increase in mood during and after physical activity. Moderate exercise is related to a range of mental and physical health benefits, and the body seems to reward people, through the experience of pleasurable moods, for engaging in physical activity at this intensity.

Intensity	Mood	Variation
Moderate	Experienced as pleasant	Most people react in a similar way
Heavy	Experienced as either pleasant or unpleasant	People vary in their response
Severe	Experienced as unpleasant	Most people react in the same way

Table 11.1 The relationship between exercise intensity and mood response
Source: Adapted from Ekkekakis et al., 2005

Heavy intensity exercise is defined as occurring between the lactate threshold and the maximal lactate steady state – the highest work rate at which blood lactate can be stabilized (Ekkekakis et al., 2005). Mood response to heavy exercise varies among individuals; some people experience it as positive, whereas others as negative. Whether people experience heavy exercise as positive or negative depends on individual differences, such as their self-efficacy or ability to deal with sensory information they receive during exercise. For example, untrained individuals might find heavy weight training a negative experience because they are not confident they can lift the weights, and they do not know how to use the internal information about muscle tension, fatigue and pain to decide when they can keep going or should stop for safety reasons. Trained people may find heavy workouts more positive because they have greater confidence they can lift the weights, and they know how to interpret muscle tension, fatigue and pain to decide when they should continue or when they should stop.

Severe exercise intensity extends from the maximal lactate steady state to individuals' maximal exercise capacity (Ekkekakis et al., 2005). Most people will experience discomfort and negative moods at this intensity. There are health risks associated with exercising at severe intensities, such as injury, increased blood pressure and depletion of energy reserves. The body seems set up to take action against operating at severe intensities for long periods of time through the negative mood response.

Once people stop exercising at heavy or severe intensities, they experience a 'rebound effect' (Ekkekakis et al., 2005). Their moods change from negative to positive. The body seems to 'reward' people for stopping intense physical activity by letting them experience pleasurable moods.

Summary

As physical activity intensity increases, there is a decrease in positive and an increase in negative mood, although people vary in their responses at given workloads. After exercise, there is a rebound effect, in which mood improves, as described by the iceberg profile.

Exercise and depression

Depression is characterized by sadness, loss of interest or pleasure, feelings of guilt or low self-worth, disturbed sleep or appetite, low energy, and poor concentration (World Health Organization, WHO, 2009). These signs can become long-lasting and substantially impair individuals' abilities to cope with life. People experiencing depression may also commit suicide. There are different types of depression, and examples include major depressive disorder, dysthymia, bipolar disorder and cyclothymia (USDHHS, 1999). Brief descriptions are presented in Table 11.2, providing some insight into what you might observe in people with each type of depression.

Major depression
<ul><li>Cardinal symptoms include depressed mood and loss of interest or pleasure</li><li>Other symptoms vary and may include weight change (loss or gain), changes in appetite (decrease or increase), changes in sleep patterns, psychomotor agitation or retardation, fatigue, feelings of worthlessness, excessive or inappropriate guilt, inability to think or concentrate, or indecisiveness</li><li>A depressive episode may last 9 months and reoccurrence of episodes is common</li></ul>
Dysthymia
<ul><li>A long-term form of depression, that may last at least two years for adults and one year in children</li><li>Individuals may display fewer than five of the symptoms needed for major depressive episode</li><li>Associated with higher rates of substance abuse and individuals are susceptible to major depression</li><li>The condition seldom remits spontaneously</li></ul>
Bipolar disorder
<ul><li>Recurrent disorder associated with one or more episodes of mania (or hypomania) or mixed depression and mania (or hypomania)</li><li>Mania may range from elation to irritability</li><li>Thought speed may increase and content may be grandiose or paranoid</li><li>Distractibility and poor concentration impair judgement</li><li>Reckless behaviour is common, examples include spending sprees, offensive and uninhibited behaviour and promiscuity</li><li>Increased subjective energy, libido and activity, but a perceived reduce need for sleep</li></ul>
Cyclothymia
<ul><li>Features manic and depressive episodes, neither of sufficient intensity or duration for bipolar depression or major depressive disorder diagnosis</li></ul>

Table 11.2 Brief descriptions of major depression, dysthymia, bipolar disorder and cyclothymia
Source: USDHHS, 1999

Depression has been called the 'common cold of mental illness', and is one of the most prevalent mental disorders (Kring et al., 2007). The American Psychiatric Association (APA, 2000) estimated the lifetime risk for major depression is 10–25% for females and 5–12% for males. Such widespread prevalence incurs a large cost to society. The WHO (2009), for example, states that depression is the leading cause of disability, and the fourth biggest contributor to the global burden of disease. Even though less than 25% of individuals have access to effective treatment, the number of people involved (121 million worldwide; WHO, 2009) means that billions of pounds are spent each year to help prevent people becoming depressed or helping them cope with the disorder.

Causes and treatment of depression

No single cause explains depression, and the interaction of biological, psychological and social factors is probably involved (Davey, 2008; Kring et al., 2007). Biological influences include genetics and abnormal brain structures and functioning. Social and psychological factors include traumatic life events, interpersonal difficulties, maladaptive beliefs, and feeling helpless. Biological, social and psychological factors probably interact with each other. Perhaps, for example, as a result of genetic factors, some people have a biological vulnerability that leads to depression after difficult social and psychological events.

A number of treatments are available for depression including medication, psychotherapy and electroconvulsive therapy (Davey, 2008; Kring et al., 2007). **Electroconvulsive therapy** involves passing an electric current through the patient's head for about half a second (Davey, 2008). Psychotherapy aims to address depression by helping individuals change their thoughts, feelings, behaviours and relationships. The UK's National Institute for Clinical Excellence (NICE, 2007) recommended treatment be tailored to the level of depression. For example, psychotherapy and exercise were two treatments for mild depression. Severe depression should be treated with medication and psychotherapy. Electroconvulsive therapy was recommended when patients displayed severe self-neglect or risk to life.

The influence of exercise on depression

There is some support for a relationship between exercise and depression (Hassmén et al. 2000). Longitudinal or prospective research, for example, provides some evidence for a link between exercise and depression. In a prospective study, investigators measure a group of individuals' levels of exercise and then over time assess the people who develop depressive symptoms. Across various prospective studies, a consistent finding is that lower levels of physical activity are associated with higher rates of depressive symptoms (Farmer et al., 1988; Motl et al., 2004). Also, as individuals vary their physical activity levels, the risk of depression changes (Motl et al., 2004). Although it might be tempting to suggest exercise is a preventive factor, prospective studies cannot determine that exercise reduces or prevents people from experiencing depression, only that the two variables coincide together (see box below). **Experiments**, which can determine cause and effect, are needed to find out if exercise can prevent and treat depression.

Thinking scientifically → **methods used to study exercise and mental health**

Researchers have undertaken a large number of studies examining the relationship between exercise and mental health, and they have used different types of research design. It can be difficult to evaluate the knowledge that has emerged from a huge number of different types of study. Here, we briefly describe three of the methods used:

- *Descriptive studies:* In descriptive studies, researchers observe people, events and things as they occur in the world without deliberately changing anything. An example includes a survey in which scientists measure how often people exercise and their levels of depression. Descriptive research can tell us if two factors are related to each other, but cannot tell us if one causes a change in the other. For example, it might indicate if exercise is related to depression, but cannot suggest if physical activity can reduce depression.

- *Experimental studies:* In experiments, scientists manipulate one factor to see if it causes a change in another variable. For example, researchers might measure the levels of depression in a number of people, and then divide them into two groups: one that exercises regularly for 12 weeks and one that does no physical activity. The scientists then measure the people's level of depression again after the 12 weeks. If the depression levels have dropped in people who exercised, but stayed the same in those who did no physical activity, scientists can conclude that exercise caused a reduction. Experiments provide the best evidence about the influence that exercise has on mental health.

- *Meta-analysis:* When lots of studies on one topic have been undertaken, such as the influence of exercise on anxiety, it can be difficult to summarize them just by reading them. Different people might come to opposite conclusions because they interpret the results in various ways. A meta-analysis is type of study that combines the results from other investigations and leads to a result that is based on objective statistical procedures instead of people's subjective judgements.

Researchers have conducted many experiments to find out if exercise can treat clinical and non-clinical levels of depression, and numerous reviews and meta-analyses of these studies exist. One of the most cited meta-analyses suggested that exercise resulted in decreased depression (North et al., 1990). In addition, the effect was found for females and males, people of various ages, and individuals of varying health status. People needing medical or psychological care demonstrated the greatest improvements. Different exercise modes were effective and included weight training, endurance activities, walking, jogging and aerobics classes. Greater improvements in depression were associated with exercise programmes that were longer lasting and had more sessions. Exercise was better than relaxation or other enjoyable activities, and as helpful as psychotherapy. Exercise was more effective when combined with psychotherapy than on its own. Similar encouraging results have continued to the present day. In one of the most recent meta-analyses, for example, exercise was more effective for clinically depressed individuals than healthy people, although both types of folk benefited (Rethorst et al,, 2009).

Although some scientists have questioned the quality of the research conducted to date, there is agreement that exercise is a useful treatment. Daley (2008), for example, suggested that although there was a need for more high-quality studies, exercise was a suitable intervention, at least in the short term, when combined with other treatments. She also described exercise as an 'all-round' treatment, because it was relatively free of negative side effects, provided a cheap alternative, could be undertaken at the individual's convenience, and provided a range of other physical and psychological benefits. Daley also pointed out challenges with using exercise. Depressed people, for example, often lack the will to complete daily routines and may not feel up to exercising. In addition, depressed individuals, particularly those who have been sedentary, may find achieving the recommended exercise levels challenging and may experience discomfort that further reduces their desire to exercise.

Summary

Although more research is needed, people who regularly exercise may be less likely to experience depression. In addition, exercise is recommended as a suitable treatment for mild-to-moderate depression, when combined with other interventions (e.g. medication or psychotherapy) and conducted under the supervision of a qualified mental health practitioner.

👁 Exercise and anxiety

In Chapter 6, you learned about competitive anxiety and its relationship with sports performance and exercise participation. Most times anxiety is an expected consequence of the situation. We would normally expect, for example, some athletes to get anxious prior to an important game. When symptoms start interfering with people's abilities to perform well or detracting from their enjoyment, then anxiety might be considered a mental health problem, and they might benefit from a sport and exercise psychologist's help. If the anxiety becomes debilitating and/or influences other areas of life, an anxiety disorder diagnosis might be suitable. Anxiety disorders involve excessive arousal that:

- may be characterized by feelings of apprehension, uncertainty and fear that are out of proportion to the threat
- may be states that individuals experience constantly
- may be non-attributable to specific threats
- may be so disabling that individuals cannot function in one or more of their life roles (Davey, 2008).

Anxiety disorders are the most common type of mental health illnesses, and 30–40% of individuals will have anxiety-based problems at some point during their lives (Davey, 2008; USDHHS, 1999). Billions of pounds are spent yearly in attempts to prevent and treat anxiety problems, and they are the most expensive type of disorders (Davey, 2008). As an illustration, Table 11.3 presents various types of anxiety-based disorders.

Panic attacks and panic disorder
<ul><li>A panic attack is a discrete period of extreme fear with physical (e.g. palpitations, trembling, chest pains) and mental (fear of dying, 'going crazy', losing control of emotions or behaviour) symptoms, and often strong desires to escape the situation</li><li>Has a sudden onset and high intensity, although typically lasts less than 30 minutes</li><li>A panic disorder is diagnosed after individuals have two or more panic attacks and persistent concerns about further episodes, or they try to avoid or minimize future occurrences</li><li>Twice as common in females than males, and age of onset is typically between late adolescence and 50</li></ul>

Specific and social phobias
■ Specific phobias consist of excessive fear of particular objects or situations, and individuals typically recognize their experiences as irrational; common examples include animals, insects, heights, elevators, flying, driving, water, storms, blood, and injections ■ Typically begin in childhood, not generally the result of single events, but social or vicarious learning may be involved ■ A social phobia (social anxiety disorder) is a marked fear of social situations and a central feature of the anxiety involves the possibility of embarrassment or ridicule ■ Adults typically recognize their fear as irrational ■ May be associated with anticipatory anxiety in the days or weeks preceding an event ■ More common in women than men and typically begins in childhood or adolescence
Generalized anxiety disorder
■ Chronic anxiety (six months' minimum) not attributable to specific objects or events, but pertains to many areas (e.g. work, relationships, finances) ■ More common in women than men, and 50% begin in childhood or adolescence ■ Has a fluctuating course associated with individuals' life stress
Obsessive-compulsive disorder
■ Involves obsessions (uncontrollable intrusive thoughts or impulses) that cause anxiety and compulsions (repetitive behaviours or mental acts) performed to reduce fear or prevent a dreaded event ■ Compulsions may occupy long periods of time (may even be several hours) ■ A common obsession with germs may be associated with hand washing (compulsion) ■ Equally common in both genders, and age of onset is adolescence to young adult life ■ Has a fluctuating course associated with individuals' life stress
Acute and post-traumatic stress disorder
■ Acute stress disorder involves anxiety and behaviour disturbances beginning within one month of an extreme trauma ■ A central feature is dissociation, or the perceived detachment of the mind from the body, although other symptoms may include avoidance of situations or stimuli that trigger memories of the trauma and intrusive recollections ■ If symptoms last more than one month, post-traumatic stress disorder is diagnosed ■ Changes associated with post-traumatic stress disorder may include decreased self-esteem, hopelessness, relationship difficulties and feeling damaged ■ More common in women than men, and develops in about 9% of individuals exposed to extreme trauma

Table 11.3 Brief descriptions of major anxiety disorders
Source: USDHHS, 1999

Causes and treatment of anxiety

There is no single explanation for why people develop anxiety disorders generally, although there is knowledge about some of the risk factors (Davey, 2008; Kring et al., 2007). For example, genes and biology seem to be involved, and parts of the brain, along with levels of neurochemicals, are associated with anxiety. The ways in which people think and interpret their world also seem to be important. For example, individuals with low perceived control, who tend to focus on negative aspects of their surroundings, and who are neurotic (or prone to excessive anxiety or emotional disturbance) seem more likely to develop anxiety problems. Also, having experienced negative life events seems to increase the risk of anxiety problems. Although scientists can identify risk factors, the level of understanding currently is not specific enough to explain why people develop specific disorders (e.g. panic attacks rather than obsessive-compulsive disorder).

Typically, anxiety treatments include psychotherapy and medication. Exposure is common to most psychotherapy approaches; psychologists agree that people need to face and work through the sources of their anxieties, typically under supervised care (Davey, 2008; Kring et al., 2007). In addition, there may be attempts to challenge individuals' beliefs about the likelihood and extent of negative outcomes resulting from the occurrence of what they dread. Medication is another common treatment, and there exists a range of drugs that can be tailored to specific issues. Side effects and withdrawal symptoms are associated with anxiety drugs, however, and the benefits of taking them seem to last only while they are being taken (Kring et al., 2007). Both medication and psychotherapy can be expensive and labour intensive. The possibility that exercise might be a low-cost alternative has led to scientists examining if physical activity can be a viable treatment.

Influence of exercise on anxiety

Similar to depression, descriptive research has suggested that increased physical activity levels in the general population are associated with lower incidences of anxiety symptoms and disorders (de Moor et al., 2006; Stephens, 1988). And like depression, although it is tempting to say that exercise is a protective factor against anxiety, such a cause-and-effect relationship cannot be drawn from descriptive research (see box above).

Perhaps people with low levels of anxiety are more likely to exercise. Experimental studies are needed.

Many experiments, which can establish cause and effect, have been conducted and, generally, there is agreement among scientists that exercise interventions result in reduced anxiety symptoms (Petruzzello et al., 1991; Wipfli et al., 2008). For example, Grove and Eklund (2004) concluded that:

- anxiety symptoms are lowered with exercise
- reductions occur for both healthy individuals and people with clinical anxiety disorders
- aerobic exercise at a moderate level has the most support.

Based on their conclusions, Grove and Eklund (2004) made a number of recommendations about exercise prescription for reducing anxiety (Table 11.4). The recommendations in Table 11.4 are similar to the guidelines for enhanced physical health – regular activity of moderate intensity for between 30–60 minutes. The similarity means that people do not have to design one exercise programme for physical health and a different one for mental health. Grove and Eklund's (2004) recommendations are also flexible and can be tailored to people's interests and preferences. For example, some people like to walk, whereas others like to run, play a team sport, mountain bike and so on. Each of these activities, if undertaken at a moderate intensity and often enough, will probably help to lower anxiety symptoms.

Use activities clients have selected
Match exercise to clients' skill levels
Focus on aerobic activities
Exercise intensity: moderate
Exercise duration: 20–50 minutes
Exercise frequency: three to five times per week
Use exercise with repetitive and rhythmical characteristics
Make use of both weight-bearing and non-weight-bearing modes

Table 11.4 Grove and Eklund's (2004) exercise recommendations for reducing anxiety

Summary

Research supports the UK's chief medical officer's observation that active people have fewer anxiety symptoms than inactive people (DH, 2004).

Also, exercise lowers both state and trait anxiety levels. Finally, physical activity has the largest effect on unfit people with high anxiety levels.

◉ Why might exercise enhance mental health?

The reasons why exercise might influence mental health are not yet known (Biddle and Mutrie, 2008). Several theories have been suggested and some have more support than others (Landers and Arent, 2007). The different theories are typically either psychological or physiological in flavour. Not all the theories are presented below, only those with the best supporting evidence (Landers and Arent, 2007).

Physiological-based explanations

Increased levels of endorphins

The **endorphins** are a range of hormones known to block pain, improve mood, and enhance a sense of wellbeing (Landers and Arent, 2007). Hormones are chemical substances the body produces to influence the activities of certain organs and processes. For example, endorphins are released during times of stress, including both aerobic and anaerobic exercise. Possibly, increased endorphins may account for the exercise 'high', or the euphoria and exhilaration sometimes experienced during moderate-to-intense aerobic activity. Also, the release of endorphins during exercise may cause the reduced anxiety, tension, anger and depression observed following physical activity. Regular exercise may:

- lead to an increased release of endorphins per session
- enhance a person's sensitivity to the hormones
- lead to a slower degradation rate (McArdle et al., 2001).

Changes in brain biology

Potentially, changes in brain biology may underlie improvements in mental health including more positive moods and intellectual abilities, such as learning and memory (Etnier et al., 1997). Some evidence suggests that regular physical activity is associated with the health, survival and generation of brain cells, along with their organization and function. Also, exercise may lead to increased blood flow to the brain (Landers and Arent, 2007).

Increased levels of monoamine neurotransmitters

Neurotransmitters are chemicals that allow nerve cells to communicate with each other or with other cells, such as muscle fibres. The **monoamines** are a group of neurotransmitters related to depression and anxiety (La Forge, 1995). Examples include dopamine, adrenaline (epinephrine in the US), noradrenaline (norepinephrine in the US) and serotonin. Antidepressant medications increase the levels of these neurotransmitters. Exercise may also increase their levels, possibly explaining why regular physical activity may reduce depression and anxiety (Landers and Arent, 2007).

Decreased stress hormone response

During times of mental and physical stress, the brain releases a range of stress hormones to help prepare the body to cope with the increased demands being made on the person (McArdle et al., 2001). Increased levels of these stress hormones are associated with depression, anxiety and negative mood. Although a single exercise session may cause the release of these stress hormones, over time, regular training leads to a reduced amount being produced at the same intensity level. Potentially, as a result of regular exercise, the body produces less stress hormones when responding to stressful events (La Forge, 1995).

Psychological-based explanations

Improved self-esteem

Self-esteem refers to the value people place on themselves, and it is an important component of mental health. Also, self-esteem is related to other mental health issues such as depression. As people engage in exercise, sports and physical activity, they may improve their skill levels, fitness levels or appearance (e.g. lose weight). With enhanced skill, fitness or appearance, they may find that their self-esteem improves (Sonstroem, 1997). Actual improvements in skill, fitness and appearance are not always needed. Self-esteem may increase if people believe that they have improved their abilities and physical conditioning (Lox et al., 2006).

Social support

Perhaps it is not physical activity, but the interactions with other people and the social support individuals experience when they do exercise that leads to improved mental health (Dishman et al., 2004). Sport and exercise psychologists have not examined the social support explanation often and more research is needed (Landers and Arent, 2007).

Summary

Although each of these explanations has some support, none of them provide a conclusive answer to why exercise might be related to mental health. For example, most of the evidence regarding changes in brain biology comes from animal research and it is not clear that findings from these studies apply to people (Landers and Arent, 2007). It is also probable that each explanation is insufficient on its own to explain why mental health is improved with exercise. Mental health involves thinking, feeling and behaviour, and none of the explanations above addresses each of these components. Instead, a combination of these explanations probably accounts for why mental health improves with exercise (Biddle and Mutrie, 2008).

Conclusions

Generally, it seems people may obtain mental health benefits from regular moderate exercise. The recommendation for people to aim for five days a week of at least 30 minutes moderate exercise so they can gain physical health benefits also seems suitable for mental health. Given the current levels of regular physical activity in the population, the challenge for exercise leaders, sports and exercise scientists, medical staff and politicians is to find ways to help people increase the amount they exercise so they can reap the mental (and physical) benefits outlined in the chapter.

Further reading

Biddle, S.J. and Mutrie, N. (2008). *Psychology of physical activity: Determinants, well-being and interventions* (2nd edn). London: Routledge.

Davey, G. (2008). *Psychopathology: Research, assessment, and treatment in clinical psychology*. Chichester: BPS Blackwell.

Lox, C.L., Martin Ginis, K.A. and Petruzzello, S.J. (2006). *The psychology of exercise: Integrating theory and practice* (2nd edn). Scottsdale, AZ: Holcomb Hathawa.

Key search terms

Anxiety, cognitive functioning, Department of Health (DH), depression, exercise, mental health, mood states, National Institute for Clinical Excellence (NICE), United States Department of Health and Human Services (USDHHS), World Health Organization (WHO)

Chapter 12

Physical health

In Chapter 11 we examined research which illustrated that exercise and physical activity can be helpful for individuals suffering from a number of mental health problems, such as anxiety and depression. People who suffer from physical health problems, such as diabetes or heart disease, not surprisingly may also suffer some adverse psychological effects of their illness. For instance, some people with physical health complaints experience a reduced quality of life, a perceived lack of control over themselves and their health, or high levels of depression or anxiety. As we will see in this chapter, research suggests that exercise can help people who suffer from physical ill health with some of these psychological effects; for example helping them to gain a sense of control, to reduce stress, anxiety and depression, and improve their perceived quality of life.

In this chapter we focus on the role of exercise in helping individuals with specific physical health complaints to deal with some of the adverse psychological consequences of these conditions and so contribute positively to their overall wellbeing. The conditions on which we focus are cancer, diabetes, heart disease and HIV. We consider the results of recent research findings from studies that have adopted a range of research approaches, including descriptive, qualitative and experimental studies.

In this chapter, we will examine:
- The role of exercise in preventing chronic disease
- The role of exercise in the lives of chronic ill health sufferers
- The influence of self-presentation on high-risk health behaviours
- The links between exercise and wellbeing in cancer, diabetes, heart disease and HIV patients

⊙ Exercise and wellbeing in chronic disease sufferers

Exercise and chronic disease prevention

Kruk (2007) conducted a review of studies published between 2004 and March 2007 that examined the links between physical activity and exercise and a number of both physical and mental health complaints: cardiovascular disease (CVD), diabetes, fall-related injuries, obesity, osteoporosis, depression and emotional distress. Her results revealed that physical activity can have a protective effect against a range of different types of cancer, with particularly strong evidence to support its effect in reducing the risk of colon and breast cancer. Physical activity has also been shown to reduce the risk of various cardiovascular diseases (e.g. hypertension/high blood pressure, stroke, coronary heart disease), with 30 minutes of moderate intensity activity on most days of the week identified as a suitable amount to reduce the risk of CVDs such as those listed.

People who are not physically active are at increased risk of developing type 2 diabetes mellitus, which is a disruption in the metabolism of carbohydrate, fat and protein, leading to an increased risk of the development of CVD. It is also associated with obesity. Similarly, a sedentary lifestyle is a risk factor for developing osteoporosis, which is a condition in which the patient suffers from brittle bones. It is a particular health risk for the elderly and postmenopausal women. Kruk (2007) discusses evidence that physical activity may help to increase bone strength and bone mineral density, thus contributing to a reduced risk of developing osteoporosis.

Some factors which influence our risk of developing diseases such as CVD or osteoporosis are not modifiable (e.g. gender, age or family history). Physical activity, however, is a lifestyle factor which can be modified, although not necessarily easily, as illustrated by the low levels of participation in physical activity across the globe. Nevertheless, the significant role played by physical activity in preventing these chronic and often fatal diseases is underscored by evidence such as that discussed by Kruk (2007). There are many reasons why people do not engage in exercise and physical activity and it is possible that some people will refrain from carrying out preventive health behaviours, including exercise, for psychological reasons. One such psychological factor is self-presentation and we consider this briefly below.

Self-presentation as a psychological barrier to disease prevention

Leary et al. (1994) examined the role of self-presentation as a psychological barrier to engaging in preventive health behaviours. As we saw in Chapter 6, self-presentation refers to the processes we use to monitor and control the images we convey to others. Among other health risks, Leary et al. discuss evidence suggesting that some people may not use condoms to reduce the risk of contracting HIV (human immuno-deficiency virus) for self-presentation reasons, such as embarrassment in purchasing them and fear of being labelled promiscuous or having a sexually transmitted disease if one carries condoms. Some people may disregard health warnings about sunbathing and tanning salons as risk factors for contracting skin cancer to present an image of a tanned individual to others. Leary et al. (1994) discuss the possibility that people who have high levels of **social physique anxiety** – a concern that others are negatively evaluating one's physique (Hart et al., 1989) – may be reluctant to exercise because of a fear of presenting an image to others of someone who is unfit, untoned and incompetent. Exercise psychologists therefore need to consider the role of self-presentation in preventing some people from exercising, and try to help to diminish these concerns in order to encourage people to exercise for the physical and mental health benefits it offers.

Exercise and wellbeing in clinical and non-clinical populations

Exercise and physical activity clearly have a role to play in reducing the risk of developing physical ill health, but from a psychological perspective, how can it help people who are suffering from physical ill health? Are the benefits comparable between people who are well (non-clinical populations) and people who are suffering from ill health (clinical populations)?

Gillison et al. (2009) conducted a useful meta-analysis of exercise interventions with clinical and well populations, focusing specifically on their effects on participants' quality of life. They drew comparisons between participants who were involved in exercise interventions for one of three different purposes:

1 *health promotion/disease prevention* – the non-clinical, well population
2 *rehabilitation* – those who had experienced a health threat but were expected to recover fully or partially
3 *disease management* – participants were exercising as part of an ongoing treatment intervention to prevent further health deterioration but their condition was not expected to improve.

Quality of life (QoL) is a multidimensional construct, and the World Health Organization (WHOQOL Group, 1998) has identified six domains of QoL that are important for both clinical and non-clinical populations: physical health, psychological state, level of independence, social relationships, environment, and spirituality, religiousness and personal beliefs.

Gillison et al.'s (2009) key findings from their meta-analysis of 56 studies were that overall QoL gains were greater in group 2 (participation in exercise for rehabilitation) than groups 1 and 3 (participation in exercise for disease prevention or management, respectively). The greatest improvements in psychological state were experienced by group 1, with the least gains in this domain experienced by patients in group 3. Although participants exercising for prevention or rehabilitation purposes reported improvements in both physical and psychological domains, those exercising for disease management only experienced improvements in physical health and in fact experienced a decrease in psychological state.

Some differences in outcome were also identified in relation to both the intensity of exercise and its mode of delivery. For both the prevention and disease management groups, greater gains were accrued in the physical domain from moderate compared with light intensity exercise. In contrast, greater gains in overall QoL were observed for light compared with moderate intensity exercise in both the rehabilitation and prevention groups, and for psychological state in the prevention group. Greater gains in overall QoL were experienced in all groups when people exercised in group compared with individual settings. Surprisingly though, more gains in the social, physical and psychological domains were accrued when people exercised individually compared with in a group setting.

These results suggest that when using exercise to improve QoL, it is important to consider the exercise intensity and mode of delivery and, of course, the reason for exercising. By doing so, we know in which QoL domains we can expect most improvement and can strive to ensure optimum improvement in people exercising for different reasons. Gillison et al. (2009) note that the decrease observed in psychological state in those exercising for disease management purposes may suggest that these people are not ready to exercise and may not appreciate the benefits of exercise for their condition. Education, monitoring and support from exercise specialists is important to ensure that any exercise intervention for this group of people is introduced at an appropriate time and in an appropriate way. This meta-analysis highlights key factors to consider when delivering exercise interventions (purpose, intensity, mode of delivery and potential outcomes), but focuses on only one psychological outcome, QoL, and does not consider specific conditions in detail, which we will do in the next section.

The role of exercise for chronic health sufferers

A qualitative study conducted by Graham et al. (2008) provides a deeper insight into the role and meaning of exercise for people with chronic illness. They interviewed 11 participants of a group-based, seated exercise programme who suffered from a range of chronic conditions such as paraplegia, arthritis and traumatic brain injury. Their findings revealed three key ways in which exercise was perceived to benefit psychological wellbeing:

1 *Exercise was seen as a vehicle for active mood management*, helping to increase feelings of energy and motivation and decrease depression, as one participant commented:

> I used to feel suicidal. I said, 'sod this for a life, what sort of life is this?' Why do that though? It mightn't be much of a life, but at least it is one. Well, it [exercise] is better than me sitting in a chair in a corner and saying, 'Oh look at me, God help me.'
> (Graham et al., 2008: 450)

2 Chronic illness can lead to a loss of previous identities, for instance socially and professionally, and *exercise helped replace these*

lost identities as participants now identified themselves as competent exercisers:

> I liked competing with people that are more able bodied than I am and I sort of say to myself, 'well, if I can compete against them!' I like to see that I'm as good as they are, or maybe better. (Graham et al., 2008: 451)

3 People with chronic illness often become isolated from others because they are no longer able to work or socialize as they did previously. *Exercise helped them to feel both connected to others and to their own bodies*, as amply illustrated in the following quotation:

> The right-hand side [of my body] is like going through a barrel of thick oil. That might seem strange. You don't know where the hand is. You roll onto your side and you would think you were lying on a set of crutches. It's not pain in the usual sense, it's a dullness. Yesterday the left arm and leg felt like a plank ... But when I use it in the [exercise] hall it helps a bit, you know? Still doesn't feel right, but at least I'm moving it, doing something with it [my arm] that means it's not just a useless weight around my neck. (Graham et al., 2008: 452)

Such qualitative evidence is clearly important in vividly capturing the participant's own experience in a way that questionnaire measures are unable to.

Summary

Physical activity and exercise can be effective in helping to prevent the onset of both physical and mental ill health; however, self-presentation concern may be one factor that prevents people from exercising and accruing its beneficial preventive effects. When administering exercise interventions, exercise professionals need to consider the purpose of the intervention (e.g. rehabilitation or disease management) and the type and mode of delivery of exercise, to ensure that different individuals can achieve optimal gains in QoL. For people suffering from chronic illness, exercise can play an important role in maintaining and developing lost identities, managing and improving mood, and reconnecting the individual with themselves and others.

⟨⊙⟩ Exercise, wellbeing and cancer

Descriptive and qualitative studies in exercise, wellbeing and cancer

Non-experimental studies have examined the feasibility and effects of exercise for cancer patients undergoing chemotherapy and at an acute stage of the disease. The studies varied slightly in some ways; some used a home-based multidimensional intervention including exercise and other elements such as stress management (Andersen et al., 2006; Wilson et al., 2006), while another used a hospital-based exercise-only intervention (Battaglini et al., 2009). None of the studies, however, included a control group who did not exercise. Collectively, their findings indicated that exercise is feasible for cancer patients suffering an acute phase of the disease and undergoing chemotherapy. Some psychological benefits were also noted by the patients, including reduced mental fatigue and improved mood (Andersen et al., 2006), decreased depression (Battaglini et al., 2009) and improved QoL in the mental health domain (Wilson et al., 2006). At the other end of the spectrum, Mosher et al. (2009) conducted telephone interviews with older, long-term (five years post-diagnosis) cancer survivors. Although exercise levels overall were quite low, those who did exercise reported improved QoL in the mental health and social functioning domains and, indeed, exceeded age-based norms for mental health.

Midtgaard et al. (2006, 2007) conducted two qualitative studies with cancer patients undergoing chemotherapy and participating in a group-based exercise intervention as part of their treatment. Results from interviews conducted in their first study (Midtgaard et al., 2006) underscored the importance of group cohesion and identity within the exercise group. Patients felt motivated and comfortable exercising with others in a similar situation to themselves, developed a sense of togetherness, and, simply but importantly, had fun while exercising and playing sport together. In their second study, Midtgaard et al. (2007) analysed the diaries of eight participants in which they wrote about their experiences of the exercise intervention. Three main themes emerged from this analysis:

- *shifting position:* participants were initially surprised with their physical capabilities and experienced a shift in focus from the burden of the illness to one of pleasure, excitement and taking personal responsibility for solving their problems

- *self-surveillance:* participating in regular exercise prompted patients to regularly monitor and reflect on their wellbeing and physical abilities, and set goals for daily living, although some participants did report anxiety about their evident lack of physical capacity
- *negotiated strength:* participants felt able to challenge previous conceptions about their physical capabilities and became hopeful that their lives would not be dominated by their illness.

Intervention research in exercise, wellbeing and cancer

Randomized controlled trials of multidimensional interventions were conducted with cancer patients by both Andersen et al. (2006) and Daubenmier et al. (2006). The first of these studies reported increases in perceived vitality, emotional functioning and mental health in the intervention group. In Daubenmeier et al.'s study, however, people in the control group also made positive lifestyle changes (e.g. increasing exercise). Nevertheless, in both groups, lifestyle improvements were related to higher QoL ratings.

Summary

Exercise has been shown to be a feasible intervention for cancer patients, even those undergoing chemotherapy and suffering an acute phase of the disease. A number of psychological benefits of exercise have been noted for cancer patients, such as improved QoL and decreased depression. Qualitative studies have revealed the importance of group cohesion and identity within the exercise group and the role of exercise in helping patients to challenge their self-perceptions and set goals for physical functioning in daily life.

◉ Exercise, wellbeing and diabetes

Perusal of the literature on exercise and diabetes tells us that there are fewer experimental intervention studies than have been conducted with cancer patients; nonetheless, descriptive studies attest to the positive psychological effects of exercise in diabetes patients. Bennett et al. (2008) compared health-related QoL between patients with type 2 diabetes and a non-clinical population prior to embarking on an exercise programme (termed 'baseline measures'). Health-related QoL was lower in the diabetes patients but fitter diabetes patients reported higher levels of health-related QoL in most of the physical domains compared with less fit diabetes patients. Higher levels of fitness are likely to be associated with higher levels of exercise and physical activity, therefore supporting the role of exercise in offsetting the negative effects of suffering from diabetes on the physical components of health-related QoL. Aman et al. (2009) and Smith and McFall (2005) conducted similar large-scale studies with teenagers (11–18 years) and adults, respectively. Compared with those who did less physical activity, diabetic teenagers who did more physical activity reported higher levels of wellbeing and QoL, more positive health perceptions and less negative psychological symptoms (Aman et al., 2009). Smith and McFall (2005) found that adults with diabetes who exercised had higher levels of QoL and those who exercised to lose weight reported similar levels of QoL to non-exercising diabetics. These two studies reinforce the suggestion that encouraging diabetic patients to exercise may help to reduce the negative effect on one's psychological health of suffering from diabetes.

Summary

There appears to be more descriptive than experimental evidence available to support the beneficial effects of exercise for diabetes patients. As with many chronic conditions, QoL tends to be lower in diabetes patients than in people who are well. Nevertheless, teenage and adult diabetics who are physically active report higher levels of QoL than those who are not physically active.

◉ Exercise, wellbeing and heart disease

Exercise, quality of life and psychosocial gains

As we have seen, patients with diabetes and cancer can gain improvements in QoL from exercise and this is also apparent for cardiovascular disease patients. Compared with control groups who did not undertake an exercise intervention, cardiac patients have been shown to experience improvements in QoL and lower levels of psychological distress and hostility (Patwala et al., 2009; Pischke et al., 2008). A meta-analysis by Conn et al. (2009) corroborates these studies' findings. The overall effect of exercise on QoL in cardiac patients was a significant improvement, which the authors suggest may stem from the improved fitness and physical function and decreased depression that are associated with physical activity.

Some insight into the role of exercise in improving cardiac patients' QoL is also offered by a qualitative study by Hudson et al. (2001), in which they interviewed 12 long-term male survivors of a cardiac event (e.g. myocardial infarction or bypass surgery). They had all taken part in a multidimensional rehabilitation programme, including exercise, and still attended supervised exercise classes 18 months to 5 years after completing their initial rehabilitation. Their cardiac illness caused them to suffer a number of significant losses: their sense of purpose, sense of self, and their lifestyle. Through their initial rehabilitation programme and continued exercise participation, however, they were able to regain these losses and gain additional benefits. Overall, they gained:

- *practical and emotional support* from exercise staff and other patients
- *increased self-esteem* through increased fitness and self-confidence
- a *renewed sense of purpose*.

These specific benefits underpinned a more global regaining of the participants' *sense of self* that had been lost as a result of their ill health and their combined losses.

Exercise programme delivery and psychological outcomes

Some researchers have examined whether or not the location or type of exercise intervention results in different QoL outcomes in cardiac patients. Jeiger et al. (2009) found the same degree of improvement in QoL in patients who exercised in a residential programme and those who took part in an outpatients programme. Greater improvements in QoL, however, were observed in patients who engaged in hospital- compared with home-based exercise (Karapolat et al., 2007). Whereas QoL improved in all but two domains in hospital-based exercisers, improvements were only seen in one domain in home-based exercisers; therefore hospital-based exercise, whether residential or not, appears more beneficial than home-based exercise for improving cardiac patients' QoL.

The type of exercise may also influence QoL outcomes for cardiac patients (Klocek, 2005). Males with congestive heart failure completed either no exercise (control group), constant workload exercise, or exercise at a progressively increasing workload for up to six months. As we might expect, the control group demonstrated no improvements in QoL over this period, but improvements were seen in both exercise groups. Importantly, improvements were much greater in the men who exercised at a progressively increasing workload than in those who exercised at the same workload for the whole intervention period.

Summary

As with other clinical populations, exercise helps to improve mental health factors in heart disease patients. Qualitative research has revealed that, as with patients suffering from a range of immobilizing chronic conditions, exercise can help cardiac patients to regain a sense of self that may be lost as a result of their illness. The location and type of exercise programme needs careful consideration to ensure that opportunities for improving QoL in cardiac patients are optimized.

Exercise, wellbeing and HIV

Descriptive studies in exercise, wellbeing and HIV

The effects of exercise on psychological state in other clinical populations extend to people who are HIV positive, as demonstrated in descriptive studies by Gielen et al. (2001) and Ramírez-Marrero et al. (2004). HIV-positive women who engaged in more health-promoting, self-care behaviours, such as exercise, reported higher levels of overall QoL and mental health (Gielen et al., 2001). Similarly, although no differences in depression were observed between physically active and physically inactive HIV-positive men and women, those who were physically active reported higher levels of life satisfaction (Ramírez-Marrero et al., 2004).

Intervention research in exercise, wellbeing and HIV

Here we consider three studies which have included experimental and control groups to reveal the effects of exercise on psychological health in people who are HIV positive. The first study conducted by Lox et al. (1995) compared the effects of aerobic exercise, weight training and a no-exercise condition. A small sample of HIV-positive men completed aerobic exercise, weight training or no exercise (control group) for three months. As we've noted previously, exercise did have a positive influence on life satisfaction and mood. Both aerobic exercise and weight training resulted in increased positive mood and decreased negative mood compared with the control group. In addition, aerobic exercise resulted in greater life satisfaction than that reported in both the weight-training and control groups. These authors also measured physical self-efficacy in the form of perceived physical ability and physical self-presentation confidence and found that, following the interventions, physical self-efficacy was greater in the aerobic exercise group compared with the weight-training group. This is a useful addition to the study, because further analysis showed that changes in physical self-efficacy were associated with changes in mood and life satisfaction. This doesn't necessarily tell us that the changes in mood and life satisfaction were caused by these increases in physical self-efficacy or vice versa. It does suggest, however, that it is wise to focus not only on improving wellbeing but also on providing opportunities for developing physical self-efficacy in patients who are HIV positive, because these psychological variables are related and changes in one may affect changes in the other.

The remaining two studies by Rojas et al. (2003) and Mutimara et al. (2008) didn't compare different types of exercise intervention but used larger mixed samples of HIV-positive men and women. For practical and ethical reasons, Rojas et al. were unable to randomly allocate patients to the exercise and control groups, however, this was possible in Mutimara et al.'s study. Both studies revealed improvements in QoL in the exercise group that weren't seen in the control group. Rojas et al.'s (2003) results revealed significant improvements in the exercise group's perceived health status, emotional wellbeing, energy and global QoL. Similar improvements were observed in psychological state, independence and social relationships in Mutimara et al.'s (2008) study. The only gender difference reported in the two studies was that women experienced greater improvements in the psychological and social QoL domains in Mutimara et al.'s study. Rojas et al. also measured and found significant reductions in anxiety and depression in both groups over the period of the study.

Mutimara et al.'s (2008) study included HIV-positive patients who had moderate-to-severe levels of body fat redistribution in the face, the lower back region, arms, breasts and abdomen. This is an effect that can occur in these patients, which can make the patient's condition visible and therefore known to other people. Not surprisingly, this can cause some distress and self-presentation concern in these patients. The exercise intervention did appear to alleviate some of this distress as patients reported improved self-esteem, life satisfaction, perceived body image and appearance, and lower emotional stress. They also reported fewer problems of feeling ashamed in public, of dressing size and style and were less embarrassed by the impact of these bodily changes as a result of their illness. They also reported feeling more confident about their health and about disclosing their HIV status to others. Thus, similar to Lox et al.'s (1995) results, this study indicates that an exercise intervention for HIV-positive patients with body fat redistribution may have implications for their interactions with others and their physical self-perceptions, as well as personal perceptions of QoL.

Summary

Individuals who are HIV positive and who engage in self-care behaviours, including exercise, benefit from higher levels of life satisfaction and QoL. Experimental studies using comparative control groups have confirmed that this is a causal relationship, that is, the increased levels of wellbeing can be attributed to exercise. These studies also demonstrate the modest advantage of aerobic exercise over weight training, and the role of exercise in helping HIV-positive patients to reduce their body image concerns and social anxiety about their condition.

◉ Conclusions

Evidence suggests that exercise can have a beneficial effect on mental health in people suffering from a range of physical ill health conditions. This can help to alleviate some of the psychological distress that is often experienced by these individuals as a result of their illness. Key mental health benefits include QoL, improved life satisfaction and improved self-perceptions. It is therefore important that exercise and health professionals are aware of these mental health benefits and integrate exercise into prevention, management and rehabilitation programmes for individuals who are suffering from chronic physical ill health.

👁 Further reading

Berger, B.G., Pargman, D. and Weinberg, R.S. (2007). *Foundations of exercise psychology* (2nd edn). Lancaster: Fitness Information Technology.
Biddle, S.J. and Mutrie, N. (2008). *Psychology of physical activity: Determinants, wellbeing and interventions* (2nd edn). London: Routledge.

👁 Key search terms

Cancer, cardiac disease, diabetes, HIV, quality of life (QoL), wellbeing

Chapter 13

Current issues

Burnout, overtraining, body image disturbance, eating disorders and drug use are issues that garner much media attention. It is easy, for example, to think of athletes who have been caught taking drugs or criticized in the press for poor performance when they were probably in overtrained states. In addition, exercise is readily promoted to help people change their body shape and feel better about their appearance, although evidence indicates that physical activity is not a magic pill. Some people believe that certain athletes may be at risk of developing eating disorders because their sports favour lean body shapes. Sport and exercise psychologists who understand these issues may be able to help clients and educate others.

In this chapter, we will examine:
- The current understanding of burnout and overtraining
- The relationship between exercise and body image
- The relationship between sport and eating disorders
- The various types of performance-enhancing drugs and why they are used

Burnout and overtraining

Definitions and theory

Sport psychologists have not been consistent in defining overtraining or related topics, such as staleness and burnout. A common theme among the definitions, however, is that athletes are not recovering from their training and other demands:

- **Overtraining** is a syndrome resulting from excessive overload (usually physical) on athletes without sufficient rest (Goodger et al., 2010).
- **Staleness** is a consequence of overtraining and refers to a long-term, that is, at least two weeks, performance drop unexplained by injury or illness (Goodger et al., 2010).
- **Burnout** refers to a withdrawal from sport, physically or psychologically, characterized by a reduced sense of accomplishment, devaluation of the activity, and exhaustion (Goodger et al., 2010).

Burnout and overtraining prevalence is poorly understood. Researchers have obtained a range of percentages, from 18 to 91%, of athletes experiencing some level of staleness, overtraining or burnout, depending on the sports studied, measures used and definitions employed. Despite inconsistent results, sport psychologists agree that overtraining is a significant problem. Richardson et al. (2008) suggested that a small but significant proportion of athletes experience severe overtraining during some stage of their careers. In addition, less severe overtraining is relatively common, and often happens at inopportune times such as during the build-up to international competitions.

Several burnout and overtraining frameworks exist, and Richardson et al.'s (2008) Overtraining Model (Figure 13.1) illustrates commonalities among the theories:

1 *Risk factors* predisposing athletes to overtraining issues are presented in stage 1 under the categories of situational factors, interpersonal factors, athlete factors and sociocultural context. Richardson et al. (2008) recognize that burnout and overtraining are not solely the result of too much training. The way the four categories interact increases or decreases the chances of overtraining occurring. For example, elite rugby union players may experience overtraining during a world cup year because they may:
   - play lots of games in the lead up – *situational factor*
   - feel obligated to comply with the demands of several coaches – *interpersonal factor*
   - fear not being selected for their country – *athlete factor*
   - feel pressured to win the tournament for their supporters – *sociocultural context.*

2 *The early warning signs* (stage 2) emerge when athletes are unable to cope with the training and non-training (e.g. media appearances) demands or there is a stress/recovery imbalance. Richardson et al. (2008) recommended monitoring various physical and psychological markers to help assess athletes' movements towards overtraining. Physical markers include fatigue, performance and niggling injuries. Psychological markers include anxiety, fear of failure and depressed mood. Although any one marker may not indicate an issue, several together may help to identify problems before they become serious.

3 Stage 3 focuses on how *athletes respond* to early warning signs. The way athletes respond is influenced by the stage 1 risk factors.

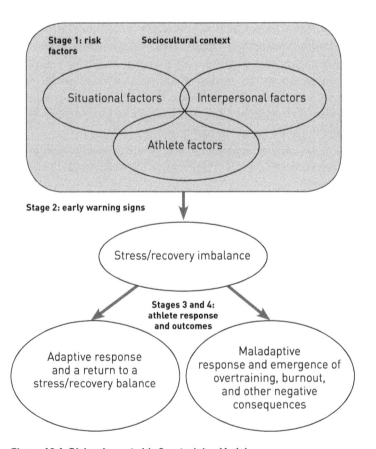

Figure 13.1 Richardson et al.'s Overtraining Model

Sometimes athletes might recognize the danger signs and find ways to reduce or deal with the demands they are facing, such as reducing overall training volume. Sometimes athletes may not recognize the signs or may feel unable to make changes. The ways that individuals respond to the initial indications influences stage 4.

4 As illustrated in stage 4, *outcomes*, when athletes respond well to early warning signs they re-establish a balance between their attempts to cope with the demands being placed on them and their need to recover. Although operating at high intensities and volumes, athletes ensure they get adequate rest. When athletes do not respond well, then overtraining markers may deteriorate and they may experience burnout, overtraining and other severe consequences, such as illness, injury, depression or fatigue. Athletes may even decide, or be forced, to cease participation.

Richardson et al.'s (2008) model is cyclical because athletes' overtraining experiences influence both the risk factors and the ways they respond to future warning signs. Some athletes, for example, may learn from their overtraining experiences, develop ways to recognize and deal with the signs and symptoms, and avoid the negative consequences.

How to help overtrained athletes

Although researchers have not often evaluated interventions for preventing or treating overtraining and burnout, sport psychologists have suggested a number of strategies and Table 13.1 presents those detailed by Goodger et al. (2010). Goodger et al.'s strategies encompass the various personal, interpersonal, situational and social risk factors highlighted by Richardson et al. (2008). On their own, each strategy may be insufficient to help athletes. Instead, using several strategies that address the various risk factors may be more effective (Cresswell and Eklund, 2006). Taken together, the strategies aim to achieve two broad objectives: ensure athletes are able to recover physically from their training and other sporting demands, and help build their confidence that they can cope with the stressors involved with participation. The elite rugby players mentioned earlier, for example, may be less likely to experience overtraining prior to the world cup if their playing schedules are managed to avoid fatigue and they remain buoyant about their abilities to cope with the demands associated with their participation.

- Identify early warning signs, such as those identified by Richardson et al. (2008)
- Increase athletes' motivation and confidence by involving them in decision-making processes
- Schedule time-outs allowing athletes to get a break from their sports and associated demands
- Manage training programmes to ensure sufficient recovery occurs
- Encourage athletes to discuss how they are feeling regarding their training load
- Educate significant others (e.g. parents, partners) about overtraining and how they might help
- Ensure athletes are enjoying their participation
- Encourage athletes to engage in suitable time and lifestyle management practices

Table 13.1 Strategies for preventing and treating overtraining and burnout
Source: Goodger et al., 2010

Summary

Burnout and overtraining occur when athletes do not recover from their training and other demands. The Richardson et al. (2008) model provides a way to illustrate the process that leads to burnout, overtraining and related negative consequences. Although few intervention programmes have been evaluated, strategies for preventing and treating overtraining revolve around adequate physical and psychological recovery.

◉ Body image

Definitions and theory

Body image refers to our mental picture of our physical self and consists of perceptual and attitudinal components (Cash, 2008). The perceptual component refers to judgements regarding body size and shape, such as our perceptions about the width of our thighs. The attitudinal component includes cognitive, affective, behavioural and global dimensions:

- The *cognitive* dimension involves people's beliefs about their bodies, such as netball players who believe being tall affords them advantages over opponents.
- The *affective* dimension refers to people's emotions about their bodies. Many individuals, for example, experience depressed mood because they are not as slender as desired.

- The *behavioural* dimension embraces the way people act due to their perceived appearance, such as some individuals who do not go swimming in public because they feel unattractive.
- The *global* dimension refers to people's overall satisfaction or dissatisfaction about their bodies.

Although difficult to establish accurately, a substantial proportion of the population are unhappy with their bodies in some way (Cash, 2002). Many people, both male and female, for example, believe they are too fat, have insufficient muscle mass, or both. **Negative body image** refers to the negative evaluations we have of our bodies along one or more of the dimensions above, and exists along a continuum (Cash, 2002). Some individuals have positive beliefs about their appearance, whereas others have negative evaluations of their bodies. One reason why many psychologists consider negative body image a health issue is because of relationships with several psychological and physical variables. As examples, low body satisfaction is associated with decreased confidence in social situations and reductions in the quality and quantity of interpersonal experiences (Cash and Fleming, 2002). Body image disturbance is a central feature in eating disorders (Garner, 2002) and body dysmorphic disorder (Phillips, 2002). Body image concerns may be associated with risky behaviours including excessive exercise and drug abuse (Cafri et al., 2008), and psychological variables, including anxiety, depression and self-esteem (Maida and Armstrong, 2005).

According to Cash (2008), four factors influence body image:

1 *Cultural socialization* refers to societal norms, such as the images portrayed in the media (e.g. magazines, movies, television, internet and computer games). Broadly, in Western culture, the dominant images typically involve slender attractive females and large muscular males.

2 *Interpersonal experiences* refer to the interactions individuals have with people around them, such as when children are bullied for being overweight.

3 *Physical attributes* influence body image. For example, some people's body satisfaction decreases with age as their physical abilities fade.

4 *Personality characteristics* also influence body attitudes. For example, individuals with perfectionist tendencies and beliefs about traditional gender roles may experience body dissatisfaction if their appearance doesn't conform to media portrayed physiques.

Much body image research has focused on the cultural socialization influence. Researchers have observed, for example, that for males and females, exposure to images of attractive individuals with ideal bodies reduces body satisfaction (Blond, 2008). In addition, negative interpersonal experiences, such as childhood bullying or low levels of social support, are associated with poor body image (Cafri et al., 2006). Throughout daily life, people receive messages that being attractive and having an athletic body are associated with rewards such as being popular, healthy or successful at work. Individuals compare their appearance with that of people around them, including celebrities and models portrayed in the media. Given the number of attractive people and models presented in the media, it is understandable many people are unhappy with their appearance. Improving appearance is a common reason why individuals start exercising (Markland and Ingledew, 2007). Many professionals in the sport and fitness industry prey on body image concerns to entice people to exercise and to sell training programmes, weight loss and gain products, and equipment.

Body image and exercise

Hausenblas and Symons-Downs (2001) found that athletes have better body images than non-athletes, a finding paralleling a common belief that because athletes train intensely and control their diets, they will develop bodies of which they will be proud. The magnitude of the difference Hausenblas and Symons-Downs found, however, was small, indicating considerable overlap: many athletes are dissatisfied, and many non-athletes are happy, with their bodies. Although training and attention to diet may lead to desirable body composition changes, physique is not the only factor influencing appearance. Body image is influenced by other factors unchanged by physical activity, including facial features, symmetry, scars and birthmarks.

Also, the sporting context may subject athletes to many appearance-related pressures. Most athletes and coaches probably accept some relationship between body shape and performance (Davis, 2002). A high power-to-weight ratio, for example, confers advantages in many sports. In subjectively scored sports, people believe that an attractive body enhances the chances of success (Davis, 2002). Coaches, teammates, families and others may place enormous pressure on athletes to obtain desirable body shapes. Such pressure may lead to reduced body satisfaction, body image disturbances, depressed moods and eating disorders.

Many exercise professionals tout exercise as a way to improve appearance, and sell training programmes designed to tighten backsides and flatten stomachs. Most of these gimmicky programmes are untested, and, for those that have been evaluated, the results are often unsupportive (Anderson et al., 2004). Instead, investigators have observed that regular physical activity may improve body satisfaction and related concepts such as decreased social physique anxiety (Hausenblas and Fallon, 2006; Reel et al., 2007). Although differing opinions exist over whether anaerobic training (e.g. weight training), aerobic exercise or a combination of both is most effective, such debate is probably of secondary importance for exercise professionals. People vary over what they would most like to change. Some individuals desire to lose fat, and aerobic exercise may be suited to their objectives. Other people want to increase muscle, and weight training is suitable for their desires. Finally, some individuals want to increase muscle and lose fat, and a combined aerobic and anaerobic intervention may be most suitable. Individuals with the lowest body satisfaction levels seem to experience the greatest benefits from exercise (Martin and Lichtenberger, 2002). Nevertheless, exercise seems to stimulate increased body image in various types of people, including males and females, and individuals across the lifespan.

Body image, however, may prevent individuals from exercising. Some people may be ashamed about their bodies and avoid exercise because they do not want to reveal themselves to others. As well as discouraging some people to exercise, body dissatisfaction may lead others to exercise excessively (Cafri et al., 2008). The observation that poor body image is associated with both the avoidance of and excessive exercise highlights the complexity of the relationship. Exercise specialists may have limited success in predicting who will and will not adhere to a training programme if they consider only body image attitudes. Instead, practitioners need to consider other aspects about each client, such as their motives and personalities.

It is not certain why exercise might enhance body image. Often people believe that physiological changes from exercise underlie body image improvements. There are mixed research results, however, and it is not clear that changes in physical conditioning account for improved body image (Martin and Lichtenberger, 2002). Instead, the influence that exercise has on body image may be mediated by enhanced subjective beliefs in physical fitness and appearance. Sonstroem's (1997) Exercise and Self-esteem Model proposes that exercise enhances physical self-efficacy, which in turn leads to improvements in various aspects of perceived physical competence, including perceived body attractiveness or body image. Across the various dimensions, enhanced perceived physical competence is associated with improved physical self-worth and, finally, self-esteem. On the basis of the Exercise and Self-esteem Model, individuals' enhanced body image results from improved physical self-efficacy. Although positive physiological changes may be associated with increased self-efficacy, they are not necessary for improvements to occur (Martin and Lichtenberger, 2002). People can experience increased self-efficacy in the absence of physiological changes; for example feedback from other people might enhance self-efficacy. Similarly, actual physiological improvement may not be associated with enhanced physical self-efficacy if individuals are not aware of them or if improvements are not satisfactory.

Summary

Body image refers to our mental pictures of our physical self, and consists of perceptual, cognitive, affective, behavioural and global dimensions. Although people's body image is influenced by their interpersonal experiences, physical attributes and psychological characteristics, most researchers highlight the ways that cultural socialization shapes individuals' perceptions of their looks and physiques. Although regular exercise may enhance body image, individuals' perceptions of their appearance may sometimes prevent them from starting a training programme or alternatively result in an overcommitment to physical activity.

◉ Eating disorders

Sport and exercise psychologists are interested in eating disorders because of the negative personal or social consequences that may result. Also, many people believe sport participation may lead to increased pressures on athletes to adopt unhealthy behaviours and attitudes that may result in an eating disorder. Table 13.2 presents an overview of the three main eating disorders: **anorexia nervosa**, **bulimia nervosa** and **binge eating disorders**. Most attention in sport has focused on anorexia and bulimia.

Estimated lifetime prevalence	Description	Main diagnostic features
Anorexia nervosa		
0.5%	Self-starvation and refusal to maintain minimal normal body weight	Refusal to maintain body weight, that is, at least 15% below normal for age and height Fear of gaining weight or becoming fat Disturbance in perceived weight, size or shape For females, the absence of three or more menstrual cycles
Bulimia nervosa		
1–3%	Recurrent episodes of binge eating followed by periods of purging or fasting	Recurrent episodes of binge eating or rapid consumption of large amounts of food Recurrent inappropriate attempts to prevent weight gain (e.g. vomiting, laxatives, exercise or fasting) Binge eating and compensatory behaviours occur two or more times a week for three months Self-evaluation disproportionately influenced by body weight and shape
Binge eating disorder		
1–3%	Recurrent episodes of binge eating without purging or fasting	Recurrent episodes of binge eating (two or more days a week for six months) Presence of marked distress regarding binge eating Binge eating is not associated with compensatory behaviour (fasting, laxatives, purging and so on)

Table 13.2 Overview of the major eating disorders
Sources: APA, 2000; Davey, 2008

Prevalence of eating disorders in sport

Among existing research, estimated eating disorder prevalence rates vary greatly. It is difficult to determine eating disorder prevalence in sport accurately. For example, prevalence rates from research may underestimate actual occurrence (Hausenblas and Carron, 1999), because people with these conditions may experience shame, guilt, anxiety or depression and may avoid participating in surveys. Athletes with eating disorders may hide their condition if they believe it might influence their selection or relationships with their coaches. In addition, some researchers doubt the adequacy of questionnaires and other techniques used to measure levels of eating disorders (Hausenblas and Carron, 1999).

Some conclusions can, however, be made:

1   Females report higher levels of eating disorder symptoms compared with males (Hausenblas and Carron, 1999). Eating disorders have traditionally been viewed as a female concern. Underreporting probably exists among males because they do not wish to be labelled as experiencing a 'female' issue.

2   Some athletes may be at greater risk of developing an eating disorder compared with non-athletes. In their meta-analysis, Hausenblas and Carron (1999) found that both male and female athletes reported greater levels of eating disorder symptoms than non-athletes, although the differences were small. There was some evidence that athletes in aesthetic or weight-dependent sports might be more likely to report symptoms than individuals in endurance or ball sports. In aesthetic sports, athletes' performances are scored by judges. Many individuals believe that performance in these sports is influenced by appearance, and athletes may experience greater pressures to attain an attractive body.

3   Athletes may have higher rates of disordered eating behaviours. Whereas eating disorders are a mental illness (see Chapter 11), disordered eating represents a mental health problem. People with disordered eating display eating disorder symptoms and may experience negative consequences, but not at a level sufficient to warrant a mental illness diagnosis.

Predisposing factors

Eating disorders are not caused by any single factor, but instead probably result from the interaction of various factors. There is not yet a complete understanding of how the factors interact (Davey, 2008). Also, the risk factors are similar for both anorexia and bulimia and it is unclear why individuals might develop one but not the other condition. There are numerous known risk factors and they may be grouped under various categories, including:

- *Biological factors:* These include genetic, hormonal and brain structure and functional abnormalities.

- *Sociocultural influences:* It seems likely that repeated exposure to media portrayals of ideal body shapes, along with negative interactions with peers (e.g. being teased) and family members (e.g. conflict) may lead to dissatisfaction with one's body, a central feature of eating disorders.
- *Adverse life experiences:* Childhood sexual abuse is one particular adverse life experience that has been implicated in eating disorder development.
- *Dispositional characteristics:* Various dispositional characteristics have been related to eating disorders; examples include perfectionism, low self-esteem and negative or depressed affect.

The reasons why athletes experience eating disorders may be different compared with the general population (Andersen and Fawkner, 2005):

1 Although poor body image may motivate individuals to exercise and play sport, there may be no changes in some anatomical features and the source of dissatisfaction may not be alleviated.
2 Some sports and types of exercise may not produce desired body changes.
3 Participation in sport and exercise may raise people's expectation beyond what is realistically possible.
4 Comparing one's self against others may result in negative evaluations and the chance for dissatisfaction may increase in sports where comparisons are part of the scoring procedures, such as diving or gymnastics.
5 Athletes may be rewarded for excessive preoccupation with their weight and appearance by coaches and others who dwell on appearance.

Andersen and Fawkner (2005) also proposed that athletes' characteristics and social factors may also play a role. They suggested, for example, that athletes with strong athletic identities may be vulnerable to eating disorders, especially if they participate in activities where thinness is desirable. Athletes are likely to experience the same risk factors as the general population. Andersen and Fawkner's (2005) review of sport-related factors helps to identify additional risk factors and these may help explain Hausenblas and Carron's (1999) finding that athletes report more eating disorder symptoms than non-athletes.

Treatments

Eating disorders are difficult to treat for a number of reasons (Davey, 2008):

1 Individuals often deny they have a problem and may see their abnormal eating and behaviour patterns as a positive way of controlling their weight and lives. Athletes, for example, might believe that they are doing what they need to do for their sport.
2 In severe cases, individuals typically need to be hospitalized because they have associated medical problems or to prevent death by starvation.
3 Many people with eating disorders also have other psychological issues, such as depression, and these other conditions also need treatment.

In the UK, the National Institute for Clinical Excellence (NICE, 2004) developed guidelines for the treatment of eating disorders. Treatment strategies included physical management, psychotherapy and medication. According to the NICE guidelines:

- *Physical management* involves monitoring and improving individuals' physical condition, such as helping people gain weight in anorexia, or mineral, vitamin, or electrolyte supplementation.
- Various types of *psychological interventions* could be employed to help patients reduce their symptoms, deal with their risk factors, and establish a healthy control over their lifestyles and diets. One such psychological intervention is family therapy, in which family members work together to reduce symptoms that may result from relationship dynamics present in the family unit.
- *Medication* is an option, such as antidepressants for bulimia; however, drugs should not be a sole or primary treatment for anorexia. Patients may experience negative side effects with drug therapy, and there is a higher dropout rate compared with psychological treatments.

The coordinated efforts of a team of specialists, including doctors, psychologists, nurses and nutritionists, is probably the best approach to treating eating disorders (Tod and Andersen, 2010). It may be also helpful if family members and close friends are aware and offer support. One way family members and friends can help individuals is by knowing the symptoms and signs associated with eating disorders. Table 13.3

provides a list of some signs that may help family and friends identify if a problem exists or is getting worse.

Physical	Psychological	Behavioural
Abdominal pain	Anxiety	Avoidance of eating
Menstrual irregularity	Body image disturbance	situations
Constipation	Depression	Secret eating
Dental decay	Adherence to society's	Excessive body checking
Hypothermia	attractiveness	Excessive weighing
Muscle atrophy/	standards	Excessive exercise
weakness	Lack of assertiveness	Sleep disturbances
Cramps	External locus of control	Substance abuse
Scarring on back on	Perfectionism	
hand	Poor self-esteem	
Weight loss/fluctuations	Social withdrawal	
	Rigidity	
	Restlessness	
	Obsessive-compulsive	
	symptoms	

Table 13.3 Some signs of eating disorders
Source: Petrie and Greenleaf, 2007

Summary

Sport and exercise psychologists are interested in eating disorders because of their consequences and the belief that some sports may expose athletes to increased risk of the condition. There is evidence that some athletes, particularly in aesthetic and weight-dependent sports, may report higher levels of eating disorder symptoms compared to the general population. In the UK, NICE (2004) recommends three possible treatment approaches including physical management, psychological interventions and medication.

◉ Performance-enhancing drugs

Given the rewards associated with elite-level sport, it is understandable that individuals may be prepared to exploit illegal avenues to help them succeed. In at least two surveys, more than 50% of athletes said they were prepared to take a drug that would guarantee sporting success, but result in their deaths within five years (Goldman et al., 1984). Although some athletes consume recreational drugs (e.g. alcohol and marijuana), we will focus on performance drugs and consider the major types, prevalence, motives for use, and ways to control use.

Major categories of banned performance-enhancing drugs

The International Olympic Committee labels the use of banned substances as doping. **Doping** refers to the use of:

- substances alien to the body or physiological substances in abnormal amounts
- abnormal methods designed to give individuals artificial or unfair enhanced competitive performances (Anshel, 2010; World Anti-Doping Agency, 2009).

Table 13.4 presents the major categories of banned drugs according to the reasons they are consumed and some possible detrimental effects. The major categories include muscle development, stimulants, blood doping, pain reduction, diuretics and other masking agents, and beta-blockers. The technique of blood doping is also banned.

Category	Purpose of use	Examples of possible side effects
Anabolic agents (including steroids and other anabolic agents)	Increase muscle size and strength, increase confidence and aggression, improve training intensity and reduce recovery time	Increased aggression, dysfunctional reproductive system, risk of cardiovascular events, changes to cholesterol levels, liver disease, changes to heart function and structure, hair loss, acne, appearance of male sex characteristics in females
Stimulants	Increase alertness and wakefulness, reduce fatigue, increase arousal and aggression	Increased anxiety, heart rate, blood pressure, sleeplessness, dehydration and heart irregularities, stroke, death
Blood doping methods	Increase endurance and stamina	Increased blood density and blood pressure, allergic reactions and infections, cardiovascular events, stroke, death
Diuretics and other masking agents	Temporary weight loss, increase muscular appearance, mask the presence of other drugs	Fatigue, drowsiness, muscle cramps, soreness, sensations of numbness, tingling and prickling, cardiac events, death

Category	Purpose of use	Examples of possible side effects
Analgesics	Reduce pain and inflammation, increase training intensity	Psychological and physical dependence, constipation, inability to concentrate, drowsiness, fear, anxiety, diabetes, bone metabolism disturbance, itchiness, suppression of hunger
Beta-blockers	Steady nerves	Lowered heart rate and blood pressure, heart failure, depression, sleeplessness, nausea, vomiting, cramps diarrhoea, weakness, sensations of numbness and tingling, light-headedness

Table 13.4 Major categories of performance-enhancing drugs according to their purpose
Sources: Based on Anshel, 2010; Bahrke, 2007; Weinberg and Gould, 2007; World Anti-Doping Agency, 2008

As well as competitive athletes, many non-athletes consume performance-enhancing drugs. Most people, for example, use steroids for cosmetic rather than performance reasons (Cohen et al., 2007). There are also other reasons why individuals use steroids, such as to enhance their performance in security jobs. The use of performance-enhancing drugs is not limited to the sports world and is an issue with which governments and the general population at large of a number of countries need to grapple.

Typically, drugs are banned for ethical, medical and legal reasons (Anshel, 2010). Ethical rationales form the core reasons for banning drugs in competitive sport. The use of performance-enhancing drugs is cheating, because it violates the rules and is counter to the values that many people believe should underpin sport. Many individuals, for example, believe competitive sport should involve equality and the comparison of athletes' 'natural' abilities untainted by artificial means. Another value is the belief that competitive sport should encourage and reward personal excellence and the striving to reach one's potential. Value-based justifications, however, are open to subjective interpretation and standards may differ from individual to individual, from place to place, or over time. For example, in the mid-19th century, many people considered physical training to be a violation of fair-play standards because such actions gave athletes an 'unnatural' advantage.

Legal justifications for banning performance-enhancing drugs reflect the laws that prohibit the use, possession and distribution of selected substances (Anshel, 2010). Different countries, however, may have different laws surrounding performance-enhancing drugs. In the US, for example, the sale and possession of steroids for non-medical use is a criminal offence. It is also illegal to purchase known counterfeits or ones not approved by the Food and Drug Administration (McArdle et al., 2001). In the UK, it is legal to possess or import steroids for personal use, but it is illegal to distribute them without a licence, or to import them for supply to others (Smith et al., 2009). In countries where specific substances are not illegal, national sporting organizations may need other justifications for introducing bans.

Drugs may be banned for medical reasons, because their use is associated with detrimental health and wellbeing for either athletes or others. For example, steroids are associated with increased aggression (e.g. road rage) and domestic violence (Choi and Pope, 1994), and one reason to ban their use is to protect the health of athletes' significant others and those people with whom they come into contact. As can be seen in Table 13.4, there are many adverse effects associated with performance-enhancing drugs, including cardiac arrest, liver dysfunction, cancer, cardiovascular disease, sterility, hypertension and premature death. Some psychological effects include dependence, anxiety, aggression, depression and attempted suicide. Individuals have argued that sporting organizations are overstepping their bounds by telling athletes what health risks they are allowed to take in their quest for competitive success. It is difficult, however, to counter arguments that drug use is acceptable when consumption is associated with the reduced health and wellbeing of those people not taking them, such as partners who are physically abused by steroid users. Not all drugs, however, are associated with such consequences.

How many athletes use drugs?

It is unlikely that the exact extent of drug use is known. Given the status of many drugs, underreporting probably occurs when researchers assess prevalence (Anshel, 2010). Most attempts have focused on athletes' and students' steroid use (Cohen et al., 2007). Estimates of high school and college students' steroid use range from 3–12% (Smith, et al., 2009). Although low, these percentages represent a large number of individuals who may be placing their current and future health at risk. The focus on athletes and students, however, may divert attention away from the typical steroid user. Recent surveys indicate that typical users are males, in their twenties and thirties, who do not play competitive sport, and who are well-educated, employed and, typically, single (Cohen et al., 2007).

Although the true prevalence of steroid (and other drug) use may be unclear, available data do provide some insights:

1 Drug use has spread from the elite sporting domain and has entered mainstream society.
2 The proportion of individuals using drugs varies with the context. For example, across the surveys, the highest steroid prevalence rates are associated with elite strength athletes, such as weightlifters and bodybuilders (Wagman et al., 1995).

Strategies for controlling drug use

The efficacy of attempts to prevent or control drug use is influenced by athletes' perceptions regarding issues such as health risks and their need to consume banned substances for sporting success. The social context is also an influence, such as the opinions and drug habits of other athletes (Anshel, 2010). Table 13.5 presents strategies that may help to prevent drug use. It is likely, however, that one technique is insufficient, and interventions involving several strategies may be most effective. In addition, most people, working alone, will struggle to reduce drug use. Instead, approaches that involve administrators, coaches, parents, teammates, sport psychologists and sport medicine specialists working together may have more influence.

▪ Develop a drug policy and communicate it to athletes
▪ Implement a random drug-testing intervention
▪ Educate athletes about the consequences of drug use
▪ Discuss the ethical, legal and medical reasons for banning drugs with athletes
▪ De-emphasize social comparison and winning
▪ Develop a culture of intolerance towards cheating
▪ Provide counselling for individuals considering drug use
▪ Learn the signs of drug use
▪ Help athletes improve their sporting abilities and teach them stress coping skills
▪ Develop athletes' self-confidence in their own abilities to succeed

Table 13.5 Strategies for reducing performance-enhancing drug use
Sources: Based on Anshel, 2010; Weinberg and Gould, 2007

Drug testing is a central strategy in any intervention and has been shown to reduce the likelihood of illegal substance use. There are four components to effective drug-testing interventions (Anshel, 2010):

1 *The athletes likely to be tested need to be made aware of the details associated with the intervention,* such as which drugs are banned and the consequences of being caught. Athletes can only be made accountable for their actions if they are aware of the intervention. It is sensible, however, to avoid announcing when testing may occur. Random testing is more likely to reduce drug use.

2 *The intervention needs to be implemented vigorously,* otherwise it may lack credibility. For example, the consequences of positive tests should apply regardless of athletes' ability levels.

3 *The intervention should be run by an independent organization,* to avoid conflicts of interests.

4 *The consequences need to be applied consistently to those who return positive tests so that athletes learn that illegal drug use is not tolerated.* In recent years, some athletes caught taking banned substances have escaped sanctions because of technical irregularities in testing procedures, highlighting the need for interventions to be implemented in transparent, legal and consistent ways. Given the rewards associated with elite sporting achievement, it is unsurprising that athletes caught cheating will defend or deny their behaviour vigorously to avoid guilty verdicts.

Summary

Doping involves the use of banned substances designed to give athletes artificial or unfair advantages over opponents. The major categories of banned substances include muscle development drugs, stimulants, blood doping, pain reduction, diuretics and other masking agents, and beta-blockers. Each category of drug is associated with detrimental health and wellbeing consequences. Performance-enhancing drugs are typically banned for ethical, legal and medical reasons. Given the sensitivity surrounding performance-enhancing drug use, it is understandable that underreporting occurs and the extent of use is unknown. Although a variety of interventions have been proposed, effective approaches to reducing drug use probably include the coordinated use of several strategies and the involvement of several individuals such as parents, coaches, teammates and sport scientists.

◉ Conclusions

Many people have benefited greatly from participating in sport and exercise. The issues discussed in this chapter, however, highlight that sometimes participation can be linked with unhealthy behaviours and detrimental consequences; for example, when athletes feel compelled to disregard their health and overtrain or take performance-enhancing drugs in their quest for sporting success. As another example, some athletes might feel pressured to achieve a body shape that is unhealthy or not realistic and become unhappy about the way they look. Such unhappiness may result in eating disorders, drug use or excessive exercise and overtraining. The possibility that some people may have negative sporting experiences serves as a reminder that sport and exercise psychology is an applied discipline. Helping individuals to avoid negative consequences and attain positive experiences, satisfaction and happiness from their sport and exercise involvement are objectives to which many sport and exercise psychologists subscribe. The more professionals are able to help athletes and exercise participants, the more they contribute to the growing acceptance of the discipline and perception that it has a meaningful contribution to make to sport, exercise and society in general.

◉ Further reading

Anshel, M.H. (2010). Drug abuse in sport: Causes and cures. In J.M. Williams (ed.) *Applied sport psychology: Personal growth to peak performance* (6th edn, pp. 463–91). Boston: McGraw-Hill.

Cash, T.F. and Pruzinsky, T. (2002). *Body image: A handbook of theory, research and clinical practice*. New York: Guilford.

Richardson, S.O., Andersen, M.B. and Morris, T. (2008). *Overtraining athletes: Personal journeys in sport*. Champaign, IL: Human Kinetics.

◉ Key search terms

Drugs, steroids, body image, burnout, overtraining, eating disorders, anorexia, bulimia

Glossary

achievement motivation A person's desire to strive for success, overcome failure and obstacles and experience pride in goal attainment.

aggression Any behaviour, verbal or non-verbal, designed to harm another living thing.

agreeableness One of the Five Factor Model dimensions, referring to the degree a person is cooperative and compassionate towards others.

amotivation The lack of any motivation towards an activity.

anger violence Refers to aggressive acts that occur when athletes react to actions they deem to be unfair.

anorexia nervosa An eating disorder that involves self-starvation and refusal to maintain minimal normal body weight.

anxiety Perception of a threat, accompanied by worry, nervousness and apprehension.

arousal Level of mental, physical and behavioural activity or excitation in the body ranging from low to high.

audience The presence of others who are attending to, and evaluating, task performance.

audience effects The influence that the presence of an audience has on individuals' psychological states, behaviour and performances.

binge eating disorder An eating disorder that involves recurrent episodes of binge eating without purging or fasting.

body image Refers to the picture we have in our mind regarding our physical self. Consists of perceptual, cognitive, emotional, behavioural and overall dimensions.

bulimia nervosa An eating disorder that involves recurrent episodes of binge eating followed by periods of purging and fasting.

burnout A withdrawal from sport, physically or mentally, characterized by a reduced sense of accomplishment, devaluation of the activity and exhaustion.

choleric One of Eysenck's personality types involving a mixture of neurotic and extraversion personality traits.

cognitive anxiety The mental aspects of anxiety: the worries, doubts and concerns we have about our performance.

cognitive strategies The psychological skills and strategies athletes use when competing.

cohesion The degree to which a group sticks together in pursuit of its goals and achieves member satisfaction.

confidence Individuals' beliefs that they have the resources to achieve success.

conscientiousness One of the Five Factor Model dimensions, referring to the degree a person is organized, diligent and scrupulous.

consideration behaviour Leadership behaviour focused on establishing positive relationships between the leader and the team.

depression A mental health illness; possible symptoms include sadness, loss of interest or pleasure, feelings of guilt or low self-worth, disturbed sleep or appetite, low energy and poor concentration.

doping The use of substances alien to the body or physiological substances in abnormal amounts, and/or abnormal methods designed to give individuals artificial or unfair competitive advantages.

ego From Freud's theory, the aspect of our personality that attempts to control the impulses of the id.

ego orientation An orientation in which success is measured through social comparison.

electroconvulsive therapy A treatment for severe depression that involves passing an electric current through a person's head for about half a second.

emotion-focused coping Attempts to modify or regulate stress-related emotions.

endorphins A range of hormones that block pain, improve mood and enhance sense of wellbeing.

experiments A type of study in which researchers manipulate one factor (independent variable) to examine its influence on another factor (dependent variable).

external imagery Refers to when athletes imagine themselves performing as if they were watching themselves on a television.

extraversion A personality characteristic in which individuals like to be centre of attention, prefer to be in social situations, focus less on themselves, and more on external events and stimuli.

extrinsic motivation The desire to participate in an activity for a tangible or intangible reward not inherent to the task.

group Two or more individuals who interact, typically with a common goal.

groupthink A type of interaction displayed by group members when trying to minimize conflict and reach a consensus without testing and evaluating ideas.

home advantage Refers to the tendency for athletes and teams to obtain better results when playing at home rather than away.

hostile aggression Aggressive behaviour in which the primary goal is to cause harm.

hypothesis A researcher's expected outcome of a study.

id From Freud's theory, the aspect of our personality that attempts to satisfy our drives.

imagery A mental process involving multisensory experiences in the absence of actual perception.

impression management Individuals' attempts to monitor and control the images they convey to others.

initiating behaviour Leadership behaviour focused on establishing clear boundaries between the leader and the followers.

instrumental aggression Aggressive behaviour in which the primary goal is to achieve an aim other than causing harm (e.g. winning a game).

internal imagery Refers to when athletes imagine themselves performing as if they were looking through their own eyes.

inter-rater reliability The degree to which different people score the same observation similarly.

intra-rater reliability The degree to which a person scores the same behaviour similarly over time.

intrinsic motivation The desire to participate in an activity for the pleasure of taking part.

introversion A personality characteristic in which individuals are less outgoing, focus more on their own thoughts and feelings, and prefer small social groups.

leader Someone who influences a team or player towards goal achievement.

mastery experience A self-efficacy source that derives from having previously attempted the task.

melancholic One of Eysenck's personality types involving a mixture of neurotic and introversion personality traits.

mental health Refers to successful mental functioning, leading to productive activities, fulfilling relationships, and the ability to cope with adversity.

mental health problem Changes in thinking, mood and/or behaviour, and distress and/or unsuccessful functioning insufficient to warrant the diagnosis of a mental health illness.

mental illness A diagnosable mental disorder characterized by changes in thinking, mood and/or behaviour, and distress and/or unsuccessful functioning.

meta-analysis A study in which investigators use statistical procedures to combine the results from existing research to determine the relationship between two variables.

modelling Social Learning Theory suggests that people learn suitable and unsuitable behaviour directly through reward and punishment, and indirectly through modelling, that is, watching how other people act and then imitating them.

monoamines A group of neurotransmitters related to depression and anxiety, such as dopamine, adrenaline (epinephrine in the US), noradrenaline (norepinephrine in the US) and serotonin.

mood states Right-now feelings that change from moment to moment.

motivation The force that impels us to achieve a goal.

motivational climate Refers to the goals and values emphasized by significant others in the social environment.

negative body image The negative evaluations we have of our bodies along one or more of the body image dimensions (perceptual, cognitive, emotional, behavioural or overall).

neuroticism A personality characteristic associated with being moody, anxious, rigid, touchy, restless, aggressive, and a tendency to experience psychological distress.

openness to experience One of the Five Factor Model dimensions, referring to an appreciation for the arts, emotions, adventures, unusual ideas, imagination, curiosity and various experiences.

overtraining A syndrome resulting from excessive overload (usually physical) on athletes without sufficient rest.

paratelic (playful) state A state in which athletes are motivated to be spontaneous and to engage with and enjoy what they are doing. They also do not concern themselves with future consequences of their behaviour.

personality The blend of characteristics (thoughts, feelings and behaviours) that make individuals unique.

phlegmatic One of Eysenck's personality types involving a mixture of introversion and stable personality traits.

play violence Refers to when athletes enjoy dominating opponents, but do not wish to cause real harm.

power violence An aggressive behaviour designed to help athletes dominate opponents.

pre-performance routine An established and practised set of thought processes and behaviours athletes carry out before performing self-paced tasks.

problem-focused coping Involves attempts to manage or change the problems that are causing stress.

psychological core The most internal and stable aspect of personality and includes attitudes, beliefs, motives, needs and values.

psychoticism From Eysenck's personality theory, a characteristic associated with being egocentric, aggressive, impersonal, cold, lacking empathy, impulsive and lacking a concern for others.

relaxation matching hypothesis The suggestion that mental strategies are more suitable for managing cognitive anxiety, whereas physical strategies are better for somatic anxiety management.

reliability The degree to which a measure is consistent over time, across items (in a questionnaire) or across people.

role-related behaviour Refers to the ways people act based on their perceptions of their social environments.

sanguine One of Eysenck's personality types involving a mixture of stable and extraversion personality traits.

science A way of learning about the world through controlled observation and experience.

scientific method A four-step process underpinning science; consists of developing a question, stating a hypothesis, collecting data, and analysing results.

self-efficacy Athletes' beliefs they can execute the behaviours needed to produce desired outcomes.

self-esteem The value people place on themselves.

self-presentation concerns The worries individuals experience about the ways they appear to others.

self-talk Statements individuals say to themselves, either out loud or in their minds.

social cohesion Refers to the degree that individuals like being part of a group and enjoy each other's company.

social facilitation Refers to the tendency for an audience to elicit the dominant response from individuals performing a task. Performance typically increases for simple and well-learned tasks. Performance typically decreases for complex and novel tasks.

Social Learning Theory A theory that suggests people learn suitable and unsuitable behaviour through direct reward and punishment, and indirectly through modelling.

social loafing Occurs when individuals make less effort to achieve a goal when they work in groups than when alone.

social physique anxiety Anxiety associated with the thought that others are negatively evaluating one's appearance.

somatic anxiety Athletes' perceptions of their physiological arousal.

sport and exercise psychology The study of people's thoughts, feelings and behaviours in sport and exercise settings.

sport confidence Athletes' beliefs about their ability to be successful in sport.

stability From Eysenck's personality theory, a characteristic associated with being calm, even-tempered, reliable, lively, carefree and leader-like.

staleness A long-term drop in performance (at least two weeks) unexplained by injury or illness.

state anxiety Athletes' right-now, moment-to-moment perceptions of threat and accompanying worries, nervousness and apprehension.

states A right-now way of behaving, thinking or feeling that may change on a moment-to-moment basis.

superego From Freud's theory, the aspect of our personality that attempts to integrate the values we have learned from our parents and society.

task cohesion Refers to the degree that individuals work well together towards the achievement of, and accept, the group's goals.

task orientation An orientation in which success is measured by self-improvement.

telic (serious) state A state in which athletes are motivated to achieve a meaningful goal, to look ahead to the future, and to contribute towards longer term goals.

theory A set of related facts that explains a topic of interest.

thrill violence Refers to when athletes act aggressively for the enjoyment of hurting others.

trait anxiety Individuals' predispositions to perceive events or situations as threatening and respond with high levels of anxiety.

traits Relatively consistent and enduring aspects of personality and behaviour.

typical responses Refers to the ways people usually act in response to people, events and situations.

validity The degree to which questionnaires (or other data collection methods) measure what they aim to measure.

verbal persuasion A self-efficacy source that involves athletes being told they can perform a task.

vicarious experience A self-efficacy source involving athletes watching models perform a task.

References

Agnew, G.A. and Carron, A.V. (1994). Crowd effects and the home advantage. *International Journal of Sport Psychology*, 25, 53–62.

Allport, F.H. (1924). *Social psychology*. Boston: Houghton Miffin.

Aman, J., Skinner, T.C., de Beaufort, C.E. et al. (2009). Associations between physical activity, sedentary behavior, and glycemic control in a large cohort of adolescents with type 1 diabetes: The Hvidoere Study Group on Childhood Diabetes. *Pediatric Diabetes*, 10, 234–9.

Andersen, C., Adamsen, L., Moeller, T. et al. (2006). The effect of a multidimensional exercise programme on symptoms and side-effects in cancer patients undergoing chemotherapy: The use of semi-structured diaries. *European Journal of Oncology Nursing*, 10, 247–62.

Andersen, M.B. and Fawkner, H.J. (2005). The skin game: Extra points for looking good. In M.B. Andersen (ed.) *Sport psychology in practice* (pp. 77–92). Champaign, IL: Human Kinetics.

Anderson, A.G., Knowles, Z. and Gilbourne, D. (2004). Reflective practice for sport psychologists: Concepts, models, practical implications, and thoughts on dissemination. *The Sport Psychologist*, 18, 188–203.

Anderson, A.G., Miles, A., Mahoney, C. and Robinson, P. (2002). Evaluating the effectiveness of applied sport psychology practice: Making the case for a case study approach. *The Sport Psychologist*, 16, 432–53.

Anderson, M.L., Foster, C., McGuigan, M.R. et al. (2004). Training vs. body image: Does training improve subjective appearance ratings? *Journal of Strength and Conditioning Research*, 18, 255–9.

Anshel, M.H. (2010). Drug abuse in sport: Causes and cures. In J.M. Williams (ed.) *Applied sport psychology: Personal growth to peak performance* (6th edn, pp. 463–91). Boston: McGraw-Hill.

APA (American Psychiatric Association) (2000). *Diagnostic and statistical manual of mental disorders: Text revision* (4th edn). Washington DC: APA.

Apter, M.J. (ed.) (2001a). *Motivational styles in everyday life: A guide to reversal theory.* Washington DC: American Psychological Association.

Apter, M.J. (2001b). An introduction to reversal theory. In M.J. Apter (ed.) *Motivational styles in everyday life: A guide to reversal theory* (pp. 3–36). Washington DC: American Psychological Association.

Arent, S.M. and Landers, D.M. (2003). Arousal, anxiety, and performance: A reexamination of the inverted-u hypothesis. *Research Quarterly for Exercise and Sport*, 74, 436–44.

Atkinson, J.W. (1974). The mainstream of achievement-orientated activity. In J.W. Atkinson and J.O. Raynor (eds) *Motivation and achievement* (pp. 13–41). New York: Halstead.

Attendances: Champions League 2008–2009 (n.d.). Retrieved 5 November 2009 from European Football Statistics website, http://www.european-football-statistics.co.uk/attn/2009/totchl.htm.

Bahrke, M.S. (2007). Muscle enhancement substances and strategies. In J.K. Thompson and G. Cafri (eds) *The muscular ideal: Psychological, social, and medical perspectives* (pp. 141–59). Washington DC: American Psychological Association.

Balmer, N.J., Nevill, A.M. and Williams, A.M. (2001). Home advantage in the Winter Olympics (1908–1998). *Journal of Sports Sciences*, 19, 129–39.

Balmer, N.J., Nevill, A.M. and Williams, A.M. (2003). Modelling home advantage in the Summer Olympic Games. *Journal of Sports Sciences*, 21, 469–78.

Bandura, A. (1977a). *Social learning theory.* Englewood Cliffs, NJ: Prentice Hall.

Bandura, A. (1977b). Self-efficacy: Toward a unifying theory of behavioral change. *Psychological Review*, 84, 191–215.

Bandura, A. (1986). *Social foundations of thought and action: A social cognitive theory.* Englewood Cliffs, NJ: Prentice Hall.

Bandura, A. (1997). *Self-efficacy: The exercise of control.* New York: Freeman.

Baron, R.A. and Richardson, D.R. (1994). *Human aggression*. New York: Plenum Press.

Battaglini, C.L., Hackney, A.C., Garcia, R. et al. (2009). The effects of an exercise program in leukemia patients. *Integrative Cancer Therapies*, 8, 130–8.

Baumeister, R.F. and Steinhilber, A. (1984). Paradoxical effects of supportive audiences on performance under pressure: The home field disadvantage in sports championships. *Journal of Personality and Social Psychology*, 47, 85–93.

Beedie, C.J., Terry, P.C. and Lane, A.M. (2000). The profile of mood states and athletic performance: Two meta-analyses. *Journal of Applied Sport Psychology*, 12, 49–68.

Behling, O. and Schriesheim, C. (1976). *Organisational behaviour: Theory, research and application*. Boston: Allyn & Bacon.

Bennett, W.L., Ouyang, P., Wu, A.W. et al. (2008). Fatness and fitness: How do they influence health-related quality of life in type 2 diabetes mellitus? *Health and Quality of Life Outcomes*, 6.

Berkowitz, L. (1969). *Roots of aggression*. New York: Atherton Press.

Biddle, S.J. and Mutrie, N. (2001). *Psychology of physical activity: Determinants, well-being and interventions*. London: Routledge.

Biddle, S.J. and Mutrie, N. (2008). *Psychology of physical activity: Determinants, well-being and interventions* (2nd edn). London: Routledge.

Blond, A. (2008). Impacts of exposure to images of ideal bodies on male body dissatisfaction: A review. *Body Image*, 5, 244–50.

Bond, C.F. and Titus, L.J. (1983). Social facilitation: A meta-analysis of 241 studies. *Psychological Bulletin*, 94, 265–92.

Brawley, L., Carron, A. and Widmeyer, W.N. (1988). Exploring the relationship between cohesion and group resistance to disruption. *Journal of Sport & Exercise Psychology*, 10, 199–213.

Bray, S.R. and Widmeyer, W.N. (2000). Athletes' perceptions of the home advantage: An investigation of perceived causal factors. *Journal of Sport Behavior*, 23, 1–10.

Bredemeier, B.J. (1994). Children's moral reasoning and their assertive, aggressive, and submissive tendencies in sport and daily-life. *Journal of Sport & Exercise Psychology*, 16, 1–14.

Bredemeier, B.J. and Shields, D. (1986a). Athletic aggression: An issue of contextual morality. *Sociology of Sport Journal*, 3, 15–28.

Bredemeier, B.J. and Shields, D. (1986b). Game reasoning and interactional morality. *Journal of Genetic Psychology*, 147, 257–75.

Butt, J., Weinberg, R. and Horn, T. (2003). The intensity and directional interpretation of anxiety: Fluctuations throughout competition and relationship to performance. *The Sport Psychologist*, 17, 35–54.

Buys, C.J. (1978). Humans would do better without groups. *Personality and Social Psychology Bulletin*, 4, 123–5.

Cafri, G., Olivardia, R. and Thompson, J.K. (2008). Symptom characteristics and psychiatric comorbidity among males with muscle dysmorphia. *Comprehensive Psychiatry*, 49, 374–9.

Cafri, G., van den Berg, P. and Thompson, J.K. (2006). Pursuit of muscularity in adolescent boys: Relations among biopsychosocial variables and clinical outcomes. *Journal of Clinical Child and Adolescent Psychology*, 35, 283–91.

Callow, N. and Hardy, L. (2005). A critical analysis of applied imagery research. In D. Hackfort, J.L. Duda and R. Lidor (eds) *Handbook of research in applied sport and exercise psychology: International perspectives* (pp. 37–58). Morgantown, WV: Fitness Information Technology.

Callow, N., Smith, M., Hardy, L. et al. (2010). Measurement of transformational leadership and its relationship with cohesion and performance level. *Journal of Applied Sport Psychology*, 21(4), 395–412.

Carducci, B.J. (2009). *The psychology of personality: Viewpoints, research, and applications* (2nd edn). Chichester: Wiley-Blackwell.

Carron, A.V. (1988). *Group dynamics in sport: Theoretical and practical issues.* London, Ontario: Spodym.

Carron, A.V., Brawley, L.R. and Widmeyer, W.N. (1997). The measurement of cohesiveness in sport groups. In J.L. Duda (ed.) *Advancements in sport and exercise psychology measurement.* Morgantown, WV: Fitness Information Technology.

Carron, A.V., Bray, S.R. and Eys, M.A. (2002). Team cohesion and team success in sport. *Journal of Sport Sciences*, 20, 119–26,

Carron, A.V., Hausenblas, H. and Eys, M.A. (2005). *Group dynamics in sport* (3rd edn). Champaign, IL: Human Kinetics.

Carron, A.V., Widmeyer, W.N. and Brawley, W.N. (1985). The development of an instrument to measure cohesion in sport teams: The Group Environment Questionnaire. *Journal of Sport Psychology*, 7, 244–66.

Cash, T.F. (2002). A 'negative body image': Evaluating epidemiological evidence. In T.F. Cash and T. Pruzinsky (eds) *Body image: A handbook of theory, research and clinical practice* (pp. 269–76). New York: Guilford.

Cash, T.F. (2008). *The body image workbook: An eight-step program for learning to like your looks* (2nd edn). Oakland, CA: New Harbinger.

Cash, T.F. and Fleming, E.C. (2002). Body image and social relations. In T.F. Cash and T. Pruzinsky (eds) *Body image: A handbook of theory, research and clinical practice* (pp. 277–86). New York: Guilford.

Cattell, R.B. and Cattell, H.E. (1995). Personality structure and the new fifth edition of the 16PF. *Educational and Psychological Measurement*, 55, 926–37.

Chantal, Y., Robin, P., Vernat, J.P. and Bernache-Assollant, I. (2005). Motivation, sportspersonship, and athletic aggression: A mediational analysis. *Psychology of Sport & Exercise*, 6, 233–49.

Chase, M.A. (2001). Children's self-efficacy, motivational intentions, and attributions in physical education and sport. *Research Quarterly for Exercise and Sport*, 72, 47–54.

Chatzisarantis, N., Hagger, M., Biddle, S. et al. (2005). On the stability of the attitude-intention relationship and the roles of autonomy and past behaviour in understanding change. *Journal of Sport Sciences*, 23, 49–61.

Chelladurai, P. (1978). A multidimentional model of leadership. Unpublished doctoral dissertation. University of Waterloo, Waterloo, Ontario.

Chelladurai, P. (1984). Discrepancy between preferences and perceptions of leadership behavior and satisfaction of athletes in varying sports. *Journal of Sport Psychology*, 6, 27–41.

Chelladurai, P. (1993). Leadership. In R.N. Singer, M. Murphy and L.K. Tennant (eds) *Handbook on research on sport psychology*. New York: Macmillan.

Choi, P.Y. and Pope, H.G. Jr (1994). Violence toward women and illicit androgenic-anabolic steroid use. *Annals of Clinical Psychiatry*, 6, 21–5.

Chow, G.M., Murray, K.E. and Feltz, D.L. (2009). Individual, team, and coach predictors of players' likelihood to aggress in youth soccer *Journal of Sport & Exercise Psychology*, 31, 425–43.

Clifton, R.T. and Gill, D.L. (1994). Gender differences in self-confidence on a feminine-typed task. *Journal of Sport & Exercise Psychology*, 16, 150–62.

Coatsworth, J.D. and Conroy, D.E. (2006). Enhancing the self-esteem of youth swimmers through coach training: Gender and age effects. *Psychology of Sport and Exercise*, 7, 173–92.

Cogan, K.D. and Petrie, T.A. (1995). Sport consultation: An evaluation of a season-long intervention with female collegiate gymnasts. *The Sport Psychologist*, 9, 282–6.

Cohen, A., Pargman, D. and Tenenbaum, G. (2003). Critical elaboration and empirical investigation of the cusp catastrophe model: A lesson for practitioners. *Journal of Applied Sport Psychology*, 15, 144–59.

Cohen, J., Collins, R., Darkes, J. and Gwartney, D. (2007). A league of their own: Demographics, motivations and patterns of use of 1,955 male adult non-medical anabolic steroid users in the United States. *Journal of the International Society of Sports Nutrition*, 4, accessed 9 September 2009, http://www.jissn.com/content/4/1/12.

Conn, V.S., Hafdahl, A.R., Moore, S.M. et al. (2009). Meta analysis of interventions to increase physical activity among cardiac subjects. *International Journal of Cardiology*, 133, 307–20.

Conroy, D.E., Silva, J.M., Newcomer, R.R. et al. (2001). Personal and participatory socializers of the perceived legitimacy of aggressive behavior in sport. *Aggressive Behavior*, 27, 405–18.

Costa, P.T. Jr and McCrae, R.R. (1992). Normal personality assessment in clinical practice: The NEO personality inventory. *Psychological Assessment*, 4, 5–13.

Cottrell, N.B., Wack, D.L., Sekerak, G.J. and Rittle, R.H. (1968). Social facilitation of dominant responses by the presence of an audience and the mere presence of others. *Journal of Personality and Social Psychology*, 9, 245–50.

Coulomb-Cabagno, G. and Rascle, O. (2006). Team sports players' observed Aggression as a function of gender, competitive level, and sport type. *Journal of Applied Social Psychology*, 36, 1980–2000.

Courneya, K.S. and Carron, A.V. (1992). The home advantage in sport competitions: A literature review. *Journal of Sport & Exercise Psychology*, 14, 28–39.

Cox, A.E. and Whaley, D.E. (2004). The influence of task value, expectancies for success, and identity on athletes' achievement behaviors. *Journal of Applied Sport Psychology*, 16, 103–17.

Cox, R.H. (2007). *Sport psychology: Concepts and applications* (6th edn). Boston: McGraw-Hill.

Craft, L.L., Magyar, T.M., Becker, B.J. and Feltz, D. L. (2003). The relationship between the Competitive State Anxiety Inventory-2 and sport performance: A meta-analysis. *Journal of Sport & Exercise Psychology*, 25, 44–65.

Cresswell, S.L. and Eklund, R.C. (2006). Athlete burnout: Conceptual confusion, current research and future research directions. In S. Hanton and S.D. Mellalieu (eds) *Literature reviews in sport psychology* (pp. 91–126). New York: Nova Science.

Crust, L. and Azadi, K. (2009). Leadership preferences of mentally tough athletes. *Personality and Individual Differences*, 47, 326–30.

Cury, F., Biddle, S., Sarrazin, P. and Famose, J.P. (1997). Achievement goals and perceived ability predict investment in learning a sport task. *British Journal of Educational Psychology*, 67, 293–309.

Daley, A. (2008). Exercise and depression: A review of reviews. *Journal of Clinical Psychology in Medical Settings*, 15, 140–7.

Daubenmier, J.J., Weidner, G., Marlin, R. et al. (2006). Lifestyle and health-related quality of life of men with prostate cancer managed with active surveillance. *Urology*, 67, 125–30.

Davey, G. (2008). *Psychopathology: Research, assessment and treatment in clinical psychology*. Chichester: BPS Blackwell.

Davidson, R.J. and Schwartz, G.E. (1976). The psychobiology of relaxation and related states: A multi process theory. In D.I. Mostofsky (ed.) *Behavior control and modification of physiological activity* (pp. 399–442). Englewood Cliffs, NJ: Prentice Hall.

Davis, C. (2002). Body image and athleticism. In T.F. Cash and T. Pruzinsky (eds) *Body image: A handbook of theory, research and clinical practice* (pp. 219–25). New York: Guilford.

Dawe, S.W. and Carron, A.V. (1990). Interrelationships among role acceptance, role clarity, task cohesion, and social cohesion. Paper presented at the Canadian Psychomotor Learning and Sport Psychology Association, Windsor, Canada.

Deci, E.L. and Ryan, R.M. (1985). *Intrinsic Motivation and Self-Determination in Human Behaviour*. New York: Plenum.

Deci, E.L. and Ryan, R.M. (1991). A motivational approach to self: Integration in personality. In R. Dienstbier (ed.) *Nebraska symposium on motivation:* vol 38, *Perspectives on motivation* (pp. 237–88). Lincoln, NE: University of Nebraska Press.

Deci, E.L. and Ryan, R.M. (2000). The 'what' and 'why' of goal pursuits: Human needs and the self-determination of behavior. *Psychological Inquiry*, 11(4), 227–68.

Deci, E.L. and Ryan, R.M. (2002). An overview of self-determination theory: An organismic-dialectical perspective. In E.L. Deci and R.M. Ryan (eds) *Handbook of Self-Determination Research*, (pp. 3–33). Rochester, NY: University of Rochester Press.

Deci, E.L., Koestner, R. and Ryan, R.M. (1999). A meta-analytic review of experiments examining the effects of extrinsic rewards on intrinsic motivation. *Psychological Bulletin*, 125, 627–700.

Deci, E.L., Vallerand, R.J., Pelletier, L.G. and Ryan, R.M. (1991). Motivation and education: The self-determination perspective. *Educational Psychologist*, 26, 325–46.

De Moor, M.H., Beem, A.L., Stubbe, J.H. et al. (2006). Regular exercise, anxiety, depression and personality: A population-based study. *Preventive Medicine*, 42, 273–9.

DH (Department of Health) (2004). *At least five a week: Evidence on the impact of physical activity and its relationship to health, A report from the Chief Medical Officer*. London: TSO.

Dishman, R.K., Wasburn, R.A. and Heath, G.W. (2004). *Physical activity epidemiology*. Champaign, IL: Human Kinetics.

Dollard, J., Doob, J., Miller, N. et al. (1939). *Frustration and aggression*. New Haven, CT: Yale University Press.

Dowie, J. (1982). Why Spain should win the World Cup. *New Scientist*, 94, 693–5.

Driskell, J.E., Copper, C. and Moran, A. (1994). Does mental practice enhance performance? *Journal of Applied Psychology*, 79, 481–92.

Duffy, L.J. and Hinwood, D.P. (1997). Home field advantage: Does anxiety contribute? *Perceptual and Motor Skills*, 84, 283–6.

Dunn, J.G. and Holt, N.L. (2004). A qualitative investigation of a personal-disclosure mutual-sharing team building activity. *The Sport Psychologist*, 18, 363–80.

Durand-Bush, N., Salmela, J.H. and Green-Demers, I. (2001). The Ottawa mental skills assessment tool (OMSAT-3*). *The Sport Psychologist*, 15, 1–19.

Edwards, T. and Hardy, L. (1996). The interactive effects of intensity and direction of cognitive and somatic anxiety and self-confidence upon performance. *Journal of Sport & Exercise Psychology*, 18, 296–312.

Edwards, T., Kingston, K., Hardy, L. and Gould, D. (2002). A qualitative analysis of catastrophic performances and the associated thoughts, feelings and emotions. *The Sport Psychologist*, 16, 1–19.

Ekkekakis, P., Hall, E.E. and Petruzzello, S.J. (2005). Variation and homogeneity in affective responses to physical activity of varying intensities: An alternative perspective on dose-response based on evolutionary considerations. *Journal of Sports Sciences*, 23, 477–500.

English Premier League Attendance: 2008/2009 (n.d.). Retrieved 5 November 2009 from ESPNsoccernet website, http://soccernet. espn.go.com/stats/attendance?league=eng.1&year=2008&cc=5739.

Escarti, A. and Guzman, J.F. (1999). Effects of feedback on self-efficacy, performance, and choice in an athletic task. *Journal of Applied Sport Psychology*, 11, 83–96.

Etnier, J.L., Salazar, W., Landers, D.M. et al. (1997). The influence of physical fitness and exercise upon cognitive functioning: A meta-analysis. *Journal of Sport & Exercise Psychology*, 19, 249–77.

Eysenck, H.J. (1988). Measurement of personality. In C.J. Kestenbaum and D.T. Williams (eds) *Handbook of clinical assessment of children and adolescents* (vol. 1, pp. 112–29). New York: New York University.

Farmer, M.E., Locke, B.Z., Mościcki, E.K. et al. (1988). Physical activity and depressive symptoms: The NHANES I epidemiologic follow-up study. *American Journal of Epidemiology*, 128, 1340–51.

Fazey, J.A. and Hardy, L. (1988). *The inverted-U hypothesis: A catastrophe for sport psychology*. British Association of Sports Sciences Monograph no. 1. Leeds: The National Coaching Foundation.

Festinger, L., Schachter, S. and Back, K.W. (1950). *Social pressures in informal groups: A study of human factors in housing*. New York: Harper.

Fiedler, F.E. (1967). *A theory of leadership effectiveness*. New York: McGraw-Hill.

Fisher, A.C. (1984). New directions in sport personality research. In J.M. Silva, III and R.S. Weinberg (eds) *Psychological foundations of sport* (pp. 70–80). Champaign, IL: Human Kinetics.

Fox, L.D., Rejeski, W.J. and Gauvin, L. (2000). Effects of leadership style and group dynamics on enjoyment of physical activity. *American Journal of Health Promotion*, 14, 277–83.

Frederick, C.M. and Ryan, R.M. (1995). Self-determination in sport: A review using cognitive evaluation theory. *International Journal of Sport Psychology*, 26, 5–23.

Freud, S. (1916/1973). Introductory lectures on psychoanalysis (J. Strachey, trans.). In J. Strachey and A. Richards (eds) *The Penguin Freud library* (vol. I, pp. 37–557). London: Penguin.

Gardner, D.E., Shields, D.L., Bredemeier, B.J. and Bostrom, A. (1996). The relationship between perceived coaching behaviors and team cohesion among baseball and softball players. *Sport Psychologist*, 10, 367–81.

Garner, D.M. (2002). Body image and anorexia nervosa. In T.F. Cash and T. Pruzinsky (eds) *Body image: A handbook of theory, research and clinical practice* (pp. 295–303). New York: Guilford.

Gee, C.J. and Leith, L.M. (2007). Aggressive behavior in professional ice hockey: cross-cultural comparison of North American and European born NHL players. *Psychology of Sport & Exercise*, 8, 567–83.

George, T.R. (1994). Self-confidence and baseball performance: A causal examination of self-efficacy theory. *Journal of Sport & Exercise Psychology*, 16, 381–99.

Gielen, A.C., McDonnell, K.A., Wu, A.W. et al. (2001). Quality of life among women living with HIV: The importance violence, social support, and self care behaviors. *Social Science and Medicine*, 52, 315–22.

Gill, D.L. (1986). *Psychological dynamics of sport*. Champaign, IL: Human Kinetics.

Gill, D.L. (2000). *Psychological dynamics of sport and exercise* (2nd edn). Champaign, IL: Human Kinetics.

Gill, D.L. and Deeter, T.E. (1988). Development of the Sport Orientation Questionnaire. *Research Quarterly for Exercise and Sport*, 59, 191–202.

Gill, D.L. and Williams, L. (2008). *Psychological dynamics of sport and exercise* (3rd edn). Champaign, IL: Human Kinetics.

Gillison, F.B., Skevington, S.M., Sato, A. et al. (2009). The effects of exercise interventions on quality of life in clinical and healthy populations; a meta-analysis. *Social Science and Medicine*, 68, 1700–10.

Goldman, B., Bush, P. and Klatz, R. (1984). *Death in the locker room: Steroids and sports*. South Bend, IN: Icarus Press.

Goodger, K., Lavallee, D., Gorely, T. and Harwood, C. (2010). Burnout in sport: Understanding the process – from early warning signs to individualized intervention. In J.M. Williams (ed.) *Applied sport psychology: Personal growth to peak performance* (6th edn, pp. 492–511). Boston: McGraw-Hill.

Goudas, M., Biddle, S., Fox, K. and Underwood, M. (1995). It ain't what you do, it's the way that you do it! Teaching style affects children's motivation in track and field lessons. *The Sport Psychologist*, 9, 254–64.

Gould, D., Dieffenbach, K. and Moffett, A. (2002). Psychological characteristics and their development in Olympic champions. *Journal of Applied Sport Psychology*, 14, 172–204.

Gould, D., Guinan, D., Greenleaf, C. et al. (1999). Factors affecting Olympic performance: Perceptions of athletes and coaches from more and less successful teams. *The Sport Psychologist*, 13, 371–94.

Graham, R., Kramer, J. and Wheeler, G. (2008). Physical illness and psychological well being among people with chronic illness and disability: A grounded approach. *Journal of Health Psychology*, 13, 447–58.

Grange, P. and Kerr, J.H. (2010). Physical aggression in Australian football: A qualitative study of elite athletes. *Psychology of Sport & Exercise*, 11, 36–43.

Green, C.D and Benjamin, L.T (2009). *Psychology gets in the game: Sport, mind, and behavior, 1880-1960*. Lincoln, NE: University of Nebraska Press.

Greer, D.L. (1983). Spectator booing and the home advantage: A study of social influence in the basketball arena. *Social Psychology Quarterly*, 46, 252–61.

Grieve, F.G., Whelan, J.P. and Meyers, A.W. (2000). An experimental examination of the cohesion-performance relationship in an interactive team sport. *Journal of Applied Sport Psychology*, 12, 219–35.

Gross, N. and Martin, W.E. (1952). On group cohesiveness. *American Journal of Sociology*, 57, 546–64.

Grove, J.R. and Eklund, R.C. (2004). Exercise and anxiety. In L.M. LeMura and S.P. von Duvillard (eds) *Clinical exercise physiology: Application and physiological principles* (pp. 605–15). Philadelphia, PA: Lippincott Williams & Wilkins.

Grove, J.R. and Heard, N.P. (1997). Optimism and sport confidence as correlates of slump-related coping among athletes. *The Sport Psychologist*, 11, 400–10.

Hagger, M.S. and Chatzisarantis, N. (2005). *The social psychology of exercise and sport*. Buckingham: Open University Press.

Hall, H.K. and Kerr, A.W. (1997). Motivational antecedents of precompetitive anxiety in youth sport. *The Sport Psychologist*, 11, 24–42.

Hanin, Y. (1989). Interpersonal and intragroup anxiety in sports. In D. Hackfort and C.D. Spielberger (eds) *Anxiety in sports: An international perspective* (pp. 19–28). Washington DC: Hemisphere.

Hanrahan, S.J., Cerin, E. and Hartel, C. (2003). Achievement goal orientations, attributional style, and motivational climate as predictors of performance and persistence. In Proceedings of the Association for the Advancement of Applied Sport Psychology Annual Conference.

Hanton, S., Jones, G. and Mullen, R. (2000). Intensity and direction of competitive state anxiety as interpreted by rugby players and rifle shooters. *Perceptual and Motor Skills*, 90, 513–21.

Hardy, J., Eys, M.A. and Carron, A.V. (2005). Exploring the potential disadvantages from high team cohesion. *Small Group Research*, 36, 166–76.

Hardy, J., Gammage, K. and Hall, C.R. (2001). A descriptive study of athletes' self-talk. *The Sport Psychologist*, 15, 306–18.

Hardy, L. (1993). A catastrophe model of performance in sport. In G. Jones and L. Hardy (eds) *Stress and performance in sport*. Hoboken, NJ: John Wiley and Sons.

Hardy, L. and Jones, G. (1994). Current issues and future directions for performance related research in sport psychology. *Journal of Sport Sciences*, 12, 61–92.

Hardy, L. and Parfitt, G. (1991). A catastrophe model of anxiety and performance. *British Journal of Psychology*, 82, 163–78.

Hardy, L., Jones, G. and Gould, D. (1996). *Understanding psychological preparation for sport: Theory and practice of elite performers.* Chichester: Wiley.

Hart, E.A., Leary, M.R. and Rejeski, W.J. (1989). The measurement of social physique anxiety. *Journal of Sport and Exercise Psychology*, 11, 94–104.

Hassmén, P., Koivula, N. and Uutela, A. (2000). Physical exercise and psychological well-being: A population study in Finland. *Preventive Medicine*, 30, 17–25.

Hausenblas, H.A. and Carron, A.V. (1999). Eating disorder indices and athletes: An integration. *Journal of Sport & Exercise Psychology*, 21, 230–58.

Hausenblas, H.A. and Fallon, E.A. (2006). Exercise and body image: A meta-analysis. *Psychology and Health*, 21, 33–47.

Hausenblas, H.A. and Symons Downs, D. (2001). Comparison of body image between athletes and nonathletes: A meta-analytic review. *Journal of Applied Sport Psychology*, 13, 323–39.

Hemery, D. (1986). *The pursuit of sporting excellence*. London: Willow.

Heuzé, J.P., Bosselut, G. and Thomas, J.P. (2007). Should the coaches of elite female handball teams focus on collective efficacy or group cohesion? *The Sport Psychologist*, 21, 383–99.

Heuzé, J.P., Sarrazin, P., Masiero, M. et al. (2006). The relationships of perceived motivational climate to cohesion and collective efficacy in elite female teams. *Journal of Applied Sport Psychology*, 18, 201–18.

Hewstone, M., Fincham, F.D. and Foster, J. (eds) (2005). *Psychology*. Oxford: Blackwell.

Highlen, P.S. and Bennett, B.B. (1983). Elite divers and wrestlers: A comparison between open- and closed-skill athletes. *Journal of Sport Psychology*, 5, 390–409.

Hill, K.L. (2001). *Frameworks for sport psychologists: Enhancing sport performance*. Champaign, IL: Human Kinetics.

Hogg, M.A. and Vaughan, G. (2005). *Social psychology*. London: Pearson Education.

Hoigaard, R., Safvenbom, R., Tonnessen, F.E. (2006). The relationship between group cohesion, group norms, and perceived social loafing in soccer teams. *Small Group Research*, 37(3), 217–32.

Hollander, E.P. (1971). *Principles and methods of social psychology* (2nd edn). New York: Oxford University Press.

Holmes, P.S. and Collins, D.J. (2001). The PETTLEP approach to motor imagery: A functional equivalence model for sport psychologists. *Journal of Applied Sport Psychology*, 13, 60–83.

Hudson, J. and Williams, M. (2001). Predicting competitive trait anxiety: The influence of competitive self-presentation concerns. *Social Behavior and Personality*, 29, 1–10.

Hudson, J., Board, E.M. and Lavallee, D. (2001). The role of cardiac rehabilitation in dealing with psychological loss among survivors of a cardiac event. *Journal of Loss & Trauma*, 6, 301–12.

Hull, C.L. (1943). *Principles of behavior*. New York: Appleton-Century-Crofts.

Janis, I. (1972). *Victims of groupthink*. Boston: Houghton-Mifflin.

Jeiger, A.J., Szmigielska, K.S., Bili´nska, M. et al. (2009). Health-related quality of life in patients with coronary heart disease after residential vs ambulatory cardiac rehabilitation. *Cardiac Rehabilitation*, 73, 476–83.

Jerome, G.J. and Williams, J.M. (2000). Intensity and interpretation of competitive state anxiety: Relationship to performance and repressive coping. *Journal of Applied Sport Psychology*, 12, 236–50.

Jones, G. and Swain, A. (1992). Intensity and direction as dimensions of competitive state anxiety and relationships with competitiveness. *Perceptual and Motor Skills*, 74, 467–72.

Jones, G., Swain, A. and Hardy, L. (1993). Intensity and direction dimensions of competitive state anxiety and relationships with performance. *Journal of Sports Sciences*, 11, 525–32.

Jones, M.V. (2003). Controlling emotions in sport. *The Sport Psychologist*, 17, 471–8.

Jones, M.V., Bray, S.R. and Bolton, L. (2001). Do cricket umpires favour the home team? Officiating bias in English club cricket. *Perceptual and Motor Skills*, 93, 359–62.

Jones, M.V., Bray, S.R. and Lavallee, D. (2007). All the world's a stage: The impact of an audience on sport performers. In S. Jowett and D. Lavallee (eds) *Social psychology in sport* (pp. 103–13). Champaign, IL: Human Kinetics.

Jones, M.V., Bray, S.R. and Olivier, S. (2005). Game location and aggression in rugby league. *Journal of Sports Sciences*, 23, 387–93.

Jurkovac, T. (1985). Collegiate basketball players' perceptions of the home advantage. Unpublished master's thesis, Bowling Green State University, Bowling Green, OH.

Kamphoff, C.S., Gill, D.L. and Huddleston, S. (2005). Jealousy in sport: Exploring jealousy's relationship to cohesion. *Journal of Applied Sport Psychology*, 17(4), 290–305.

Karapolat, H., Eyigör, S., Zoghi, M. et al. (2007). Comparison of hospital-supervised exercise versus home-based exercise in patients after orthotopic heart transplantation: Effects on functional capacity, quality of life, and psychological symptoms. *Transplantation Proceedings*, 39, 1586–8.

Kavussanu, M. and Roberts, G.C. (2001). Moral functioning in sport: An achievement goal perspective. *Journal of Sport & Exercise Psychology*, 23, 37–54.

Kerr, J.H. (1985). The experience of arousal: A new basis for studying arousal effects in sport. *Journal of Sports Sciences*, 3, 169–79.

Kerr, J.H. (2004). *Rethinking aggression in sport*. Abingdon: Routledge.

Kerr, J.H. and Vanschaik, P. (1995). Effects of game venue and outcome on psychological mood states in rugby. *Personality and Individual Differences*, 19, 407–10.

Kerr, J.H., Yoshida, H., Hirata, C. et al. (1997). Effects on archery performance of manipulating metamotivational state and felt arousal. *Perceptual and Motor Skills*, 84, 819–28.

Kingston, K.M. and Hardy, L. (1994). Effects of different types of goals on processes that support performance. *The Sport Psychologist*, 11, 277–93.

Klocek, M., Kubinyi, A., Bacior, B. and Kawecka-Jaszcz, K. (2005). Effect of physical training on quality of life and oxygen consumption in patients with congestive heart failure. *International Journal of Cardiology*, 103, 323–9.

Koestner, R. and Losier, G.F. (2002). Distinguishing three ways of being internally motivated: A closer look at introjection, identification and intrinsic motivation. In E.L. Deci and R.M. Ryan (eds) *Handbook of Self-Determination Research* (pp. 101–22). New York: University of Rochester Press.

Koning, R.H. (2005). Home advantage in speed skating: Evidence from individual data. *Journal of Sports Sciences*, 23, 417–27.

Krane, V. and Williams, J.M. (2010). Psychological characteristics of peak performance. In J.M. Williams (ed.) *Applied sport psychology: Personal growth to peak performance* (6th edn, pp. 169–88). Boston: McGraw-Hill.

Kring, A.M., Davison, G.C., Neale, J.M. and Johnson, S.L. (2007). *Abnormal psychology* (10th edn). Hoboken, NJ: Wiley.

Kruk, J. (2007). Physical activity in the prevention of the most frequent chronic diseases: An analysis of the recent evidence. *Asian Pacific Journal of Cancer Prevention*, 8, 325–38.

La Forge, R. (1995). Exercise-associated mood alterations: A review of interactive neurobiologic mechanisms. *Medicine, Exercise, Nutrition and Health*, 4, 17–32.

Landers, D.M. and Arent, S.M. (2007). Physical activity and mental health. In G. Tenenbaum and R.C. Eklund (eds) *Handbook of sport psychology* (3rd edn, pp. 469–91). Hoboken, NJ: Wiley.

Landers, D.M. and Boutcher, S.H. (1998). Arousal-performance relationships. In J.M. Williams (ed.) *Applied sport psychology: Personal growth to peak performance* (pp. 197–218). Mountain View, CA: Mayfield.

Lane, A.M. (2007). The rise and fall of the iceberg: Development of a conceptual model of mood-performance relationships. In A.M. Lane (ed.) *Mood and human performance: Conceptual, measurement and applied issues* (pp. 1–33). New York: Nova.

Lane, A.M., Sewell, D.F., Terry, P.C. et al. (1999). Confirmatory factor analysis of the Competitive State Anxiety Inventory-2. *Journal of Sports Sciences*, 17, 505–12.

Latané, B., Williams, K.D. and Harkins, S.G. (1979). Many hands make light the work: The causes and consequences of social loafing. *Journal of Personality and Social Psychology*, 37, 822–32.

Leary, M.R. (1992). Self-presentational processes in exercise and sport. *Journal of Sport & Exercise Psychology*, 14, 339–51.

Leary, M.R. and Kowalski, R.M. (1990). Impression management: A literature review and two-component model. *Psychological Bulletin*, 107, 34–47.

Leary, M.R., Tchividjian, L.R. and Kraxberger, B.E. (1994). Self-presentation can be hazardous to your health: Impression management and health risk. *Health Psychology*, 13, 461–70.

Lerner, B.S. and Locke, E.A. (1995). The effects of goal setting, self-efficacy, competition, and personal traits on the performance of an endurance task. *Journal of Sport & Exercise Psychology*, 17, 138–52.

Lirgg, C.D., George, T.R., Chase, M.A. and Ferguson, R.H. (1996). Impact of conception of ability and sex-type of task on male and female self-efficacy. *Journal of Sport & Exercise Psychology*, 18, 426–34.

Locke, E.A. and Latham, G.P. (2002). Building a practically useful theory of goal setting and task motivation: A 35-year odyssey. *American Psychologist*, 57, 705–17.

Long, T., Pantaleon, N., Bruant, G. and d'Arripe-Longueville, F. (2006). A qualitative study of moral reasoning of young elite athletes. *The Sport Psychologist*, 20, 330–47.

Lorenz, K. (1966). *On aggression*. New York: Harcourt, Brace & World.

Lorimer, R. and Jowett, S. (2008). Empathic accuracy in coach–athlete dyads who participate in team and individual sports. *Psychology of Sport and Exercise*, 10(1), 152–8.

Lorimer, R. and Jowett, S. (2010). Feedback of information in the empathic accuracy of sport coaches. *Psychology of Sport and Exercise*, 11, 12–17.

Loughead, T.M. and Hardy, J. (2005). An examination of coach and peer leader behaviors in sport. *Psychology of Sport and Exercise*, 6, 303–12.

Lox, C.L., McAuley, E. and Tucker, R.S. (1995). Exercise as an intervention for enhancing subjective wellbeing in an HIV-1 population. *Journal of Sport & Exercise Psychology*, 17, 345–62.

Lox, C.L., Martin Ginis, K.A. and Petruzzello, S.J. (2006). *The psychology of exercise: Integrating theory and practice* (2nd edn). Scottsdale, AZ: Holcomb Hathaway.

McArdle, W.D., Katch, F.I. and Katch, V.L. (2001). *Exercise physiology: Energy, nutrition, and human performance* (5th edn). Philadelphia, PA: Lippincott, Williams & Wilkins.

McClelland, D.C. (1961). *The achieving society.* New York: Free Press.

McClelland, D.C., Atkinson, J.W., Clark, R.W. and Lowell, E.L. (1953). *The achievement motive.* New York: Appleton-Century-Crofts.

McClure, B.A. and Foster, C.D. (1991). Group work as a method of promoting cohesiveness within a women's gymnastics team. *Perceptual and Motor Skills*, 73, 307–13.

McEnroe, J. with Kaplan, J. (2002). *You cannot be serious.* London: Little Brown.

McGowan, E., Prapavessis, H. and Wesch, N. (2008). Self-presentational concerns and competitive anxiety. *Journal of Sport & Exercise Psychology*, 30, 383–400.

McKnight, P., Williams, J.M. and Widmeyer, W.N. (1991). The effects of cohesion and identifiability on reducing the likelihood of social loafing. Presented at the Association for the Advancement of Applied Sport Psychology Annual Conference, Savannah, GA.

Mahoney, M.J. and Avener, M. (1977). Psychology of the elite athlete: An exploratory study. *Cognitive Therapy and Research*, 1, 135–41.

Maida, D.M. and Armstrong, S.L. (2005). The classification of muscle dysmorphia. *International Journal of Men's Health*, 4, 73–91.

Males, J.R. and Kerr, J.H. (1996). Stress, emotion and performance in elite slalom canoeists. *The Sport Psychologist*, 10, 17–37.

Malmo, R.B. (1959). Activation: A neuropsychological dimension. *Psychological Review*, 66, 267–386.

Markland, D. and Ingledew, D.K. (2007). Exercise participation motives: A self-determination theory perspective. In M.S. Hagger and N.L. Chatzisarantis (eds) *Intrinsic motivation and self-determination in exercise and sport* (pp. 23–34). Champaign, IL: Human Kinetics.

Martens, R. (1977). *Sport competition anxiety test*. Champaign, IL: Human Kinetics.

Martens, R. and Landers, D.M. (1969). Coaction effects in a muscular endurance task. *Research Quarterly*, 40, 733–7.

Martens, R. and Landers, D.M. (1972). Evaluation potential as a determinant of coaction effects. *Journal of Experimental Social Psychology*, 8, 347–59.

Martens, R., Burton, D., Vealey, R.S. et al. (1990a). Development and validation of the Competitive State Anxiety Inventory-2 (CSAI-2). In R. Martens, R.S. Vealey and D. Burton (eds) *Competitive anxiety in sport*. Champaign, IL: Human Kinetics.

Martens, R., Vealey, R.S. and Burton, D. (eds) (1990b). *Competitive anxiety in sport*. Champaign, IL: Human Kinetics.

Martin, K.A. and Lichtenberger, C.M. (2002). Fitness enhancement and changes in body image. In T.F. Cash and T. Pruzinsky (eds) *Body image: A handbook of theory, research and clinical practice* (pp. 414–21). New York: Guilford.

Martin, R. and Davids, K. (1995). The effects of group development techniques on a professional athletic team. *Journal of Social Psychology*, 135(4), 533–5.

Martin, S.B., Kellmann, M., Lavallee, D. and Page, S.J. (2001). The Sport Psychology Attitudes – Revised form Manual. Unpublished test manual. Denton, TX: University of North Texas.

Maxwell, J.P., Visek, A.J. and Moores, E. (2009). Anger and perceived legitimacy of aggression in male Hong Kong Chinese athletes: Effects of type of sport and level of competition. *Psychology of Sport & Exercise*, 10, 289–96.

Maynard, I.W., Hemmings, B. and Warwick-Evans, L. (1995b). The effects of a somatic intervention strategy on competitive state anxiety and performance in semiprofessional soccer players. *The Sport Psychologist*, 9, 51–64.

Maynard, I.W., Smith, M.J. and Warwick-Evans, L. (1995a). The effects of a cognitive intervention strategy on competitive state anxiety and performance in semiprofessional soccer players. *Journal of Sport & Exercise Psychology*, 17, 428–46.

Michaels, J.W., Blommel, J.M., Brocato, R.M. et al. (1982). Social facilitation and inhibition in a natural setting. *Replications in Social Psychology*, 2, 21–4.

Midtgaard J., Rorth M., Stelter R. and Adamsen L. (2006). The group matters: An explorative study of group cohesion and quality of life in cancer patients participating in physical exercise intervention during treatment. *European Journal of Cancer Care*, 15, 25–33.

Midtgaard, J., Stelter, R., Rørth, M. and Adamsen, L. (2007). Regaining a sense of agency and shared self-reliance: The experience of advanced disease cancer patients participating in a multidimensional exercise intervention while undergoing chemotherapy – analysis of patient diaries. *Scandanavian Journal of Psychology*, 48, 181–90.

Miller, B.W., Roberts, G.C. and Ommundsen, Y. (2005). Effect of perceived motivational climate on moral functioning, team moral atmosphere perceptions, and the legitimacy of intentionally injurious acts among competitive youth football players. *Psychology of Sport & Exercise*, 6, 461–77.

Moore, J.C. and Brylinsky, J.A. (1993). Spectator effect on team performance in college basketball. *Journal of Sport Behavior*, 16, 77–84.

Morgan, W.P. (1980). The trait psychology controversy. *Research Quarterly for Exercise and Sport*, 51, 50–76.

Morgan, W.P. (1985). Affective beneficence of vigorous physical activity. *Medicine & Science in Sports & Exercise*, 17, 94–100.

Moritz, S.E., Feltz, D.L., Fahrbach, K.R. and Mack, D.E. (2000). The relation of self-efficacy measures to sport performance: A meta-analytic review. *Research Quarterly for Exercise and Sport*, 71, 280–94.

Mosher, C.E., Sloane, R., Morey, M.C. et al. (2009). Associations between lifestyle factors and quality of life among older long-term breast, prostate, and colorectal cancer survivors. *Cancer*, 115, 4001–9.

Motl, R.W., Birnbaum, A.S., Kubik, M.Y. and Dishman, R.K. (2004). Naturally occurring changes in physical activity are inversely related to depressive symptoms during early adolescence. *Psychosomatic Medicine*, 66, 336–42.

Mullen, B. and Cooper, C. (1994). The relation between group cohesiveness and performance: An integration. *Psychological Bulletin*, 115, 210–22.

Murphy, S., Nordin, S. and Cumming, J. (2008). Imagery in sport, exercise, and dance. In T.S. Horn (ed.) *Advances in sport psychology* (3rd edn, pp. 297–324). Champaign, IL: Human Kinetics.

Murray, H.A. (1943). *Thematic apperception test manual.* Cambridge, MA: Harvard University Press.

Mutimura, E., Stewart, A., Crowther N.J. et al. (2008). The effects of exercise training on quality of life in HAART-treated HIV-positive Rwandan subjects with body fat redistribution. *Quality of Life Research*, 17, 377–85.

Myers, N.D., Vargas-Tonsing, T.M. and Feltz, D.L. (2005). Coaching efficacy in intercollegiate coaches: sources, coaching behavior, and team variables. *Psychology of Sport and Exercise*, 6, 129–43.

Naylor, K. and Brawley, L. (1992). Social loafing: Perceptions and implications. Paper presented at the Joint Meeting of the Canadian Association of Sport Sciences and the Canadian Psychomotor of Learning and Sport Psychology Association Conference, Sashkatoon, Saskatchewan.

Nelson, L.R. and Furst, M.L. (1972). An objective study of the effects of expectation on competitive performance. *Journal of Psychology*, 81, 69–72.

Nevill, A., Balmer, N. and Wolfson, W. (eds) (2005). The extent and causes of home advantage: Some recent insights. Special issue. *Journal of Sports Sciences*, 23(4).

Nevill, A.M. and Holder, R.L. (1999). Home advantage in sport: An overview of studies on the advantage of playing at home. *Sports Medicine*, 28, 221–36.

Nevill, A.M., Newell, S.M. and Gale, S. (1996). Factors associated with home advantage in English and Scottish soccer matches. *Journal of Sports Sciences*, 14, 181–6.

NICE (National Institute for Clinical Excellence) (2004). *Eating disorders*. London: NICE.

NICE (National Institute for Clinical Excellence) (2007). *Depression (amended): Management of depression in primary and secondary care*. London: NICE.

Nicholls, J.G. (1984). Achievement motivation: Conceptions of ability, subjective experience, task choice, and performance. *Psychological Review*, 91, 328–46.

North, T.C., McCullagh, P. and Tran, Z.V. (1990). Effect of exercise on depression. *Exercise & Sport Science Reviews*, 18, 379–415.

Ommundsen, Y., Roberts, G.C., Lemyre, P.N. and Treasure, D. (2003). Perceived motivational climate in male youth soccer: Relations to social-moral functioning, sportspersonship and team norm perceptions. *Psychology of Sport & Exercise*, 4, 397–413.

Paskevich, D.M. (1995). Conceptual and measurement factors of collective efficacy in its relationship to cohesion and performance outcome. Unpublished doctoral dissertation, University of Waterloo, Canada.

Patterson, M.M., Carron, A.V. and Loughead, T.M. (2005). The influence of team norms on the cohesion-self-reported performance relationship: A multi-level analysis. *Psychology of Sport and Exercise*, 6(4), 479–93.

Patwala, A.Y., Woods, P.R., Sharp, L. et al. (2009). Maximizing patient benefit from cardiac resynchronization therapy with the addition of structured exercise training: A randomized controlled study. *Journal of the American College of Cardiology*, 53, 2332–9.

Pelletier, L.G., Fortier, M.S., Vallerand, R.J. and Brière, N.M. (2001). Associations between perceived autonomy support, forms of self regulation and persistence: A prospective study. *Motivation and Emotion*, 25(4), 279–306.

Pelletier, L.G., Fortier, M.S., Vallerand, R.J. et al. (1995). Toward a new measure of intrinsic motivation, extrinsic motivation and amotivation in sports; The Sport Motivation Scale (SMS). *Journal of Sport and Exercise Psychology*, 17, 35–53.

Perkins, D., Wilson, G.V. and Kerr, J.H. (2001). The effects of elevated arousal and mood on maximal strength performance in athletes. *Journal of Applied Sport Psychology*, 13, 239–59.

Perry, J.D. and Williams, J.M. (1998). Relationship of intensity and direction of competitive trait anxiety to skill level and gender in tennis. *The Sport Psychologist*, 12, 169–79.

Petrie, T.A. and Greenleaf, C.A. (2007). Eating disorders in sport: From theory to research to intervention. In G. Tenenbaum and R.C. Eklund (eds) *Handbook of sport psychology* (3rd edn, pp. 352–78). Hoboken, NJ: Wiley.

Petruzzello, S.J., Landers, D.M., Hatfield, B.D. et al. (1991). A meta-analysis on the anxiety-reducing effects of acute and chronic exercise: Outcomes and mechanisms. *Sports Medicine*, 11, 143–82.

Phillips, K.A. (2002). Body image and body dysmorphic disorder. In T.F. Cash and T. Pruzinsky (eds) *Body image: A handbook of theory, research and clinical practice* (pp. 312–21). New York: Guilford.

Pischke, C.R., Scherwitz, L., Weidner, G. and Ornish, D. (2008). Long-term effects of lifestyle changes on wellbeing and cardiac variables among coronary heart disease patients. *Health Psychology*, 27, 584–92.

Potocky, M. and Murgatroyd, S. (1993). What is reversal theory? In J.H. Kerr, S. Murgatroyd and M.J. Apter (eds) *Advances in reversal theory*. Lisse: Swets & Zeitlinger.

Prapavessis, H. and Carron, A.V. (1996). The effect of group cohesion on competitive state anxiety. *Journal of Sport and Exercise Psychology*, 18, 64–74.

Prapavessis, H. and Carron, A.V. (1997). Sacrifice, cohesion and conformity to norms in sport teams. *Group Dynamics*, 1(3), 231–40.

Prapavessis, H. and Grove, J.R. (1994). Personality variables as antecedents of precompetitive mood state temporal patterning. *International Journal of Sport Psychology*, 25, 347–65.

Prapavessis, H., Carron, A.V. and Spink, K.S. (1996). Team-building in sport. *International Journal of Sport Psychology*, 27, 269–85.

Raglin, J.S. and Morris, M.J. (1994). Precompetition anxiety in women volleyball players: A test of ZOF theory in a team sport. *British Journal of Sports Medicine*, 28, 47–51.

Ramírez-Marrero, F.A., Smith, B.A., Meléndez-Brau, N. and Santana-Bagur, J.L. (2004). Physical and leisure activity, body composition, and life satisfaction in HIV-positive Hispanics in Puerto Rico. *Journal of the Association of Nurses in AIDS Care*, 15, 68–77.

Reel, J.J., Greenleaf, C., Baker, W.K. et al. (2007). Relations of body concerns and exercise behavior: A meta-analysis. *Psychological Reports*, 101, 927–42.

Reinboth, M. and Duda, J.L. (2004). Relationship of the perceived motivational climate and perceptions of ability to psychological and physical well-being in team sports. *The Sport Psychologist*, 18, 237–51.

Reinboth, M. and Duda, J.L. (2006). Perceived motivational climate, need satisfaction and indices of well-being in team sports: A longitudinal perspective. *Psychology of Sport and Exercise*, 7, 269–86.

Reis, H.T., Sheldon, K.M., Gable, S.L. et al. (2000). Daily well-being: The role of autonomy, competence, and relatedness. *Personality and Social Psychology Bulletin*, 26(4), 419–35.

Rethorst, C.D., Wipfli, B.M. and Landers, D.M. (2009). The antidepressive effects of exercise: A meta-analysis of randomized trials. *Sports Medicine*, 39, 491–511.

Richardson, S.O., Andersen, M.B. and Morris, T. (2008). *Overtraining athletes: Personal journeys in sport*. Champaign, IL: Human Kinetics.

Robazza, C., Bortoli, L. and Hanin, Y. (2004). Precompetition emotions, bodily symptoms, and task-specific qualities as predictors of performance in high-level karate athletes. *Journal of Applied Sport Psychology*, 16, 151–65.

Rojas, R., Schlicht, W. and Hautzinger, M. (2003). Effects of exercise training on quality of life, psychological wellbeing, immune status, and cardiopulmonary fitness in an HIV-1 positive population. *Journal of Sport & Exercise Psychology*, 25, 440–55.

Romand, P., Panteleon, N. and Cabagno, G. (2009). Age differences in individuals' cognitive and behavioral moral functioning responses in male soccer teams. *Journal of Applied Sport Psychology*, 21, 49–63.

Rovio, E., Eskola, J., Kozub, S.A. et al. (2009). Can high group cohesion be harmful? A case study of a junior ice-hockey team. *Small Group Research*, 40(4), 421–35.

Ruder, M.K. and Gill, D.L. (1982). Immediate effects of win-loss on perceptions of cohesion in intramural and intercollegiate volleyball teams. *Journal of Sport & Exercise Psychology*, 4, 227–34.

Ryan, R.M. and Deci, E.L. (2000). Intrinsic and extrinsic motivations: Classic definitions and new directions. *Contemporary Educational Psychology*, 25(1), 54–67.

Sage, G. (1984). *Motor learning and control.* Dubuque, IA: Brown.

Sage, G.H. (1975). An occupational analysis of the college coach. In D.W. Ball and J.W. Loy (eds) *Sport and social order* (pp. 408–55). Reading, MA: Addison-Wesley.

Sarrazin, P., Vallerand, R.J., Guillet, E. et al. (2002). Motivation and dropout in female handballers: A 21-month prospective study. *European Journal of Social Psychology*, 32, 395–418.

Savoy, C. (1993). A yearly mental training program for a college basketball player. *The Sport Psychologist*, 7, 173–90.

Schlenker, B.R. (1980). *Impression management: The self-concept, social identity, and interpersonal relations.* Monterey, CA: Brooks/Cole.

Schwartz, B. and Barsky, S.F. (1977). The home advantage. *Social Forces*, 55, 641–61.

Senécal, J., Loughead, T.M. and Bloom, G.A. (2008). A season-long team-building intervention program: Examining the effect of team goal setting on cohesion. *Journal of Sport & Exercise Psychology*, 30, 186–99.

Shaw, M.E. (1981). *Group dynamics: The psychology of small group behaviour* (3rd edn). New York: McGraw-Hill.

Sherif, M. and Sherif, C.W. (1956). *An outline of social psychology.* New York: Harper.

Shields, D.L. and Bredemeier, B.J. (2001). Moral development and behavior in sport. In R. Singer, H. Hausenblas and C. Janelle (eds) *Handbook of sport psychology* (2nd edn, pp. 585–603). New York: Wiley.

Short, S. and Ross-Stewart, L. (2009). A review of self-efficacy based interventions. In S.D. Mellalieu and S. Hanton (eds) *Advances in applied sport psychology: A review* (pp. 221–80). London: Routledge.

Simonton, D.K. (2008). Genius, creativity and leadership. In T. Rickards, M.A. Runco and S. Moger (eds) *The Routledge companion to creativity* (pp. 247–55). London: Routledge.

Singer, R.N. (2002). Preperformance state, routines, and automaticity: What does it take to realize expertise in self-paced events? *Journal of Sport & Exercise Psychology*, 24, 359–75.

Skinner, B.F. (1978). *Reflections on behaviorism and society*. Englewood Cliffs, NJ: Prentice Hall.

Smith, D., Hale, B., Rhea, D. et al. (2009). Big, buff and dependent: Exercise dependence, muscle dysmorphia and anabolic steroid use in bodybuilders. In L.J. Katlin (ed.) *Men and addictions: New research* (pp. 1–36). New York: Nova Science.

Smith, D.W. and McFall, S.L. (2005). The relationship of diet and exercise for weight control and the quality of life gap associated with diabetes. *Journal of Psychosomatic Research*, 59, 385–92.

Smith, M.D. (1980). Hockey violence: Interring some myths. In F.W. Straub (ed.) *Sport psychology: An analysis of athlete behavior* (2nd edn). Ithaca, NY: Mouvement.

Smith, R.E. and Smoll, F.L. (1997). Coach-mediated team building in youth sports. *Journal of Applied Sport Psychology*, 9, 114–32.

Smith, R.E., Smoll, F.L. and Hunt, E. (1977). A system for the behavioral assessment of athletic coaches. *Research Quarterly for Exercise and Sport*, 48, 401–7.

Smith, R.E., Schutz, R.W., Smoll, F.L. and Ptacek, J.T. (1995). Development and validation of a multidimensional measure of sport-specific psychological skills: The athletic coping skills inventory-28. *Journal of Sport & Exercise Psychology*, 17, 379–98.

Smoll, F.L. and Smith, R.E. (1989). Leadership behaviours in sport: A theoretical model and research paradigm. *Journal of Applied Social Psychology*, 19, 1522–51.

Smoll, F.L., Smith, R.E., Barnett, N.P. and Everett, J.J. (1993). Enhancement of children's self-esteem through social support training for youth sport coaches. *Journal of Applied Psychology*, 78, 602–10.

Sonstroem, R.J. (1997). The physical self-system: A mediator of exercise and self-esteem. In K.R. Fox (ed.) *The physical self: From motivation to well-being* (pp. 3–26). Champaign, IL: Human Kinetics.

Spielberger, C.D. (1966). Theory and research on anxiety. In C.D. Spielberger (ed.) *Anxiety and behavior* (pp. 3–22). New York: Academic Press.

Spink, K.S., Wilson, K.S. and Odnokon, P. (2010). Examining the relationship between cohesion and return to team in elite athletes. *Psychology of Sport and Exercise*, 11(1), 6–11.

Stefani, R. (2007). Measurement and interpretation of home advantage. In J. Albert and R.H. Koning (eds) *Statistical thinking in sports* (pp. 203–16). London: CRC Press.

Stephens, T. (1988). Physical activity and mental health in the United States and Canada: Evidence from four population surveys. *Preventive Medicine*, 17, 35–47.

Stogdill, R.M. (1948). Personal factors associated with leadership: Survey of literature. *Journal of Psychology*, 25, 35–71.

Straub, W.F. (1975). Team cohesiveness in athletics. *International Journal of Sport Psychology*, 6, 125–33.

Suinn, R.M. (1987). Behavioral approaches to stress management in sport. In J.R. May and M.J. Asken (eds) *Sport psychology* (pp. 59–75). New York: PMA.

Swain, A. and Jones, G. (1992). Relationships between sport achievement orientation and competitive state anxiety. *The Sport Psychologist*, 6, 42–54.

Swain, A. and Jones, G. (1993). Intensity and frequency dimensions of competitive state anxiety. *Journal of Sports Sciences*, 11, 533–42.

Take a seat: Study puts Indy's capacity at 257,325 (27 May 2004). Retrieved 5 November 2009 from USAToday.com website, http://www.usatoday.com/sports/motor/irl/indy500/2004-05-27-attendance-count_x.htm.

Terry, P.C., Walrond, N. and Carron, A.V. (1998). The influence of game location on athletes' psychological states. *Journal of Science and Medicine in Sport*, 1, 29–37.

Terry, P.C., Carron, A.V., Pink, M.J. et al. (2000). Perceptions of group cohesion and mood in sport teams. *Group Dynamics: Theory and Practice*, 4, 234–43.

Thirer, J. and Rampey, M. (1979). Effects of abusive spectator behavior on the performance of home and visiting intercollegiate basketball teams. *Perceptual and Motor Skills*, 48, 1047–53.

Thomas, J.R., Nelson, J.K. and Silverman, S.J. (2005). *Research methods in physical activity* (5th edn). Champaign, IL: Human Kinetics.

Thomas, O., Hanton, S. and Maynard, I. (2007a). Anxiety responses and psychological skill use during the time leading up to competition: Theory to practice I. *Journal of Applied Sport Psychology*, 19, 379–97.

Thomas, O., Maynard, I. and Hanton, S. (2004). Temporal aspects of competitive anxiety and self-confidence as a function of anxiety perceptions. *The Sport Psychologist, 18*, 172–87.

Thomas, O., Maynard, I. and Hanton, S. (2007b). Intervening with athletes during the time leading up to competition: Theory to practice II. *Journal of Applied Sport Psychology*, 19, 398–418.

Thomas, P.R., Murphy, S.M. and Hardy, L. (1999). Test of performance strategies: Development and preliminary validation of a comprehensive measure of athletes' psychological skills. *Journal of Sports Sciences*, 17, 697–711.

Thuot, S.M., Kavouras, S.A. and Kenefick, R.W. (1998). Effect of perceived ability, game location, and state anxiety on basketball performance. *Journal of Sport Behavior*, 21, 311–21.

Ticketing (n.d.). Retrieved November 5, 2009 from London 2012 website, http://www.london2012.com/plans/ticketing/index.php.

Tod, D. and Andersen, M.B. (2010). When to refer athletes for counseling and psychotherapy. In J.M. Williams (ed.) *Applied sport psychology: Personal growth to peak performance* (6th edn, pp. 443–62). Boston: McGraw-Hill.

Treasure, D.C., Monson, J. and Lox, C.L. (1996). Relationship between self-efficacy, wrestling performance, and affect prior to competition. *The Sport Psychologist*, 10, 73–83.

Triplett, N. (1898). The dynamogenic factors in pacemaking and competition. *American Journal of Psychology*, 9, 505–23.

Tucker, L.W. and Parks, J.B. (2001). Effects of gender and sport type on intercollegiate athletes' perceptions of the legitimacy of aggressive behaviors in sport. *Sociology of Sport Journal*, 18, 403–13.

Tuckman, B.W. (1965). Developmental sequence in small groups. *Psychological Bulletin*, 63, 384–99.

Tuckman, B.W. and Jensen, M.C. (1977). Stages of small-group development revisited. *Group and Organization Studies*, 2, 419–27.

UK Sport (2009). *Home advantage: The performance benefits of hosting major sporting events.* London: UK Sport.

USDHHS (United States Department of Health and Human Services) (1999). *Mental health: A report of the surgeon general.* Rockville, MD: USDHHS, Substance Abuse and Mental Health Services

Administration, Centre for Mental Health Services, National Institutes of Health, National Institute of Mental Health.

Vallerand, R.J. and Thill, E.E. (1993). *Introduction à la psychologie de la motivation. (Introduction to the psychology of motivation)*. Laval, Canada: Éditions Études Vivantes.

Van Raalte, J.L. and Cornelius, A.E. (2007). The relationship between hazing and team cohesion. *Journal of Sport Behavior*, 30(4), 491–507.

Vealey, R.S. (1986). Conceptualization of sport-confidence and competitive orientation: Preliminary investigation and instrument development. *Journal of Sport Psychology*, 8, 221–46.

Vealey, R.S. (2001). Understanding and enhancing self-confidence in athletes. In R.N. Singer, H.A. Hausenblas and C.M. Janelle (eds) *Handbook of sport psychology* (2nd edn, pp. 550–65). New York: Wiley.

Vealey, R.S. (2002). Personality and sport behavior. In T.S. Horn (ed.) *Advances in sport psychology* (2nd edn, pp. 43–82). Champaign, IL: Human Kinetics.

Vealey, R.S. and Chase, M.A. (2008). Self-confidence in sport. In T.S. Horn (ed.) *Advances in sport psychology* (3rd edn, pp. 65–97). Champaign, IL: Human Kinetics.

Vealey, R.S., Hayashi, S.W., Garner-Holman, M. and Giacobbi, P. (1998). Sources of sport-confidence: Conceptualization and instrument development. *Journal of Sport & Exercise Psychology*, 20, 54–80.

Wagman, D.F., Curry, L.A. and Cook, D.L. (1995). An investigation into anabolic androgenic steroid use by elite U.S. powerlifters. *Journal of Strength and Conditioning Research*, 9, 154–69.

Wallace, H.M., Baumeister, R.F. and Vohs, K.D. (2005). Audience support and choking under pressure: A home disadvantage? *Journal of Sports Sciences*, 23, 429–38.

Wankel, L. (1984). Audience effects in sport. In J.M. Silva and R.S. Weinberg (eds) *Psychological foundations of sport* (pp. 293–314). Champaign, IL: Human Kinetics.

Weinberg, R.S. and Gould, D. (2007). *Foundations of sport and exercise psychology* (4th edn). Champaign, IL: Human Kinetics.

Weinberg, R.S. and Williams, J.M. (2010). Integrating and implementing a psychological skills training program. In J.M. Williams (ed.) *Applied sport psychology: Personal growth to peak performance* (6th edn, pp. 361–91). Boston: McGraw-Hill.

Weinberg, R.S., Gould, D., Yukelson, D. and Jackson, A. (1981). The effect of preexisting and manipulated self-efficacy on a competitive muscular endurance task. *Journal of Sport Psychology*, 4, 345–54.

Weiss, M.R. and Chaumeton, N. (1992). Motivational orientations in sport. In T.S. Horn (ed.) *Advances in Sport Psychology* (pp. 61–99). Champaign, IL: Human Kinetics.

Weiss, M.R. and Friedrichs, W.D. (1986). The influence of leader behaviors, coach attributes, and institutional variables on performance and satisfaction of collegiate basketball team. *Journal of Sport Psychology*, 8, 332–46.

Wells, C.M., Collins, D. and Hale, B.D. (1993). The self-efficacy-performance link in maximum strength performance. *Journal of Sports Sciences*, 11, 167–75.

WHO (World Health Organization) (2009). Depression. Retrieved 21 May 2009, http://www.who.int/topics/depression/en/.

WHOQOL Group (1998). The World Health Organization quality of life assessment (WHOQOL): Development and general psychometric properties. *Social Science & Medicine*, 46, 1569–85.

Widmeyer, W.N., Brawley, L.R. and Carron, A.V. (1990). The effects of group size in sport. *Journal of Sport and Exercise Psychology*, 12, 177–90.

Williams, J.M. and Straub, W.F. (2010). Sport psychology: Past, present, future. In J.M. Williams (ed.) *Applied sport psychology: Personal growth to peak performance* (6th edn, pp. 1–17). Boston: McGraw-Hill.

Williams, L. and Gill, D.L. (2000). Aggression and prosocial behavior. In D.L. Gill (ed.) *Psychological dynamics of sport and exercise* (pp. 239–54). Leeds: Human Kinetics.

Wilson, P. and Eklund, R.C. (1988). The relationship between competitive anxiety and self-presentational concerns. *Journal of Sport & Exercise Psychology*, 20, 81–97.

Wilson, R.W., Taliaferro, L.A. and Jacobsen, P.B. (2006). Pilot study of a self-administered stress management and exercise intervention during chemotherapy for cancer. *Support Care Cancer*, 14, 928–35.

Wipfli, B.M., Rethorst, C.D. and Landers, D.M. (2008). The anxiolytic effects of exercise: A meta-analysis of randomized trials and dose-response analysis. *Journal of Sport & Exercise Psychology*, 30, 392–410.

Woodman, T. and Hardy, L. (2003). The relative impact of cognitive anxiety and self-confidence upon sport performance: A meta-analysis. *Journal of Sports Sciences*, 21, 443–57.

World Anti-Doping Agency (2008). *The 2009 prohibited list: International standard*. Montreal, QC: World Anti-Doping Agency.

World Anti-Doping Agency (2009). *World anti-doping code*. Montreal, QC: World Anti-Doping Agency.

Wright, E.F., Jackson, W., Christie, S.D. et al. (1991). The home course disadvantage in golf championships: Further evidence for the undermining effect of supportive audiences on performance under pressure. *Journal of Sport Behavior*, 14, 51–60.

Wright, E.F., Voyer, D., Wright, R.D. and Roney, C. (1995). Supporting audiences and performance under pressure: The home-ice disadvantage in hockey championships. *Journal of Sport Behavior*, 18, 21–8.

Yerkes, R.M. and Dodson, J.D. (1908). The relation of strength of stimulus to rapidity of habit formation. *Journal of Comparative and Neurological Psychology*, 18, 459–82.

Zajonc, R.B. (1965). Social facilitation. *Science*, 149, 269–74.

Zajonc, R.B., Heingartner, A. and Herman, E.M. (1969). Social enhancement and impairment of performance in the cockroach. *Journal of Personality and Social Psychology*, 13, 83–92.

Index

Entries in **bold** refer to glossary definitions

Reading guide

This table identifies where in the book you'll find relevant information for those of you studying or teaching A-level. You should also, of course, refer to the Index and the Glossary, but navigating a book for a particular set of items can be awkward and we found this table a useful tool when editing the book and so include it here for your convenience.

Topic	Edexcel	WJEC	OCR	Page
Aggression	x		x	44–57
Anxiety	x	x		75–91
Arousal	x	x	x	58–74
Attribution – internal factor	x	x		92
Audience effects	x	x		120–4
Catastrophe Theory	x			65, 79–82
Cognitive Evaluation Theory	x			40
Drive Theory	x			59–60
Effects of exercise – mental health		x		166
Effects of exercise – physical health		x		166
Evaluation-apprehension theory	x			123
Explanations of motivation	x	x	x	30–43
Frustration-Aggression Theory		x		46
Gender differences	x			97, 133–46
Goal setting	x			88–9
Imagery	x			102–4
Instinct Theory			x	46

Topic	Edexcel	WJEC	OCR	Page
Optimal level of arousal	x			61
Participation	x			12, 34, 152, 161, 169
Personality	x		x	13–29
Qualitative data	x			56, 115, 164
Quantitative data	x			113
Reinforcement	x			18, 50, 52, 140
Self-efficacy	x			93-5
Socialization	x			179–80
Social Learning Theory		x	x	7, 46–7
State anxiety			x	75–6
Team membership – external factor		x		52
Trait anxiety			x	61–2, 75–6
Ways of improving motivation	x	x	x	41
What makes a good coach?	x			139–42

Printed and bound in Great Britain by
CPI Group (UK) Ltd, Croydon, CR0 4YY